CITY

ANDREA BENNETT

Contents

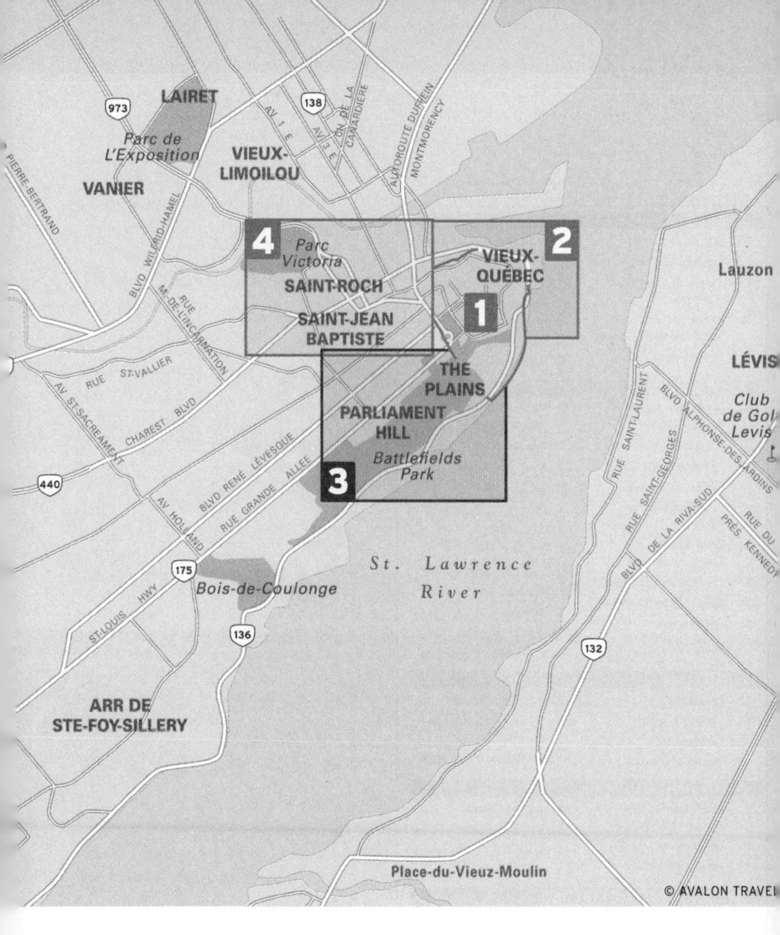
LAIRET
Parc de L'Exposition
VANIER
VIEUX-LIMOILOU
4
Parc Victoria
SAINT-ROCH
SAINT-JEAN BAPTISTE
2
VIEUX-QUÉBEC
1
THE PLAINS
PARLIAMENT HILL
3
Battlefields Park
Lauzon
LÉVIS
St. Lawrence River
Bois-de-Coulonge
ARR DE STE-FOY-SILLERY
Place-du-Vieuz-Moulin
© AVALON TRAVEL

Maps

SIGHTS

- 4 Parc de L'Artillerie
- 5 Les Fortifications
- 37 Musée de L'Amérique Francophone
- 40 Basilique-Cathédrale Notre-Dame-de-Québec
- 41 Séminaire de Québec
- 52 Musée des Ursulines
- 58 Place d'Armes
- 59 Château Frontenac
- 64 Terrasse Dufferin
- 71 Parc du Cavalier-du-Moulin
- 76 La Citadelle

RESTAURANTS

- 1 Restaurant Monastère des Augustines
- 6 Il Teatro
- 13 Le Petite Coin Latin
- 18 Les Trois Garçons
- 20 Café-Boulangerie Paillard
- 22 Chez Boulay Bistro Boréal
- 23 Les Frères de la Côte
- 24 Casse-Crêpe Breton
- 25 Chez Ashton
- 28 Tournebroche Bistro Gourmet
- 31 Masaru Sushi
- 33 Chez Temporel
- 39 Le Café Buade
- 54 Aux Anciens Canadiens
- 56 Conti Caffe
- 57 Le Continental
- 60 Le Champlain
- 65 Le Saint-Amour
- 66 Apsara
- 68 Bello Ristorante
- 70 Café Bistro L'Omelette

NIGHTLIFE

- 12 Le Sapristi
- 15 Bar Ste-Angèle
- 16 Le Bistro Plus
- 17 Pub St-Alexandre
- 30 Pub Saint Patrick
- 46 Le Charles Baillairgé Jazz Bar
- 61 1608 Wine & Cheese Bar

ARTS AND CULTURE

- 2 Le Monastère des Augustines Museum
- 7 Le Capitole
- 10 Palais Montcalm
- 44 Morrin Centre
- 51 Musée du Fort
- 55 Galerie d'Art Brousseau And Brousseau

SPORTS AND ACTIVITIES

- 9 Patinoire de la Place d'Youville
- 75 Glissades de la Terrasse Dufferin

SHOPS

- 11 Première Issue
- 14 Délices Érable & Cie
- 19 Librairie Pantoute
- 21 Confiserie c'Est Si Bon
- 26 Le Spa du Manoir
- 29 Magasin Général P.L. Blouin
- 32 Bibi et Compagnie
- 34 Zimmermann
- 35 Boutique Artisans Canada
- 36 La Maison Simons
- 38 La Boutique de Noël
- 42 La Maison Darlington
- 50 Artisans de la Cathédrale
- 53 Galerie d'art Les Trois Colombes
- 62 Lambert & Co.

HOTELS

- 3 Monastère des Augustines
- 8 Hotel du Capitole
- 27 Hôtel Manoir Victoria
- 43 Auberge Internationale de Québec
- 45 Hôtel Le Champlain
- 47 Hôtel Clarendon
- 48 Hôtel Ste-Anne
- 49 Auberge Place d'Armes
- 63 Fairmont Le Château Frontenac
- 67 Chez Hubert
- 69 Hôtel Le Clos Saint-Louis
- 72 Hôtel Cap Diamant
- 73 La Marquise de Bassano
- 74 Hôtel Château Bellevue

SEE MAP 4

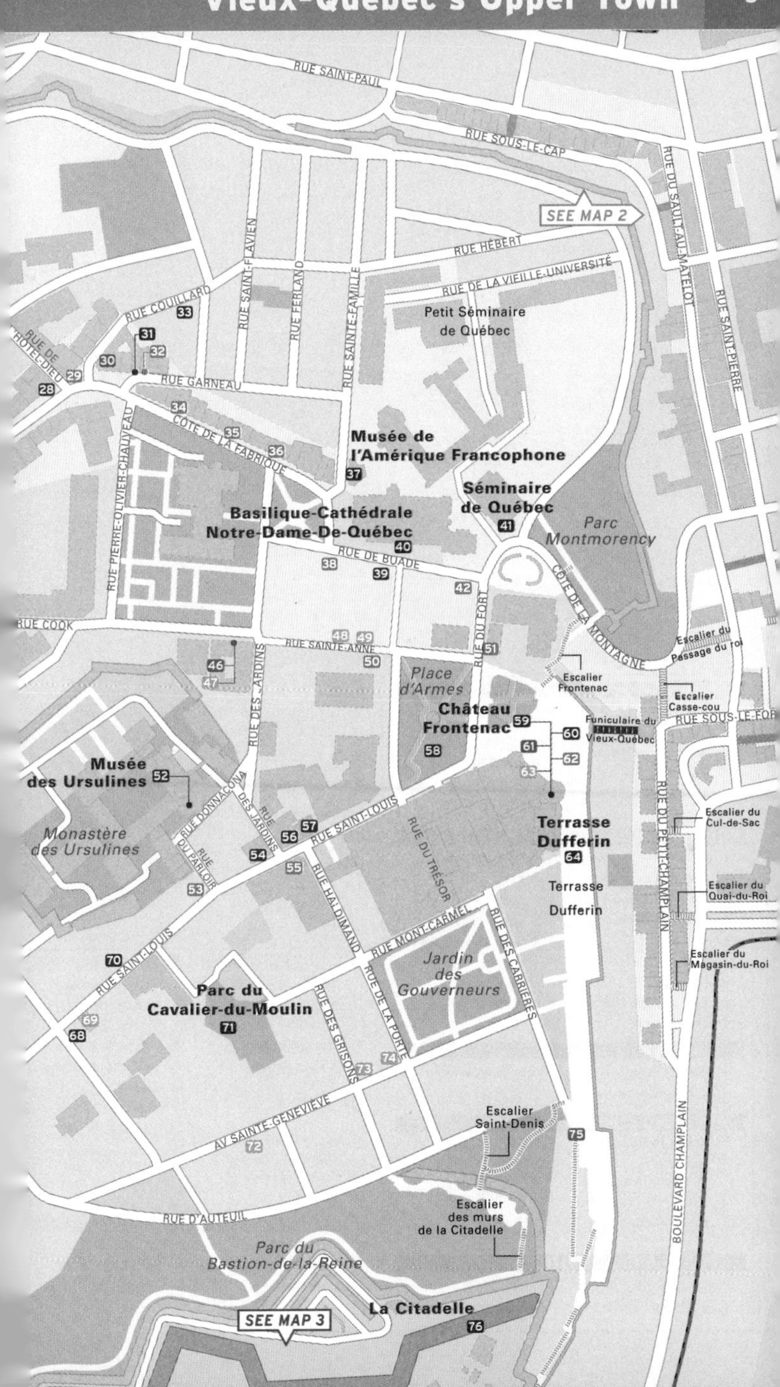
Rue Saint-Paul
Rue Sous-le-Cap
SEE MAP 2
Rue du Sault-au-Matelot
Rue Hébert
Rue de la Vieille-Université
Rue Saint-Flavien
Rue Ferland
Rue Sainte-Famille
Petit Séminaire de Québec
Rue Saint-Pierre
Rue Couillard
Rue de l'Hôtel-Dieu
Rue Garneau
Côte de la Fabrique
Musée de l'Amérique Francophone
Séminaire de Québec
Parc Montmorency
Basilique-Cathédrale Notre-Dame-De-Québec
Rue Pierre-Olivier-Chauveau
Rue de Buade
Côte de la Montagne
Rue du Fort
Rue Cook
Rue Sainte-Anne
Escalier du Passage du roi
Escalier Frontenac
Escalier Casse-cou
Place d'Armes
Château Frontenac
Funiculaire du Vieux-Québec
Rue Sous-le-Fort
Rue des Jardins
Musée des Ursulines
Monastère des Ursulines
Rue Donnacona
Rue du Parloir
Rue Saint-Louis
Rue du Trésor
Terrasse Dufferin
Rue du Petit-Champlain
Escalier du Cul-de-Sac
Escalier du Quai-du-Roi
Rue Haldimand
Rue Mont-Carmel
Rue des Carrières
Jardin des Gouverneurs
Escalier du Magasin-du-Roi
Parc du Cavalier-du-Moulin
Rue des Grisons
Rue de la Porte
Av Sainte-Geneviève
Escalier Saint-Denis
Boulevard Champlain
Rue d'Auteuil
Escalier des murs de la Citadelle
Parc du Bastion-de-la-Reine
La Citadelle
SEE MAP 3
28 29 30 31 32 33 34 35 36 37 38 39 40 41 42 46 47 48 49 50 51 52 53 54 55 56 57 58 59 60 61 62 63 64 68 69 70 71 72 73 74 75 76

MAP 2

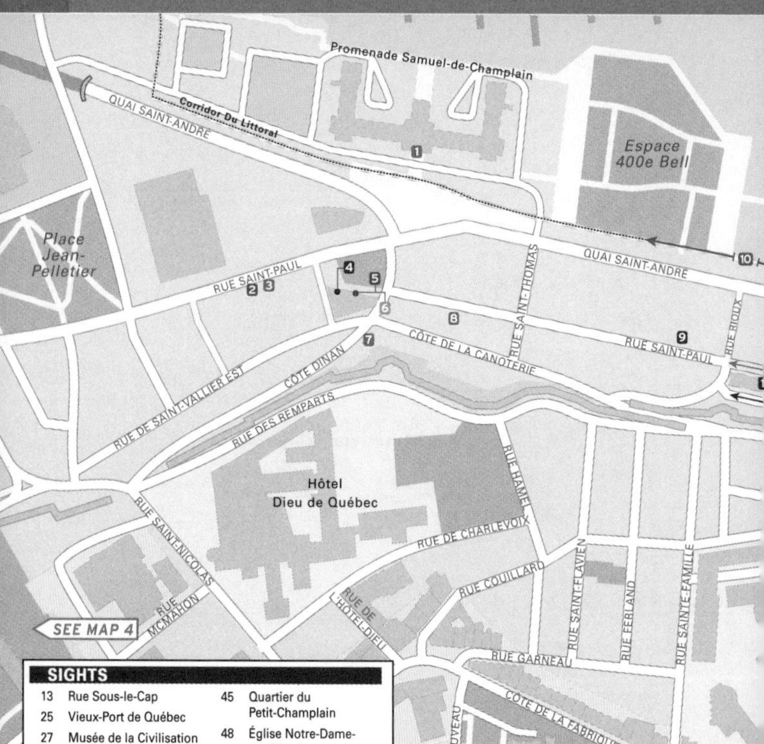

SIGHTS

13 Rue Sous-le-Cap
25 Vieux-Port de Québec
27 Musée de la Civilisation
37 Place Royale
40 La Fresque des Québécois
45 Quartier du Petit-Champlain
48 Église Notre-Dame-des-Victoires
54 Funiculaire du Vieux-Québec

RESTAURANTS

4 Légende
9 Chez Rioux et Pettigrew
11 Les Cafés du Soleil
14 Buffet de l'Antiquaire
16 Café St-Malo
17 SSS
18 L'Échaudé
19 Café Bistro du Cap
22 Laurie Raphaël
24 Café du Monde
30 Toast!
32 Chez Muffy
34 Restaurant l'Initiale
41 Café La Maison Smith
43 La Pizz
56 Lapin Sauté
57 Le Cochon Dingue

NIGHTLIFE

5 Taverne Belley
44 L'Oncle Antoine
50 Le Pape-Georges

ARTS AND CULTURE

3 Galerie Michel Guimont
7 Galerie Madeleine Lacerte
23 Musée Naval de Québec
26 La Caserne Dalhousie
35 Galeries d'art Beauchamp and Beauchamp
36 Galerie Perreault
61 Le Théâtre du Petit Champlain

SPORTS AND ACTIVITIES

2 Cyclo Services
10 Corridor du Littoral
38 Echo Sports
39 Croisières Aml

SHOPS

1 Marché du Vieux Port
8 Machin Chouette
12 Rue Saint-Paul
15 Antiquités Bolduc
42 Boutique des Métiers d'Art
46 Quartier du Petit-Champlain
47 Richard Robitaille Signature
49 Atelier la Pomme
51 Pot en Ciel
52 Boutique Bilodeau
53 La Fudgerie
55 Pauline Pelletier
58 Charlevoix Pure Laine
59 Le Capitaine d'Abord
60 Oclan
62 Madame Gigi Confiserie
63 Soierie Huo
64 La Petite Cabane à Sucre de Québec

HOTELS

6 Hôtel Belley
20 L'Hôtel Le Germain
21 Hôtel Port-Royal
28 Auberge Saint-Pierre
29 Hôtel 71
31 Hôtel Le Priori
33 Auberge Saint-Antoine

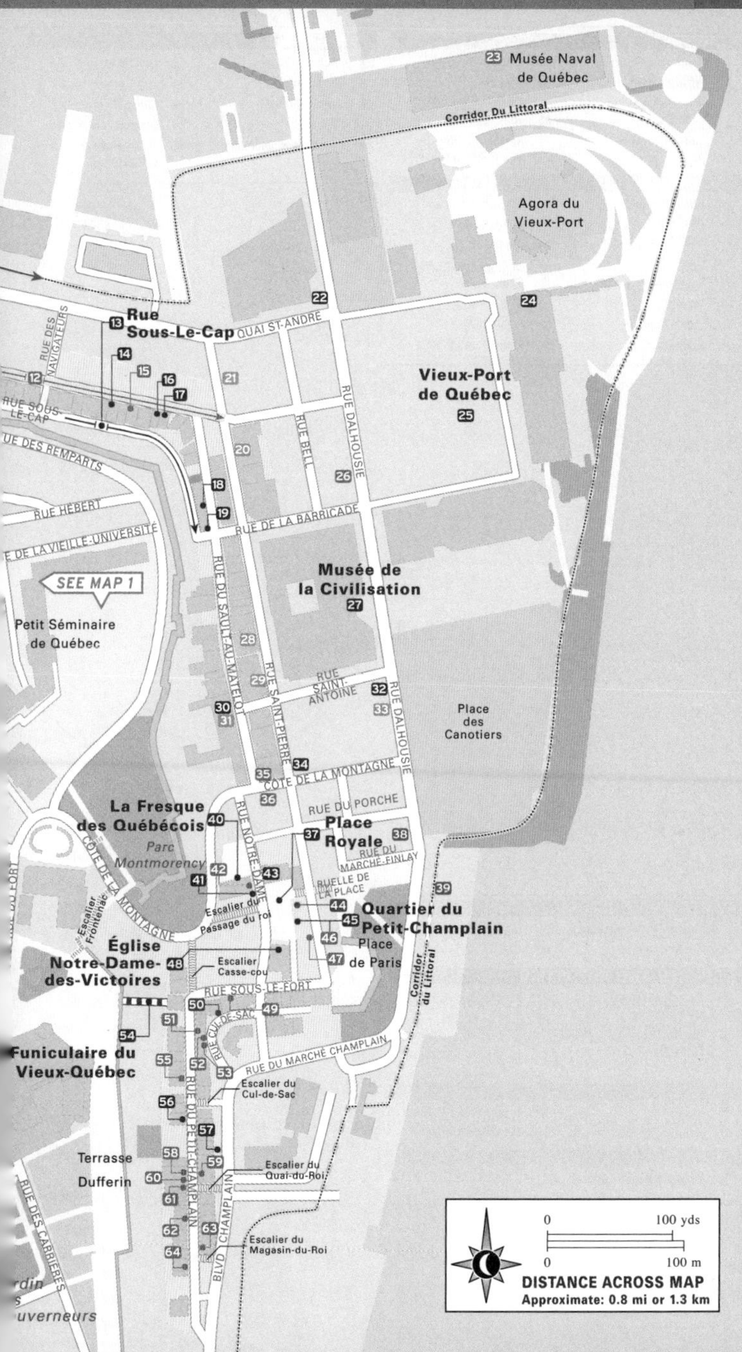
23 Musée Naval de Québec
Corridor Du Littoral
Agora du Vieux-Port
22
24
13 Rue Sous-Le-Cap
QUAI ST-ANDRE
RUE DES NAVIGATEURS
14
15
12
16
17
21
RUE SOUS-LE-CAP
Vieux-Port de Québec
25
RUE DES REMPARTS
20
RUE BELL
RUE DALHOUSIE
26
18
19
RUE HEBERT
RUE DE LA BARRICADE
RUE DE LA VIEILLE-UNIVERSITÉ
SEE MAP 1
Musée de la Civilisation
27
Petit Séminaire de Québec
RUE DU SAULT-AU-MATELOT
28
29
RUE SAINT-PIERRE
RUE SAINT-ANTOINE
32
33
Place des Canotiers
30
31
34
35
CÔTE DE LA MONTAGNE
36
RUE DU PORCHE
La Fresque des Québécois
40
RUE NOTRE-DAME
Place Royale
37
38
Parc Montmorency
42
RUE DU MARCHÉ-FINLAY
41
43
RUELLE DE LA PLACE
39
CÔTE DE LA MONTAGNE
Escalier Frontenac
Escalier du Passage du roi
44
45
Quartier du Petit-Champlain
46
Place de Paris
47
Église Notre-Dame-des-Victoires
48
Escalier Casse-cou
Corridor du Littoral
RUE SOUS-LE-FORT
50
49
51
RUE CUL-DE-SAC
54
Funiculaire du Vieux-Québec
55
52
53
RUE DU MARCHÉ CHAMPLAIN
RUE DU PETIT-CHAMPLAIN
Escalier du Cul-de-Sac
56
57
Terrasse Dufferin
58
59
60
Escalier du Quai-du-Roi
61
RUE DES CARRIÈRES
62
63
BLVD. CHAMPLAIN
64
Escalier du Magasin-du-Roi
0 100 yds
0 100 m
DISTANCE ACROSS MAP
Approximate: 0.8 mi or 1.3 km

SIGHTS

1 Fontaine de Tourny
2 Hôtel du Parlement
3 Observatoire de la Capitale
12 La Grande-Allée
14 Manège Militaire
34 Parc des Plaines d'Abraham
36 Tours Martellos
41 Musée National des Beaux-Arts du Québec

NIGHTLIFE

7 Société Cigare
8 Le Maurice
9 Le Dagobert
10 Brasserie Inox
11 Les Voûtes Napoléon
22 Le Jules et Jim
24 Pub Galway
26 Rideau Rouge
28 Blaxton Pub and Grill
45 Le Charlotte Ultra Lounge

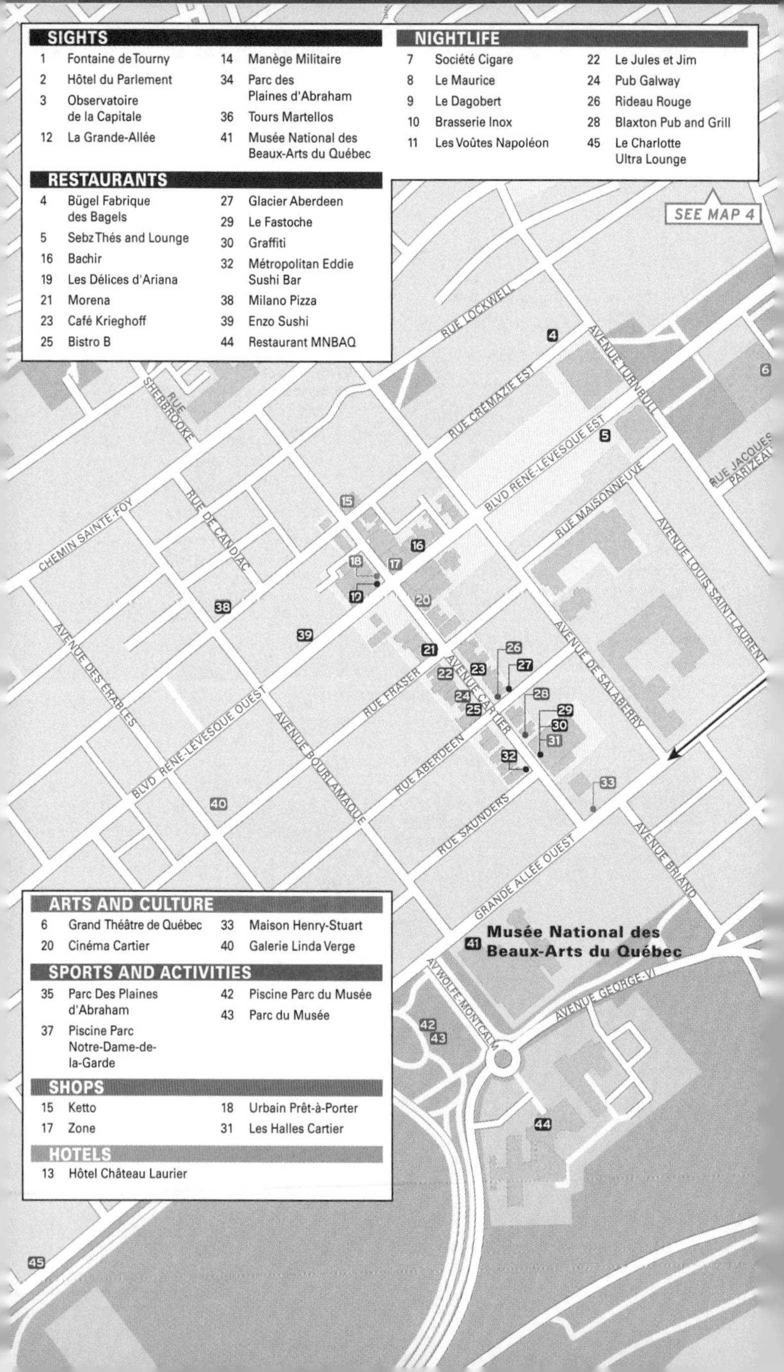

RESTAURANTS

4 Bügel Fabrique des Bagels
5 Sebz Thés and Lounge
16 Bachir
19 Les Délices d'Ariana
21 Morena
23 Café Krieghoff
25 Bistro B
27 Glacier Aberdeen
29 Le Fastoche
30 Graffiti
32 Métropolitan Eddie Sushi Bar
38 Milano Pizza
39 Enzo Sushi
44 Restaurant MNBAQ

SEE MAP 4

ARTS AND CULTURE

6 Grand Théâtre de Québec
20 Cinéma Cartier
33 Maison Henry-Stuart
40 Galerie Linda Verge

SPORTS AND ACTIVITIES

35 Parc Des Plaines d'Abraham
37 Piscine Parc Notre-Dame-de-la-Garde
42 Piscine Parc du Musée
43 Parc du Musée

SHOPS

15 Ketto
17 Zone
18 Urbain Prêt-à-Porter
31 Les Halles Cartier

HOTELS

13 Hôtel Château Laurier

Fontaine de Tourny
Hôtel du Parlement
Observatoire de la Capitale
La Grande-Allée
Manège Militaire
Parc de l'Amérique-Française
Parc des Champs-de-Bataille
Parc des Plaines d'Abraham
Tours Martellos
Parc Notre-Dame de la Garde
Escalier Cap-Blanc
SEE MAP 2
RUE SAINT-GABRIEL
RUE SAINT-PATRICK
RUE DU MARCHÉ-BERTHELOT
RUE RENÉ-JALBERT
RUE LOUIS-ALEXANDRE-TASCHEREAU
RUE DES PARLEMENTAIRES
AVENUE HONORÉ-MERCIER
CÔTE DE LA CITADELLE
RUE SCOTT
RUE DE LOMÉ
RUE BERTHELOT
RUE DE LA CHEVROTIÈRE
RUE DU BON-PASTEUR
RUE JACQUES-PARIZEAU
PLACE GEORGE-V OUEST
RUE DE L'AMÉRIQUE-FRANÇAISE
RUE DE CLAIRE-FONTAINE
GRANDE ALLÉE EST
AVENUE WILFRID-LAURIER
AVENUE GEORGE-VI
AVENUE ONTARIO
RUE CHAMPLAIN
BOULEVARD CHAMPLAIN
Corridor Du Littoral
0 100 yds
0 100 m
DISTANCE ACROSS MAP
Approximate: 1.1 mi or 1.8 km

SIGHTS

20 Rue Saint-Joseph
40 Jardin Saint-Roch
52 Église Saint-Jean-Baptiste
72 Rue Saint-Jean
73 St. Matthew Church and Cemetery

RESTAURANTS

4 L'Affaire est Ketchup
5 Tora-Ya Ramen
7 Le Clocher Penché
9 Le Cercle
11 Le Croquembouche
12 Nektar Caféologue
14 La Boîte à Pain
15 Le Bureau de Poste
18 Brûlerie Saint-Roch
26 Camellia Sinensis
32 Yuzu Sushi Bar
47 Chez Victor
50 Au Bonnet d'Âne
55 Buvette Scott
56 Crêperie Le Billig
59 Librairie St-Jean-Baptiste
60 Le Paingrüel
61 Le Moine Échanson
63 Sushi To Go
67 Le Hobbit
68 Tutto Gelato
74 Snack Bar St-Jean
78 Saveurs du Monde
79 Le Comptoir

NIGHTLIFE

1 La Barberie
6 Macfly
8 Le Deux 22
16 La Korrigane
30 Taverne Jos Dion
33 Mo
39 La Revanche
42 Mælstrøm Saint-Roch
43 La Cuisine
44 Les Salons d'Edgar
45 Scanner Bistro
54 Le Sacrilège
57 Fou-Bar
65 Bar Le St-Matthew
66 Pub Nelligan's
76 La Ninkasi
77 Le Drague

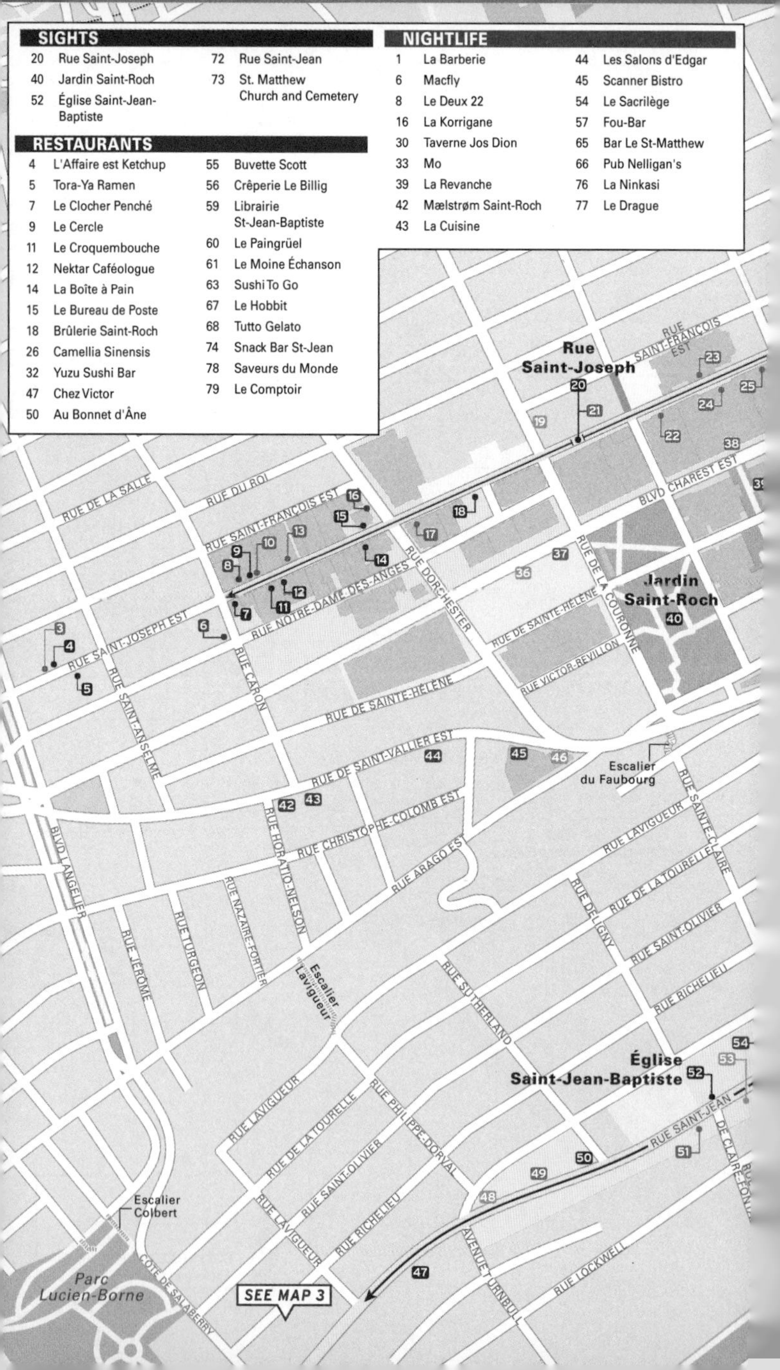

SEE MAP 3

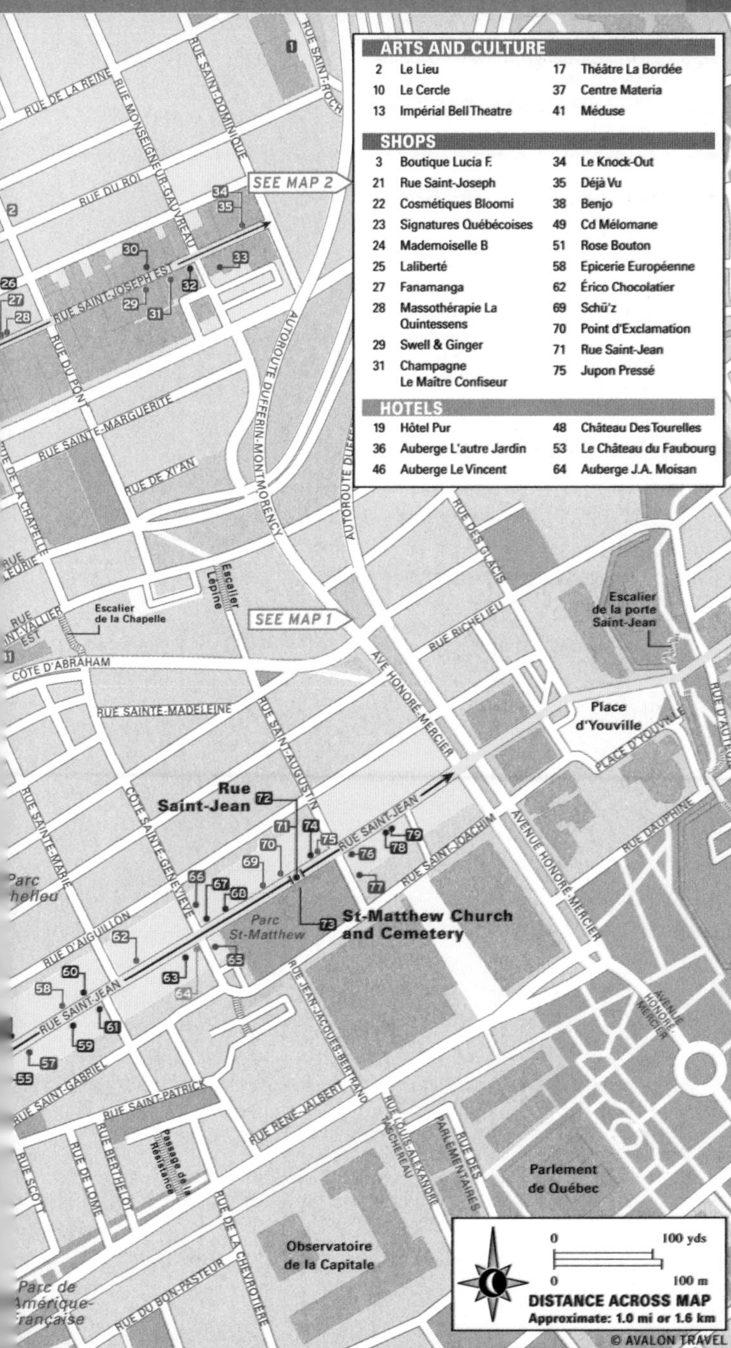
ARTS AND CULTURE
2 Le Lieu
10 Le Cercle
13 Impérial Bell Theatre
17 Théâtre La Bordée
37 Centre Materia
41 Méduse
SHOPS
3 Boutique Lucia F.
21 Rue Saint-Joseph
22 Cosmétiques Bloomi
23 Signatures Québécoises
24 Mademoiselle B
25 Laliberté
27 Fanamanga
28 Massothérapie La Quintessens
29 Swell & Ginger
31 Champagne Le Maître Confiseur
34 Le Knock-Out
35 Déjà Vu
38 Benjo
49 Cd Mélomane
51 Rose Bouton
58 Epicerie Européenne
62 Érico Chocolatier
69 Schü'z
70 Point d'Exclamation
71 Rue Saint-Jean
75 Jupon Pressé
HOTELS
19 Hôtel Pur
36 Auberge L'autre Jardin
46 Auberge Le Vincent
48 Château Des Tourelles
53 Le Château du Faubourg
64 Auberge J.A. Moisan
SEE MAP 2
SEE MAP 1
RUE DE LA REINE
RUE MONSEIGNEUR-GAUVREAU
RUE SAINT-DOMINIQUE
RUE SAINT-ROCH
RUE DU ROI
RUE SAINT-JOSEPH EST
RUE DU PONT
AUTOROUTE DUFFERIN-MONTMORENCY
RUE SAINTE-MARGUERITE
RUE DE XI'AN
RUE DES GLACIS
Escalier Lépine
Escalier de la Chapelle
CÔTE D'ABRAHAM
RUE RICHELIEU
Escalier de la porte Saint-Jean
AVE HONORÉ-MERCIER
RUE SAINTE-MADELEINE
Place d'Youville
PLACE D'YOUVILLE
RUE D'AUTEUIL
RUE SAINT-AUGUSTIN
Rue Saint-Jean
CÔTE SAINTE-GENEVIÈVE
RUE SAINT-JEAN
RUE SAINTE-MARIE
RUE SAINT-JOACHIM
AVENUE HONORÉ-MERCIER
RUE DAUPHINE
Parc St-Matthew
St-Matthew Church and Cemetery
RUE D'AIGUILLON
RUE JEAN-JACQUES-BERTHAND
RUE SAINT-GABRIEL
RUE SAINT-PATRICK
RUE RENÉ-JALBERT
RUE LOUIS-ALEXANDRE TASCHEREAU
RUE DES PARLEMENTAIRES
Passage de la Résistance
RUE SCOTT
RUE DE LOME
RUE BERTHELOT
RUE DE LA CHEVROTIÈRE
Parlement de Québec
Observatoire de la Capitale
RUE DU BON-PASTEUR
0 100 yds
0 100 m
DISTANCE ACROSS MAP
Approximate: 1.0 mi or 1.6 km
© AVALON TRAVEL

MAP 5

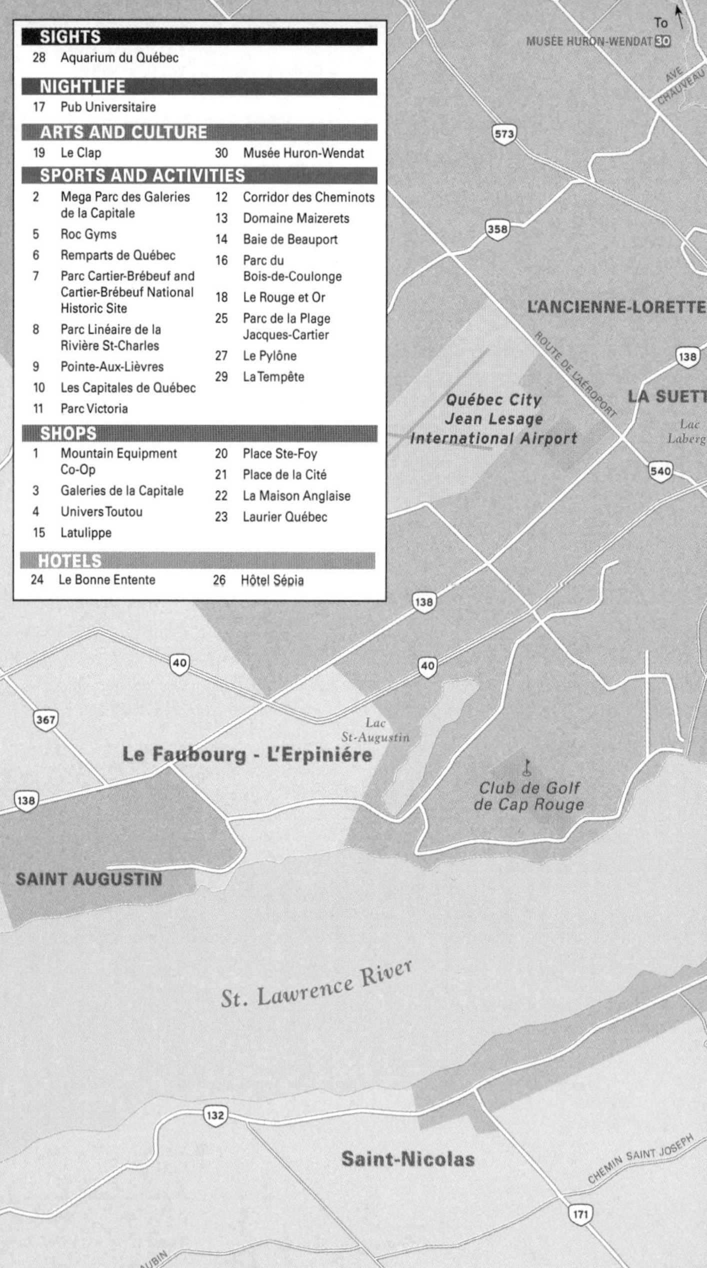
SIGHTS
28 Aquarium du Québec
NIGHTLIFE
17 Pub Universitaire
ARTS AND CULTURE
19 Le Clap
30 Musée Huron-Wendat
SPORTS AND ACTIVITIES
2 Mega Parc des Galeries de la Capitale
5 Roc Gyms
6 Remparts de Québec
7 Parc Cartier-Brébeuf and Cartier-Brébeuf National Historic Site
8 Parc Linéaire de la Rivière St-Charles
9 Pointe-Aux-Lièvres
10 Les Capitales de Québec
11 Parc Victoria
12 Corridor des Cheminots
13 Domaine Maizerets
14 Baie de Beauport
16 Parc du Bois-de-Coulonge
18 Le Rouge et Or
25 Parc de la Plage Jacques-Cartier
27 Le Pylône
29 La Tempête
SHOPS
1 Mountain Equipment Co-Op
3 Galeries de la Capitale
4 Univers Toutou
15 Latulippe
20 Place Ste-Foy
21 Place de la Cité
22 La Maison Anglaise
23 Laurier Québec
HOTELS
24 Le Bonne Entente
26 Hôtel Sépia
To
MUSÉE HURON-WENDAT 30
AVE CHAUVEAU
573
358
L'ANCIENNE-LORETTE
ROUTE DE L'AÉROPORT
138
Québec City Jean Lesage International Airport
LA SUETTE
Lac Laberge
540
138
40
40
367
Lac St-Augustin
Le Faubourg - L'Erpiniére
138
Club de Golf de Cap Rouge
SAINT AUGUSTIN
St. Lawrence River
132
Saint-Nicolas
CHEMIN SAINT JOSEPH
171
CHEMIN AUBIN
20

LEBOURGNEUF
LAIRET
VIEUX-LIMOILOU
VANIER
AUTOROUTE DUFFERIN MONTMORENCY
SAINT-ROCH
SAINT-JEAN-BAPTISTE
VIEUX-QUÉBEC
Lévis
Québec City
PARLIAMENT HILL
Battlefields Park
St. Lawrence River
SILLERY
SAINTE-FOY
PLACE-DU-VIEUZ-MOULIN
CHEMIN DES ÎLES
ST LOUIS
AQUARIUM DU QUÉBEC
SAINT-ROMUALD
SAINT-JEAN-CHRYSOSTOME
Place-Normandie
RUE DE L'EGLISE
Moulin-Gosselin
0 1.5 mi
0 1.5 km
DISTANCE ACROSS MAP
Approximate: 18.7 mi or 30 km

DISCOVER Québec City

The province of Québec is a place all its own: It's a country within a country with its own traditions, architecture, and language. Perched on a cliff above the St. Lawrence River, Québec City is the soul of the province—the first city to be founded in Canada, the seat of the Québec government, and the self-proclaimed "Capitale Nationale."

The historic landmarks and 17th-century architecture are captivating. But what will impress you the most is the infectious energy that the people exude. Temperatures drop below freezing in winter, but bars and restaurants are still packed, windows steaming with that unmistakable joie de vivre.

You can still walk the narrow, cobblestone streets of Vieux-Québec's Lower Town or pose next to one of the many cannons that line the city's walls. But a youthful revolution in the old working-class neighborhoods is bringing a daring new quality of art and culture to this historic city.

Clockwise from top left: Église Notre-Dame-des-Victoires; water fountain in front of the Hôtel de Ville; Bonhomme de Neige, the beloved mascot of Carnaval de Québec; the Terrasse Dufferin.

Planning Your Trip

Where to Go

Vieux-Québec's Upper Town

Les Fortifications surround Vieux-Québec's Upper Town, a 400-year-old neighborhood where the history of the winding streets and the original architecture remain safe from the ravages of time. These walls protect the **Château Frontenac,** Québec City's most famous sight, and the **Séminaire de Québec,** one of the city's oldest sights.

Vieux-Québec's Lower Town

The stone Normandy-style buildings and cobblestone streets of **Place Royale** mark the country's birthplace. History is unavoidable here, from the narrow lanes of **Quartier du Petit-Champlain** to the historic **Vieux-Port,** with its converted warehouses, antiques shops, and boutique hotels.

Parliament Hill and the Plains

Just outside the city's fortifications, you'll find the **Parc des Plaines d'Abraham,** the site of France's historic defeat by the British. The seat of the provincial government is to its north, housed in **Hôtel du Parlement.** Running alongside the government building are the nightclubs and bars of **La Grande-Allée,** the city's nightlife destination. Also in the Plains of Abraham is **Musée National des Beaux-Arts du Québec,** which holds the largest existing collection of Québec art.

view of Vieux-Québec's Lower Town

the Hôtel du Parlement

Saint-Jean-Baptiste and Saint-Roch

Once working-class neighborhoods, Saint-Jean-Baptiste and Saint-Roch are now **trendy, bohemian neighborhoods,** home to the city's coolest kids, and the area where you'll find the best bars, browse independent boutiques, and catch the latest bands. It's also a major **arts hub,** and the contemporary arts complex **Méduse** is located here.

Greater Québec City

In the areas surrounding the center of the city, find kid-friendly destinations like the **Aquarium du Québec** and the beautiful, sprawling gardens of **Parc du Bois-de-Coulonge.** The slopes of **Mont-Sainte-Anne** are fun for the whole family.

Excursions

Less than a half-hour drive from the city, you'll find **Chute Montmorency,** an impressive natural wonder, and the picturesque towns of **Île d'Orléans** and **Côte-de-Beaupré** (home of the massive Basilique Sainte-Anne-de-Beaupré). An hour north, the **Charlevoix** region has some of the most spectacular scenery in the region.

Know Before You Go

When to Go

Though **summer** is the busiest time to visit, it's also the best time to explore the city's neighborhoods, and you'll get to experience fun summer events like the Festival d'Été du Québec.

It's no surprise that prices drop considerably **October-April,** so if you can handle a bit of cold, your pocketbook will thank you. Québec City **winters** can be particularly freezing, but **December-March** is an ideal time to visit if you love skiing or other winter recreational activities. October is especially pretty thanks to the changing fall foliage, and even February has a couple of bright spots with the Carnaval de Québec's unadulterated celebration of snow.

Passports and Visas

All visitors must have a **valid passport** or other accepted secure documents to enter the country; even those entering from the United States by road or train must have these documents.

Citizens of the United States, Australia, New Zealand, Israel, Japan, and most Western European countries don't need visas to enter Canada for stays up to 180 days. U.S. permanent residents are also exempt.

Nationals from South Africa, China, and about 150 other countries must apply for a **temporary resident visa** (TRV) in their home country. Full details can be found at **Citizen and Immigration Canada. Single-entry visitor visas** are valid for six months and cost $100, while **multiple-entry visas** last for up to 10 years, as long as a single stay doesn't last for longer than six months, and cost $100. A separate visa is required if you intend to work in Canada.

Transportation

If you're arriving by **air,** direct flights are available to Québec City's **Aéroport International Jean-Lesage de Québec,** which is about 15 kilometers from downtown. The best way to get to downtown is by taxi; a public bus connects downtown with the airport, but it runs during the early morning and late afternoon only.

If you're coming by **train** you'll arrive at Québec City's **Gare du Palais** near the Vieux-Port. Those arriving by **bus** in Québec City will also arrive at the Gare du Palais.

Québec City's **transit system** is limited to buses, but they are fast and efficient in getting you up those steep hills. **Taxis** are useful when the winter hits, though they can be hard to flag down, depending on the area. Although **driving** the city streets is straightforward enough, if you're not used to ice and snow, it's better to leave it to the pros.

The Best of Québec City

Four days is the perfect length of time to visit Québec City, allowing you to dedicate enough time to experience the city's historic center with a few side trips.

Day 1

Drop off your luggage at your hotel in Vieux-Québec's Upper Town, then head directly to **Café-Boulangerie Paillard** for some fresh croissants. Browse the shops and historical buildings on **Côte de la Fabrique** until it brings you to **Terrasse Dufferin** in the shadow of **Château Frontenac.** Snack on a beaver tail pastry as you stroll the promenade and look out over the St. Lawrence, then head into the château for a guided tour.

Tour the historic **Citadelle** and then wander through the winding streets and alleys of **Upper Town.**

For dinner, take your pick of the restaurants along **rue St-Louis** or splurge at **Le Champlain.** After dinner, walk along **Les Fortifications** and finish the night at a *boîte à chansons,* such as **Le Pape-Georges,** or with a nightcap at the cozy **Bar Ste-Angèle.**

Day 2

After breakfast at **Crêperie Le Billig** take **L'Escalier Casse-Cou** or ride the **Funiculaire du Vieux-Québec** down to one of the oldest streets in North America, **rue du Petit-Champlain.** Browse the independent boutiques and follow the cobblestone lanes, which will eventually lead you to **Place Royale.** Take a peek at **La Fresque des Québécois** and see if you can point out the famous characters. Whether you fail the test or not, head to the

L'Escalier Casse-Cou, or the Breakneck Stairs

Château Frontenac viewed from Lower Town

Get Outside

No matter where you are in the province or how low the temperature drops, you're never far from serious outdoor fun.

- **Baie de Beauport,** just outside of the city, is a great place to canoe, kayak, sail, or play beach volleyball.
- **Parc des Plaines d'Abraham** is the place in the city to run, walk, bike, or even swim. Come winter you can cross-country ski, ice skate, or snowshoe.
- A 20-minute drive out of the city will bring you to the bird-watching and hiking heaven that is **Cap-Tourmente.**
- **Corridor du Littoral** follows the coast of the river and is ideal for cycling day trips.
- **Domaine Maizerets** is great for biking, skating, cross-country skiing, snowshoeing, and tobogganing.
- Some of the best skiing in the country is just an hour's drive away at **Le Massif.**
- Ski station **Mont-Sainte-Anne** is busiest throughout winter, but in summer, the area offers camping and mountain-biking trails.
- **Parc de la Plage Jacques-Cartier,** just outside of the city, offers picnicking spots and 2.5 kilometers of hiking trails.
- **Parc du Bois-de-Coulonge,** the residence of lieutenant-governors 1870-1966, is a sprawling park, easily accessible from downtown. It offers hiking, self-guided tours, beautiful gardens, and impressive river views.
- **Parc Linéaire de la Rivière Saint-Charles,** with 32 kilometers of trails to choose from, offers opportunities for biking, rollerblading, snowshoeing, cross-country skiing, and ice-skating.

Parc du Bois-de-Coulonge

Musée de la Civilisation and brush up on your history. If the weather is nice, head up the external stairs of the museum and take a quiet moment to relax on the rooftop *terrasse.*

After visiting the museum, head west along **rue St-Paul** to browse antiques stores. Or skip the stores and take the well-hidden **rue Sous-le-Cap** until it brings you to **Galerie Madeleine Lacerte.** Check out the latest exhibit and then cross the street for a drink at **Taverne Belley** and watch the locals playing petanque.

On your way to **Saint-Roch,** stop to admire the graffiti murals on the highway overpass, then head for a bistro dinner at **L'Affaire Est Ketchup.** Cap the night off with a show at **Le Cercle.**

Day 3

Have a hearty breakfast at **Le Petit Coin Latin,** then head to the **Fontaine de Tourny** and take a trip around the statues at the **Hôtel du Parlement.** Stroll the rolling hills of the **Parc des Plaines d'Abraham** and make a stop at the **Tours Martello.** Continue through the park all the way to the **Musée National des Beaux-Arts du Québec.** After seeing the latest exhibit, grab lunch at **Morena** on avenue Cartier.

Follow Cartier south, down the sloping hill, and take a right on **rue St-Jean,** where you can spend the rest of the afternoon popping in and out of stores and drinking coffee at the many cafés. Don't miss **J.A. Moisan,** the oldest grocery store in North America, or the quiet shade of **St. Matthew's Church and Cemetery.**

While you've got the European vibe going, why not continue with a French wine and regional cuisine at **Le Moine Échanson.** After your meal, head over to **La Grande-Allée** for a taste of sophisticated nightlife at **Le Charlotte Ultra Lounge.**

Day 4

Head down to **Cyclo Services** and rent bikes for the day. Pack your bags with sandwiches, goodies, and perhaps a bottle of wine from the **Marché du Vieux-Port** and then take the **Corridor du Littoral,** heading northeast 12 kilometers to the impressive **Chute Montmorency.**

Leave your bike and follow the path closest to the falls and cool off in the mist. Climb the stairs to the top for a view of the falls and mythic

Chute Montmorency as seen from the suspension bridge over the falls

Île d'Orléans. After you've taken in the view, go for lunch on-site at **La Terrasse du Manoir,** then get back on your bike and return to the city.

Ride about nine kilometers southwest and make a stop at the historical **Domaine Maizerets** park. Unwrap your picnic dinner and enjoy it among the ancient trees and lily-pad ponds. Then, get back on your bike and ride another three kilometers back to the city. Once there, leave the bikes at the rental place and head for a late-night stroll around the Vieux-Port. Finally, treat yourself to a pastry or gelato at a shop in Lower Town—you've earned it.

Head back to your hotel for a good night's rest before leaving the next morning.

Romantic Weekend Getaway

For a short, romantic getaway, Québec City is considered one of the most romantic cities in North America. The winding cobblestone streets, classic New France architecture, and overall charming ambience have a tendency to bring out the amorous side in visitors. But nothing seems forced about it—instead, it carries its romantic status quite naturally.

Day 1

Check into your suite at the plush **Auberge Saint-Antoine** and then go exploring along the cobblestone streets of **Quartier du Petit-Champlain.** Stop for a coffee or a cool drink on the corner terrace of **Lapin Sauté** and be charmed by the traditional music of street performers. Head to **Place Royale** and check out the small but beautiful chapel in **Église Notre-Dame-des-Victoires.**

view from the Lapin Sauté patio

Winter Pursuits and Cold Comforts

Life in Québec City completely changes once winter hits. And though it might seem like the perfect season to hibernate, the mounting snow is no excuse to stay indoors. Whether you're in the city or the country, there's a variety of things to do when the mercury drops.

- Drive an hour north to **Le Massif,** the highest ski mountain in the province. The ski runs offer 49 different trails and have the most breathtaking views of the St. Lawrence River.
- Bundle up and head to **Château Frontenac** for some serious winter sledding down the **Glissades de la Terrasse Dufferin.**
- The sweet treat known as ***tire sur la neige*** (maple syrup frozen on snow) can be found at just about every corner come winter.
- A typical après-ski meal of **raclette** is the perfect end-of-the-day fare. It can be procured in the cozy confines of restaurant **Le Petit Coin Latin.**

Glissades de la Terrasse Dufferin

- **Carnaval de Québec,** which takes place between the end of January and early February, is two weeks of outdoor fun, from snow sculpture competitions and outdoor dance parties to dog-sled races and canoe races over the icy St. Lawrence River.

Browse antiques and galleries on **rue St-Pierre** and **rue St-Paul.** Stroll among the boats and quays of the **Vieux-Port,** then head to Quai Chouinard and board the Croisières AML boat ***Louis Jolliet*** for one of their many cruises—ranging from a 1.5-hour sightseeing cruise to a four-hour, five-course meal cruise featuring fireworks.

From the river, enjoy views of **Chute Montmorency, Île d'Orléans,** and the city, perched on Cap Diamant. If you didn't opt for a dinner cruise, toast to your good health with some bubbles at the on-board bar.

Day 2

Breakfast at **Chez Muffy** and then take the **Funiculaire du Vieux-Québec** to **Terrasse Dufferin.** Snap the requisite shots of **Château Frontenac** before taking the stairs at the far end to the **Parc des Plaines d'Abraham.** Stroll through the park to the **Musée National des Beaux-Arts du**

1608 Wine & Cheese Bar in the Fairmont Le Château Frontenac

Québec. After browsing the largest existing collection of Québec art, pick up some gourmet treats at **Les Halles Cartier,** then grab a cab to **Parc du Bois-de-Coulonge.** Picnic overlooking the St. Lawrence River, then wander the grounds, and don't miss the arboretum close to the shore.

Hail a cab back to Upper Town and shop the independent boutiques along **rue St-Jean.** Freshen up back at the hotel and cab it to your reservation in the glass dining room at **Le Saint-Amour.** After dinner, take a moonlight walk through the streets of Upper Town, stopping to admire the view at the **Parc du Cavalier-du-Moulin.** Then grab a cozy nook at the Fairmont Le Château Frontenac's **1608 Wine & Cheese Bar** for a nightcap.

Day 3

Rise early and drive to the base of the **Chute Montmorency,** about 20 minutes outside of Québec City, where you'll board the **Train de Charlevoix** for a leisurely trip upriver. Take in the stunning views of the **Charlevoix** region and the St. Lawrence from this luxury locomotive. Disembark at **Baie-Saint-Paul,** check out the modern and ecofriendly hotel **Le Germain Charlevoix Hotel & Spa** before exploring the town's cultural heritage at the many galleries and artisanal shops. If all that walking makes you thirsty, grab a local microbrew at **Le Saint-Pub.**

Hop back on the train, heading 40 minutes farther north to the majestic **Fairmont Le Manoir Richelieu** in **La Malbaie** for an overnight stay. Located on the banks of the river, it's one of the prettiest spots in the region and a perfect place to kick back for the night. When you're settled in your room, relax next to the outdoor pool and get a massage at the in-house spa.

In the evening have dinner at **Vices Versa,** and get a taste of the local cuisine.

Old Québec Walking Tour

- **Total distance:** 3.5 kilometers (2.2 miles)

- **Walking time:** 55 minutes

This walk is designed to give you an introduction to three of Québec City's neighborhoods: Upper Town (Haute-Ville), Parliament Hill and the Plains, and Lower Town (Basse-Ville). Québec City is inescapably hilly, and this walk includes hills, slopes, and steps. If you have minor mobility issues, it would be a good idea to set aside more time for the walk. Visitors with more significant mobility issues should cut the first section of the walk and begin, instead, at La Citadelle.

Old Québec Walking Tour

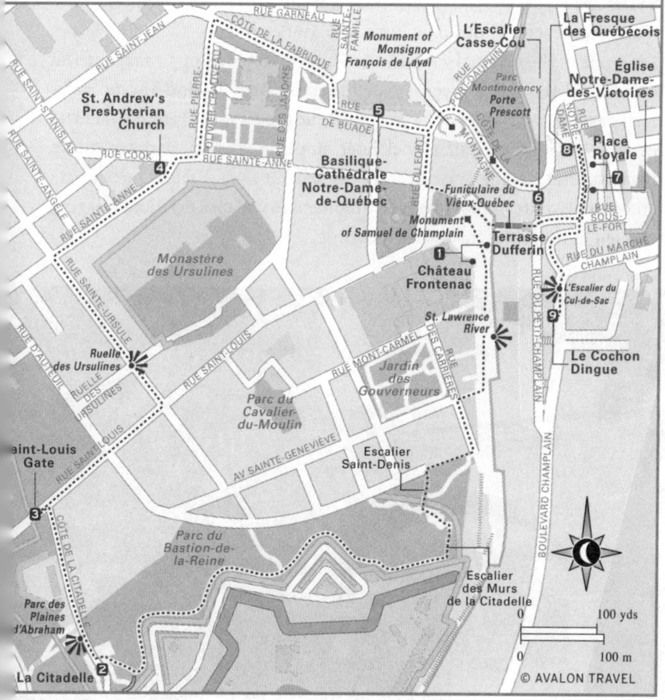

Stop 1

Start at the **monument of Samuel de Champlain,** who founded Québec, on **Terrasse Dufferin.** In front of Champlain, you'll get a great view of the **St. Lawrence River.** To your right, you'll see the **Château Frontenac.** Walk south along the boardwalk for about 220 meters, keeping the St. Lawrence on your left. At your feet, you'll notice skylights peeking down at the relics of Vieux-Québec's barricades.

Stop 2

Walk to the end of the boardwalk and take the stairs going up. There's a brilliant view over the St. Lawrence as well as Upper Vieux-Québec and Lower Vieux-Québec here. You've reached the east end of **La Citadelle,** a 300-year-old star-shaped fortification that is still an active military base. Zigzag southwest along the trail at the edge of the Citadelle until you reach a small access road, Côte de la Citadelle. Here, you can enter the Citadelle to take a guided tour if time allows. Look southwest—you've reached the edge of the **Parc des Plaines d'Abraham,** site of a historic battle between the French and British in 1759—before continuing 225 meters down Côte de la Citadelle until you reach rue St-Louis.

Stop 3

When you reach rue St-Louis, turn left. You've reached the **Saint-Louis Gate,** one of the original gates in **Les Fortifications.** Stop to snap a selfie with one of the wall's green-capped turrets. Turn around and proceed northeast for two blocks until you reach rue Ste-Ursule. Hang a left at rue Ste-Ursule and, then, half a block later, stop and take a peek down **ruelle des Ursulines,** an alleyway—it'll appear on your right. Vieux-Québec's architecture is quite impressive; take a moment to collapse time and imagine yourself in the age of the town's founding.

Saint-Louis Gate

Stop 4

Continue following rue Ste-Ursule to rue Ste-Anne. Take a right. Walk one block until you reach a T junction with rue Cooke. On your left, you'll see **St. Andrew's Presbyterian Church** (built in 1810). St. Andrew's, the site of the oldest English-speaking congregation in Canada, is also home to an impressive organ, 19th-century stained-glass windows, and a moderately quirky layout: Its pews surround the pulpit in a semi-circular formation. This church's original congregants were military men, mostly from the 78th Fraser Highlanders, who fought, most famously, at the Battle of the Plains of Abraham.

Stop 5

Turn right at the T junction and take an immediate left onto rue Pierre Olivier Chavreau. Walk one block, and then take Côte de la Fabrique right. Take Côte de la Fabrique one block until it loops around and meets rue de Buade (you'll pass rue des Jardins on your right). Turn left at rue de Buade and walk 20 meters: look to your left and you'll see the **Basilique-Cathédrale Notre-Dame-de-Québec** (1647, 1759, 1922) on your left. This church features a number of build dates as it was bombarded and torched in 1759 during the British siege and burned down again in 1922. The seat of the Catholic church in Canada, this church is stunning and ornate and features three Casavantes organs, as well as a crypt where over 900 people are buried. Be sure to visit both the church and the museum.

Stop 6

At the end of the block, rue de Buade reaches a T junction with rue Porte Dauphin/rue du Fort. Take a left onto rue Porte Dauphin, passing the **monument of Monsignor François de Laval,** a statue commemorating the first Roman Catholic Bishop of Québec. Take an immediate right onto Côte de la Montagne. In 20 meters, cross Côte de la Montagne and enter **Parc Montmorency,** a small park and national historical site that is home to a handful of cannons, statues, and monuments. Walk 30 meters to the ramparts at the eastern edge of the park for another view of the river. Exit the park the way you entered and continue down Côte de la Montagne for about 100 meters. You'll pass under **Porte Prescott** (another one of the city's gates) before you reach a set of steep wooden stairs—**L'Escalier Casse-Cou**—on your right. This is one of the most iconic spots to take a picture of Québec City. Take L'Escalier Casse-Cou down to the Lower Town.

IF YOU HAVE MOBILITY ISSUES:

You can avoid L'Escalier Casse-Cou and take the funicular instead. When rue de Buade reaches a T junction with rue Porte Dauphin/rue du Fort, take a right onto rue du Fort instead of a left onto rue Porte Dauphin. Walk one block and head left to the **Funiculaire du Vieux-Québec,** 40 meters away.

Place Royale

Stop 7

At the bottom of L'Escalier Casse-Cou, turn left onto rue Sous-le-Fort, part of the **Quartier du Petit-Champlain,** one of the city's most picturesque neighborhoods. A block away, turn left onto rue Notre-Dame. On your right is **Église Notre-Dame-des-Victoires** (1687-1723). Follow along the side of the building to take a gander at its stained-glass windows, its front entrance, and the Place Royale. This church is quaint, small, and warm; if you're visiting in early January, be sure to join the congregation for the Feast of Sainte-Geneviève. Take a moment to enjoy, as well, the historic **Place Royale,** where Samuel de Champlain first founded l'Abitation de Québec in 1608.

Stop 8

Walk an additional 50 meters down Rue Notre-Dame to reach **La Fresque des Québécois,** a giant mural full of important historical city and provincial figures. Retrace your steps back down rue Notre-Dame one block past rue Sous-le-Fort and take a right onto rue du Cul-de-Sac. Follow the curve of rue du Cul-de-Sac 50 meters until you reach a T junction with boulevard Champlain. Take a right. Walk 15 meters until you reach a set of stairs, **L'Escalier du Cul-de-Sac,** on your right. Look upward (but don't climb!): You'll be looking up at the massive, imposing Château Frontenac, where you began your walk.

Stop 9

Continue an additional 20 meters down boulevard Champlain until you reach **Le Cochon Dingue** on your right. Open daily from morning to night, it's a great place to stop and have a meal (you can never go wrong with *steak frites*)—and a glass of wine.

Sights

Look for ★ to find recommended sights

Highlights

★ **Most Iconic Sight:** The most photographed hotel in the world, **Château Frontenac** has become an indelible image of Québec City (page 34).

★ **Best Views:** Stroll along the top of **Les Fortifications** for the most stunning views of the city from both within and outside of the historic walls (page 36).

★ **Best Museum:** Dedicated to the history of Québec, **Musée de la Civilisation** offers an in-depth look at Québécois culture (page 45).

★ **Most Historic Sight:** The site of the first settlement in Québec, **Place Royale** is the birthplace of both the French-Canadian nation and Canada itself (page 47).

★ **Most Picturesque Neighborhood:** Once home to Irish immigrants and dock workers, **Quartier du Petit-Champlain** has been revived and rejuvenated by a co-op of artists (page 48).

★ **Most Unusual City Street: Rue Sous-le-Cap** is a charming three-meter-wide street that runs along the cliff face and is lined with tiny old cottages (page 49).

★ **Best Collection of Québécois Art:** With a 19th-century prison incorporated into its design, the **Musée National des Beaux-Arts du Québec** beautifully mixes history and art (page 54).

★ **Most Patriotic Site:** The **Parc des Plaines d'Abraham** is the site of the historic 1759 battle between the French and British, an event that changed the course of North American history (page 56).

★ **Most Historical City Street:** Learn about the city's history in the older buildings that line **rue St-Jean** as you wander down what is now one of the busiest commercial streets in the city (page 59).

the majestic Château Frontenac

The only fortified city left in North America, Québec City is like no other place on the continent. Constructed on the top of Cap Diamant, a cliff that looks out over the St. Lawrence River (Fleuve St-Laurent in French), the city is defined by its natural hills and cliffs, though from afar it's not always easy to notice. Québec City is the cradle of Canadian society, where in 1608 the first settlers arrived and established a colony on the territory of the Abenaki, Haudenosaunee, Malécties, and Huron-Wendat First Nations. Led by Samuel de Champlain, the French built the first habitation on the site that's now called Place Royale. It was under French rule until 1759, when it fell to the British at the Battle of the Plains of Abraham, but this political feat did not alter the existing French-Canadian culture and way of life. Despite 100 years of British rule and the eventual founding of the Canadian Dominion, the city's ties to the early settlers remain remarkably intact. It's this lineage and incredible architectural heritage that give it its own unique (albeit European) feel.

Québec City is divided into two main areas, Haute-Ville (Upper Town) and Basse-Ville (Lower Town). They are easy to differentiate thanks to their geography. Upper Town constitutes the area on the top of the cliff, while Lower Town constitutes everything below it. In Upper Town you'll find Les Fortifications, the walled defenses that encircle Upper Town, and many of the biggest sights, including Château Frontenac and La Citadelle.

Directly below, between the cliff and the river, is Vieux-Québec's Basse-Ville (Old Québec's Lower Town). This is where the first European settlement was established, near Place Royale, and where historical areas like

Previous: Quartier du Petit-Champlain in Lower Town; Terrasse Dufferin and Château Frontenac.

the Vieux-Port (Old Port) and the Quartier du Petit-Champlain are situated. Getting from the lower to the upper part of the city isn't complicated, provided the winding, hilly streets aren't sheets of ice. Taking L'Escalier Casse-Cou (Breakneck Stairs) is the easiest way, but the funicular and the Métrobus system offer some good alternatives.

Though separated by a cliff, Vieux-Québec is quite small and dense, so it's easy to cover by foot. In fact the best way to get around the city, in winter or summer, is by walking. Expect to get quite a workout, though, thanks to the hilly geography. No matter where you are in the city, if you want to get down or up, there are likely stairs involved, or at the very least, a city bus. (Travelers with mobility issues may want to plan in advance—the funicular and accessible city buses should get you where you need to go.) Due to the density of the city, even peripheral areas like the Plains (just outside of the walls in Upper Town) and Saint-Roch (the city's coolest post code, located in Lower Town) are only a 15-minute walk from Vieux-Québec.

Of course, Québec is a vastly different city with a completely different landscape in winter than in summer. Many sites close during the winter or have truncated hours. What constitutes the different seasons, however, is a complicated matter. A good general rule of thumb is the following: Summer hours usually run from June 24, Saint-Jean-Baptiste Day and the province's national holiday, to Labor Day, the first Monday in September. Winter hours, meanwhile, could start as early as Labor Day or Canadian Thanksgiving (the second Monday of October) and run until May or June. Many of these dates fluctuate according to the weather, so make sure to double-check hours if there's a particular sight you want to visit.

There are so many interesting historical sites just about everywhere you turn in Québec City—even a stroll down Faubourg Saint-Jean-Baptiste is a lesson in the city's evolution—you'll find plenty to do, and see.

Vieux-Québec's Upper Town Map 1

BASILIQUE-CATHÉDRALE NOTRE-DAME-DE-QUÉBEC

On this site, high above the St. Lawrence River, explorer Samuel de Champlain built Québec's first church in 1647. Later, in 1664, the Basilique-Cathédrale Notre-Dame-de-Québec became the first parish church in North America. It was given the title of cathedral 10 years later, when the diocese of Québec was established with the arrival of Monsignor de Laval, the first bishop of New France.

Destroyed by fire during the English conquest in 1759, it was entirely reconstructed a few years later, only to be remodeled again in 1843, by Thomas Baillairgé. Inspired by Sainte-Geneviève in Paris, Baillairgé (whose father, François, designed the church's interior) gave it a neoclassical facade. That, too, had to be reconstructed when the church was once again ravaged by fire—arsonists used the fire to steal priceless paintings—in 1922.

Confession: Québec City's Love Affair with Churches

If you weren't convinced about the Catholic Church's involvement in the development of New France, you will be after a trip to Québec City. There are so many churches in the city that a single trip alone couldn't cover them all. Most are free and open to the public for both prayer and sightseeing.

- **Chalmers-Wesley United Church:** A neo-Gothic Protestant church, this one was completed in 1853 and was designed by architect John Wells. Its steeple is the tallest inside the walls of Old Québec at 164 feet above the sidewalk (78 rue Ste-Ursule).
- **Chapelle Bon-Pasteur:** Designed by Charles Baillairgé in 1868, the slanting roof hides an ornate baroque-style interior (1080 rue de la Chevrotière).
- **Église Saint-Dominique:** Run by Dominican monks, this church and former monastery boasts a stunning wood-beamed ceiling reminiscent of medieval architecture (175 La Grande-Allée).
- **Holy Trinity Anglican Cathedral:** Inspired by St-Martin-in-the-Fields in London, this was the first Anglican cathedral to be built outside of the British Isles (31 rue des Jardins).
- **Sanctuaire Notre-Dame-du-Sacré-Coeur:** Tucked back from the road, this slender, neo-Gothic church was built in 1910 by François-Xavier Berlinguet and is renowned for its stained-glass windows and marble plaques that line the walls (71 rue Ste-Ursule).
- **St. Andrew's Presbyterian Church:** This congregation had its start among the Scottish Fraser Highlanders that were part of Wolfe's Army in 1759 (106 rue Ste-Anne).

During this rebuilding period, however, the builders tried to stay as true as possible to the original building, working off of François Baillairgé's original 18th-century drawings for the interior. Despite having been rebuilt a number of times, the bell tower and portions of the walls are from the original structure.

Long and narrow, the interior is a soft buttery yellow with a high arched ceiling, lined with windows and intricate moldings. A stunning gold-plated baldaquin stands at the altar, and other items include paintings of the Virgin Mary that date back to the French regime, the bishop's original throne, and a chancel lamp that was a gift of Louis XIV.

Between 1654 and 1898, over 900 people were buried in the crypt below the church, including 20 bishops and four governors. It's also rumored that Samuel de Champlain himself is buried nearby; archaeologists have been searching for the grave for over 50 years. In 2014, when the church celebrated its 350th anniversary, a holy door was installed (the only one of its kind in North America, and one of eight across the world). This holy door will be open on Jubilee years. Guided tours of the crypt and basilica are available but must be reserved in advance, so call ahead.

MAP 1: 16 rue de Buade, 418/692-2533, www.notre-dame-de-quebec.org; 7am-4pm Mon.-Fri., 7am-6pm Sat., 8am-5pm Sun. Nov.-Apr.; 7am-7pm Mon.-Sat., 8am-7pm Sun. May-Oct.; free

★ CHÂTEAU FRONTENAC

Proudly holding the title of "most photographed hotel in the world," Château Frontenac, operated now as the Fairmont Le Château Frontenac, is one of the most stunning buildings in Québec. The fortress-like architecture and its location on the top of the Cap Diamant, a bluff overlooking the St. Lawrence, give it an especially majestic feel.

Built in 1893, it is part of a chain of "château style" hotels that were constructed across the country by the Canadian Pacific Railway. Since Québec was one of the North American ports before the long trip across the Atlantic, the hotel was designed to rival any European counterpart and grab the attention of travelers. The building's architect, Bruce Price, drew from both the Middle Ages and Renaissance and used elements like the turrets found on Scottish castles and the bastion towers of French châteaus.

Named after Louis de Buade de Frontenac, who was governor of New France twice between 1672 and 1698, the hotel sits on the site of what was once Château Saint-Louis, the official residence of the governor of New France and later home of the British governors. The ruins of the many incarnations of the residence lie just in front of the hotel.

It has been the temporary residence of everyone from Queen Elizabeth II to Charles Lindbergh, as well as the setting for Alfred Hitchcock's *I Confess,* but the hotel's proudest moment took place in 1943. It was the site of the Québec Conference of World War II, where U.S. president Franklin D. Roosevelt, British prime minister Winston Churchill, and Canadian prime minister William Lyon Mackenzie King discussed the eventual invasion of France.

MAP 1: 1 rue des Carrières, 418/692-1751, www.fairmont.com/frontenac-quebec; 24 hours daily; free

LA CITADELLE

The largest British fortress in North America, La Citadelle is also the largest defense on the continent to have never seen battle. Covering 2.3 square kilometers and perched on the edge of the cape at the highest point in the city, overlooking the St. Lawrence, this strategically placed defense is an imposing figure, standing out along the rolling plains and the copper roofs of Vieux-Québec.

Built under the direction of British officer Lieutenant-Colonel Elias Walker Durnford, the design is entirely French. Modeled in the style of military engineer Vauban, it is shaped like a four-pointed star and as such has no blind spots. Construction on the Citadelle started in 1820, took 30

A Tour of One's Own: Best Walking Tours

There's more than one way to see the city, but the best way to see it is on foot. Here are a few fun, kookier ways to get to know the town.

If you like to be spooked, **Ghost Tours of Québec** (418/692-9770, www.ghosttoursofquebec.com) is for you. Reservations are recommended for these nighttime tours that whisk participants down darkened streets while talking about the city's 400-year-old history and all the ghosts and hauntings that go with it. Guides will even take visitors into one of the most haunted buildings in the city, though taking a pass and staying outside is totally okay. Learn about the previous job experience needed to qualify for the job of executioner in the 1600s, or how the murder of an American in Québec could be the source of an unexplained haunting.

Founded in 2007, **Cicerone Tours** (418/977-8977, www.cicerone.ca) offers tours by guides who wear period costumes (including, often, fur hats) as they show you around their city. An hour-long guided tour of the Château Frontenac includes information about the site's history, historical figures, and architecture; a December-based Christmas magic tour offers a window on Québec's historical and current Christmas traditions, and takes you to the Christmas Market to sample local offerings. Their signature tour, clocking in at 2.5 hours, provides a mix of history and culture, with a dash of local food tasting to keep you going.

If you love the history but hate the gore (well, some of it anyway), **Les Tours Voir Québec** (866/694-2001, www.toursvoirquebec.com) hits up all the important sights on their Grand Tour. The architecture, the events, the history—it's all here, along with a few lesser-known sights. If you're not quite full yet, take a second helping and try their Food Tour, which looks at the influence of British, French, and indigenous cooking in the kitchen. Of course, a taste of local wine, beer, chocolate, cheeses, pastries, and crêpes will only give you a better idea of exactly how this whole mix has come together.

Fed up with walking? **Tours Ludovica** (418/655-5836, www.toursludovica.com) does the work while you sit back and relax. Guides ride around on bikes while visitors sit and enjoy the scenery, in a sort of mash-up between a rickshaw and a horse-drawn carriage. Going off map, Tours Ludovica offers tours of lesser-known areas like Saint-Roch, Saint-Sauveur, and Limoilou. A ride out to Saint-Sauveur lets visitors take in the historical architecture of a neighborhood that—had Samuel de Champlain's plans gone through—would have become a large city called Ludovica. You'll find many old seminaries and other church buildings as well as the Hôpital Général de Québec, the city's original hospital and the oldest building in the city. Up-and-coming Limoilou can also be explored by pedicab; let the guide lead you through the history of this emerging neighborhood before hopping out to grab a coffee at one of the sidewalk cafés.

years to complete, and incorporated two existing buildings from the French regime, the oldest of which is a battery dating back to 1750. The winding gate that is used as entrance into the Citadelle is also the only real gate remaining from the French regime, and is reminiscent of what all gates into the city were once like.

Though it never saw any action, the Citadelle continues to be the official residence of the Royal 22e Régiment, the only Francophone infantry regiment in the Canadian Forces Regular Force. The low stone barracks are a mix of English and French influences, with symmetric casement windows and doors and pitched tin roofs. A museum, completed in 2014, commemorates the regiment's 100th anniversary. Housed in a historic building on the site, the museum is dedicated to the regiment's distinguished military history. Starting with the early days and Québec's most important battles, the exhibits continue up to the modern day with the regiment's tour in Bosnia and other United Nations missions. One exhibit is dedicated to the war heroes of the 22e Régiment who fought in World Wars I and II, summarizing their duties, showing personal artifacts, and in one case showing a spy's various identity cards.

As early as the 1860s there was talk of tearing down the Citadelle, but Governor General Lord Dufferin refused, instead pointing to the fortifications' historical importance. Since that time, his residence became the official residence of the governor general of Canada. It is here too that Georges Vanier, the first French-Canadian governor general and a war hero, was laid to rest in a battery turned chapel.

Since it is still an active military residence, the only way to get inside the Citadelle is to take a tour. Both the regiment and city get equal tour time, and though there's a lot to see, the most interesting aspects, such as the barracks and doors that lead inside the walls, are off-limits.

MAP 1: 1 Côte de la Citadelle, 418/694-2815, www.lacitadelle.qc.ca; bilingual tours 10am-4pm daily Nov.-Apr., 9am-5pm daily May-Oct.; $16 adults, $14 seniors and students, $6 youth aged 11-17, children 10 and under free

★ LES FORTIFICATIONS

Québec is the only fortified city in North America, and its walls encircle the entirety of Upper Town, covering 4.6 kilometers, which you can walk for free. The fortifications offer some of the most stunning views of the city and environs and are a great place to hang out in the summer and have a picnic or take a break from sightseeing. One of the best places to start is at the **Saint-Louis Gate** on rue St-Louis, as it's here that you're mostly likely to recognize the ramparts. As you walk along the walls, every angle of the city can be explored, from the defenses of La Citadelle to the lookouts over the river. Lined with cannons and grass-covered in spots, the stone walls of Les Fortifications frame the city in a way that transports visitors back to the days when they were a practical defense against attacks. Along this part, surrounding the Citadelle, you'll find the best views.

Built in a classic urban style, the fortifications are characterized by the geometry of flanking and the adaptation of the walls to the city's topography, which sees the walls grow in height and depth at different parts. Though Québec was a bustling city by 1700, its defense system was inadequate, and the city was a maze of temporary and permanent structures. It wasn't until the siege of Louisbourg, a fort in Cape Breton off the coast of

Clockwise from top left: Basilique-Cathédrale Notre-Dame-de-Québec; Musée de l'Amérique Francophone; Saint-Louis Gate in Les Fortifications.

Nova Scotia, in 1745, that serious consideration was given to the state of the fortifications. It was Governor Beauharnois who, following Chaussegros de Léry's designs, authorized a new stretch of fortification that permanently closed the city to the open countryside.

In the late 19th century, citizens complained about the impracticality of the gates, complaining that they stopped circulation and were a nuisance—the gates would close at curfew, and, up until the British troops left, the ramparts were for military and pedestrian use only. Though Lord Dufferin, then governor general of Canada, understood their complaints, he also saw the historical importance of the fortifications—during the summer-long siege of Québec, it was these walls that kept the citizens from British invasion—and instead suggested the gates be dismantled and then rebuilt to make them wider.

The Interpretation Centre of Les Fortifications is by the Saint-Louis Gate, beneath the city's ramparts. It offers information about the history of the city's defenses as well as exhibits and guided tours, which depart from Terrasse Dufferin.

MAP 1: 2 rue d'Auteuil, 418/648-7016, www.pc.gc.ca/en/lhn-nhs/qc/fortifications; Interpretation Centre 10am-5pm daily late May-late June, 10am-6pm daily late June-early Sept., 10am-5pm daily early Sept-early Oct.; Interpretation Centre $4 adults, $3.50 seniors, $2 children; tours $9.80 adults, $7.30 seniors, $4.90 children

MUSÉE DE L'AMÉRIQUE FRANCOPHONE

Entering the modernized foyer of the museum, you're almost not prepared for the historic chapel that you enter shortly after. Full of green marble pillars, beautiful stained-glasses windows, golden busts of important members of Québec's history, and a 1753 organ, the chapel's most alluring feature is the baroque music that is played throughout the day.

After a bit of maze-like wandering—through the chapel, into an elevator, and across an outdoor walkway—you arrive at the building that houses the Musée de l'Amérique Francophone, an old building that once belonged to the Séminaire de Québec. The first exhibit on the ground floor looks at the history of the seminary itself, with artifacts like old keys, chalices, and furniture that once belonged to the seminary.

Moving on to the museum's permanent collection, visitors get a well-rounded view of the history and trajectory of the Francophone population, not just in Canada but within the whole of the continent. It retraces the roots of Francophone explorers and guides who helped explore the United States and found American cities like Detroit, Pittsburgh, Buffalo, and St. Louis.

The design of the exhibit is modern and easy to navigate, even in high season when there are more crowds. For the most part, however, it's rarely overcrowded and visitors can wander the exhibits at their leisure.

MAP 1: 2 Côte de la Fabrique, 418/692-2843, www.mcq.org; 10am-5pm Sat.-Sun. early Sept.-late Dec., 10am-5pm daily late-Dec.-early Jan. (closed Christmas Day), 10am-5pm Sat.-Sun. early Jan.-late June, 10am-5pm daily late June-early Sept.; $8 adults over 31, $5.50 adults 17-30, $2 youth 12-17, children under 12 free; guided group visits available for $4.50 pp

MUSÉE DES URSULINES

Founded in 1639 by Marie de l'Incarnation, an Ursuline nun, and Madame Marie-Madeline de Chauvigny de la Peltrie, a rich widow, the Couvent des Ursulines is among the oldest schools in North America. Girls still study at this institution, now joined by boys (though their education is segregated). The site now also boasts a museum and a chapel alongside the schoolrooms and courtyard playgrounds.

The first Ursuline nuns landed in Québec on August 1, 1639, and soon started teaching, though at the time the French-Canadian population was so small, the majority of their students were First Nations girls. Just outside of the convent's walls is the Musée des Ursulines de Québec, which tells the story of these pioneer women who were both teachers and students. Newly reopened and renovated, the new permanent collection, The Young Ladies' Academy, allows visitors into the heart of the boarding school and the daily lives of the nuns and pupils that passed through the convent's halls. Artifacts from the time of the French regime are also on view, including teaching materials, personal objects, and sacred artwork.

When French governor Montcalm died after the Battle of the Plains of Abraham, he was buried in the convent chapel by night so as not to arouse suspicion. For a long time his skull was part of the museum's permanent collection, to the delight of visiting schoolchildren.

Despite the simple, austere pews found in the small Ursuline chapel, it has some of the most beautiful sculpted wood in Québec. The carvings were created by master craftsman Pierre-Noël Levasseur between 1723 and 1739, and it was the Ursulines themselves who gilded the carvings, which now adorn the nave of the chapel. The tomb of founder Marie de l'Incarnation can also be found here. The chapel is open to the public from May to October, and entry is free.

MAP 1: 12 rue Donnacona, 418/694-0694, www.museedesursulines.com; 10am-5pm Tues.-Sun. May-Sept., 1pm-5pm Tues.-Sun. Oct.-Apr.; $10 adults, $8 seniors and students, $5 youth 13-17, children under 13 free

PARC DE L'ARTILLERIE

The position of the Parc de l'Artillerie, looking out over the west of the city and across the St. Charles River, has made it a strategic military site since the late 17th century. Four vastly different buildings trace the city's history from the French regime right up to the 1940s. Of the four buildings that make up the site, the Dauphine Redoubt is the most striking, with

Clockwise from top left: Séminaire de Québec; Musée des Ursulines; Parc de l'Artillerie.

massive white supports that plunge down the side of a hill. Built in 1712 and completed in 1748, it was army barracks both before and after the British conquest and eventually became the home of the superintendent. During the summer, characters in period costume bring the barracks to life with demonstrations and tours through the rooms, which have been decorated to reflect various periods in the building's evolution.

Kitty-corner to the Redoubt is the interpretation center, a former foundry used to make an arsenal for the Canadian military from the Boer War up to World Wars I and II, and even the Korean War. The site now holds a 200-year-old scale model of Québec. Constructed 1806-1808, by draftsman Jean-Baptiste Duberger and John By, a military engineer, it was sent to England in 1810 to convince the British government that the city needed new fortifications. Alongside uncovered ruins, there are artifacts that were found on and around the site, including toothbrushes, children's toys, and belt buckles.

MAP 1: 2 rue d'Auteuil, 418/648-7016, www.pc.gc.ca; 10am-5pm daily late May-late June, 10am-6pm daily late June-early Sept., 10am-5pm daily early Sept-early Oct.; $4 adults, $3.50 seniors, $2 children

PARC DU CAVALIER-DU-MOULIN

This tiny little park tucked away at the end of a quiet residential street is one of the city's best-kept secrets. Passing through the park's wrought-iron gates, visitors enter onto Mont-Carmel, the spot of an old windmill (*moulin* in French). Originally a military outpost, the 1,500-square-meter park was one of the few defenses constructed by the French military in the 17th century. This defensive outpost was then named "cavalier," a nod to its solitary position. In 1663, the windmill was erected here and included in the military fortification. By 1700, with the building of the first surrounding walls, *le cavalier du moulin* was no longer needed.

Nowadays the park acts as a window onto history, allowing visitors to imagine a city that once had nothing but fields beyond this hillock. It's adorned with a cannon to remind people of its past life as a military defense; the cannon juts out over the hill, directed at the houses and winding streets beyond.

MAP 1: Rue Mont-Carmel; 24 hours daily; free

PLACE D'ARMES

The history of Place d'Armes is the history of Québec. In this public square, safely behind the defenses, the military would perform their various parades and military inspections. When construction of the Citadelle was undertaken in 1820, however, the military moved and the regular parades went with it, moving instead to the Parc de l'Esplanade in front of the fortress and running alongside the city walls.

Though it lost its military importance, the square continued to be a popular meeting place, and in 1915 a monument was erected to the notion of faith. Dedicated to the Récollets, the first religious community to live

Sky High: Édifice Price

Completed in 1931, **Édifice Price** (65 rue Ste-Anne) is the only skyscraper in Vieux-Québec. Built as the headquarters for Price Brothers Limited, one of the biggest printing companies in Québec at the time, it was designed by Montréal firm Ross and Macdonald. Despite heavy criticism from the public, the government ignored accusations that it wasn't protecting Québec's historical area—two historical houses were demolished to make way for the new building—and gave the company a building permit anyhow.

the art deco Édifice Price

The 82-meter-tall, 18-floor art deco building is reminiscent of the Empire State Building in New York, though much smaller. The design uses setbacks to gradually taper the building's width. Unlike the Empire State Building, the roof is classical in design, with a château-style steepled copper roof that blends well with its surroundings. The interior includes bas-reliefs that depict the origins of the Price company, which was forced into bankruptcy during the Depression.

Since 2001, the 16th and 17th floors have become the official residence of the premier of Québec, and the two-floor apartment includes a 14-guest dining room, two bedrooms, and offices. Decorated to reflect the province's history, it boasts maple hardwood floors, traditional Québec-style furnishings, and paintings by local artists.

in New France, the monument today stands in the shadow of the Château Frontenac at the center of a bustling square surrounding by busy restaurants and cafés.

MAP 1: Between rue du Trésor and rue du Fort

SÉMINAIRE DE QUÉBEC

Established in 1663 by Monsignor François de Laval, the first bishop of New France, to train young men for the priesthood, this seminary was expanded five years later to include the Petit Séminaire, which, in a push to Gallicize the indigenous population, accepted both First Nations and French students to study at the Collège des Jésuites. It continued to be the training ground of future priests right up until the conquest, when its connection to the priesthood was somewhat lost. The studies instead began to focus on the liberal arts, and the school began accepting students who didn't want to become priests. By 1852 the college part of the Séminaire de Québec became the University of Laval. Today, it remains both a school and seminary, with Laval's school of architecture located on the site and priests who continue to live here and dedicate their lives to the church.

Laid out according to 17th-century principles, the *séminaire* has various wings, all of which center around interior courtyards (you can enter one through the Musée de l'Amérique Francophone). Though the time periods vary there is continuity in the architecture, with stone masonry covered with stucco, casement windows, steep roofs with dormers, and raised firewalls evident in all of the buildings. The bursar's wing in particular is interesting. Designed between 1678 and 1681 and restored in 1866 after a fire, its vaulted kitchen is still intact, along with the chapel of Monsignor Briand, who was bishop of Québec from 1766 to 1784.

Before—or after—you wander around the *séminaire*'s grounds, visit the Musée de l'Amérique Francophone to see religious relics and other items in the museum's Séminaire de Québec collection.

MAP 1: 1 rue des Remparts, 418/692-3981, www.seminairedequebec.org; free

TERRASSE DUFFERIN

Along the front of Château Frontenac, looking out over the St. Lawrence River and across to Lévis, is the wide boardwalk of Terrasse Dufferin. Created in 1879 by the governor general of Canada, Lord Dufferin, the 671-meter-long promenade was designed by Charles Baillairgé, the same designer behind the kiosks and street lamps that line the boardwalk.

It was during his summer stay at the Citadelle, now at the opposite end of the promenade, that Lord Dufferin conceived of the idea to build the boardwalk, a place for residents and visitors to take their daily stroll. The use of wooden planks gives the whole thing an air of summer, even in the middle of winter. Though he left his post in 1879, Dufferin himself inaugurated the project and put down the first stone.

Beneath the *terrasse* lie the ruins of the former Saint-Louis Fort and Château, which was destroyed by fire in 1834. Visitors are able to visit the excavation site thanks to a Parks Canada interpretation center cleverly hidden by the boardwalk. Only a few steps down and you're face-to-face with the foundations of the original building and some of the artifacts they uncovered here.

During the winter, a huge slide is built at the Citadelle end of the *terrasse* and children of all ages line up to take a super-fast ride down *les glissades* overlooking the frozen river.

MAP 1: Intersection of rue des Carrières and Place d'Armes

ÉGLISE NOTRE-DAME-DES-VICTOIRES

The oldest stone church in Québec, Église Notre-Dame-des-Victoires was built on Place Royale in 1688, on the site of l'Abitation, Québec's first building. In the basement of the church you can still see one of the building's walls, and archaeological digs have uncovered one of the building's original turrets in the church's facade. The king's storehouse also stood on this site, and this particular location attracted François de Laval, the bishop of New France. For years Laval requested a chapel be built on the site of the king's storehouse, an extension of Upper Town's Notre-Dame-de-Québec church, but it was his successor, Monsignor de Saint Vallier, who would see the work completed in 1723.

Designed by Claude Baillif, the church was originally named l'Enfant Jesus, but its name was changed twice. In 1690 the British admiral Phipps was defeated by Governor Frontenac, and the church was renamed Notre-Dame-de-la-Victoire. In 1711, the city was again saved when the fleet of Admiral Walker, on its way to attack Québec, was shipwrecked in the St. Lawrence. This time the name change was easy; they made it plural. Despite two failed attempts, the British would eventually destroy the church in 1759 during the siege of Québec. The subsequent reconstructions were meticulous and took place 1762-1766 under the eye of Jean Baillairgé.

The interior itself is rather austere, with a few pews and a tiny, circular staircase leading up to the organ. Designed by students of Thomas Baillairgé (Jean's grandson), it was constructed in 1854-1857 and features several paintings from the 17th, 18th, and 19th centuries. The oldest part of the church is the tabernacle; originally found in the Sainte-Geneviève Chapel, it dates from 1724. Unique to Québec, the frescos on either side of the main altar retrace the history of the church and city, and were done by local painter and decorator Jean-M. Tardivel. The most striking church accent, however, is the single ex-voto, a model of a vessel that arrived in 1664, transporting the Carignan Regiment and the Marquis de Tracy, which hangs suspended over the pews.

MAP 2: Place Royale, 32 rue Sous-le-Fort, 418/692-1650, www.notredamedequebec.org; midnight-7pm Wed.-Sat., 9:30am-7pm Sun.; tours May-Oct., reservations required mid-Oct.-Apr.; free

LA FRESQUE DES QUÉBÉCOIS

Reaching nearly three stories tall and at a size of 420 square meters, La Fresque des Québécois is the largest and most historical trompe l'oeil in the city. Unveiled in 1999, it took 12 artists to complete the immense mural that cleverly shows the city's history and its important figures. Sixteen important Québécois are featured in the painting, including historical figures like Jacques Cartier, Samuel de Champlain, and Lord Dufferin, as well as cultural icons like singer/songwriter Félix Leclerc and politician

Louis-Joseph Papineau. Also shown in the mural are typical Québécois buildings through whose windows the important figures peek. One of the gates figures prominently, as do the famous L'Escalier Casse-Cou (Breakneck Stairs) and the province's four seasons.

A popular tourist sight (it's fun to try to slip yourself in among the historical figures), it kicked off a trompe l'oeil craze around the city, and many buildings are now covered in historically clever murals.

MAP 2: Place Royale, on the west side of rue Notre-Dame, located between rue du Marché Finlay and rue du Porche

FUNICULAIRE DU VIEUX-QUÉBEC

The only funicular of its kind in North America, the Funiculaire du Vieux-Québec was built in 1879 and designed by William Griffith. Wood-covered and steam-powered, it operated six months a year as an alternative to horse and buggy, transporting passengers and merchandise from Lower Town to Upper Town. The arrival of electrical power in 1907 meant it could work year-round, which it did until 1945, when the wooden structure caught fire and was subsequently rebuilt with metal shelters. It lets passengers off and on at Terrasse Dufferin.

Transportation is still its main function, though today it transports more tourists than merchandise since it allows incomparable views of Lower Town, the port, and Lévis, across the water.

The entrance of the funicular is in a house, built in 1683 by Québec architect Baillif, that once belonged to one of the country's first European explorers, Louis Jolliet. Jolliet, along with Father Jacques Marquette, was the first European to explore and map the Mississippi River. Jolliet lived here until his death in 1700.

MAP 2: 16 rue du Petit-Champlain, 418/692-1132, www.funiculaire.ca; 7:30am-10:30pm daily Dec.-Mar., 7:30am-11pm daily Apr.-mid-June, 7:30am-11:30pm daily mid-June-early Sept., 7:30am-11pm daily early Sept.-Oct.; $3

★ MUSÉE DE LA CIVILISATION

In the heart of the port district, not far from the shores of the St. Lawrence and surrounded by historical buildings, the modern facade of the Museum of Civilization strikes out against its surroundings. Designed by Moshe Safdie, the architect behind Montréal's Habitat 67, the front of the museum is built into an incline, tucking the museum away and adding a touch of nature, with a glass roof and greenery sprouting from along the sides. Inaugurated in 1988, the museum is dedicated to the history, present, and future of Québec civilization, as well as that of cultures from around the world.

Inside, the harmony with the surroundings continues with a large open lobby, full of glass and light. The three-story building accommodates 10 exhibits simultaneously, three of which are permanent exhibits rooted in the region's history. The People of Québec...Then and Now is an overview of the history of this nation within a nation, from the first explorers to Expo

Clockwise from top left: Musée de la Civilisation; Funiculaire du Vieux-Québec; Place Royale.

Crossing the St. Lawrence: Québec-Lévis Ferry

One of the best views of the city is from across the river in the city of Lévis. Get there by hopping on the **Québec-Lévis Ferry** located right on the port (10 rue des Traversiers, 877/787-7483, www.traversiers.gouv.qc.ca; $3.55 adult, $3 senior, $2.40 child, $8.40 car). The views of the city are stunning, especially at night, and the 10-minute trip on the commuter ferry will give you a new appreciation for the city's geography. The ferry runs daily all year long, several times an hour 6:30am-6pm and hourly 6pm-2:30am.

67. It's a fun exhibition with bits of pop culture—like videos of iconic TV presenters and shows from the 1980s and 1990s—placed within context next to religious iconography, old tramway signs, sabers, and World War II ration boxes. Presented in conjunction with the National Film Board of Canada (the NFB), historic films, political speeches, and important cultural events are shown on film here.

With a focus on curiosity and the senses, the interactive, family-friendly Observe. More Than Meets the Eye exhibition employs trompe l'oeil, traps, and illusions to get kids and parents alike to rethink whether the old koan, "seeing is believing," is true.

Those wanting to learn more about Québec's First Nations will enjoy This Is Our Story, which looks at the 11 different tribes that inhabit the province and includes videos, artifacts—a birch canoe, a tepee, Inuit sculpture—as well as a look at the history and migration patterns of the particular tribes.

MAP 2: 85 rue Dalhousie, 418/643-2158, www.mcq.org; 10am-5pm daily mid-June-early Sept., 10am-5pm Tues.-Sun. early Sept.-mid-June; $16 adults over 30, $10 adults 18-30, $5 youth 12-17, children 11 and under free

★ PLACE ROYALE

For all intents and purposes this is the birthplace of Canada—or more specifically the birthplace of French-Canadian civilization in Canada. It's also probably the most picturesque spot in the city, aside from Château Frontenac.

It was here that Samuel de Champlain, founder of Québec, built l'Abitation, the first European settlement in Québec, and though the structure itself is long gone, slate stones mark where the building once stood. As early as 1623, the square started to take on a life of its own alongside the settlement's second habitation. A military parade ground, marketplace, and the surrounding houses burned to the ground during a fire that destroyed Lower Town in 1682. Place Royale got its name in 1686 when Intendant Jean Bochart de Champigny erected a bust of King Louis XIV in its center. As in all towns in France, it was the custom to have a square dedicated to royalty, but unlike in France, there was nothing ceremonious about the square or

Bunge du Canada

A number of imposing silos occupy the far end of Québec City's port. Known as the **Bunge of Canada** (300 rue Dalhousie), these grain silos have been in operation for more than 40 years, enabling Canadian and American shippers to store a massive amount of grain before sending it overseas. They are some of the few silos in the eastern region of the country and a reminder of the city's history as a bustling and crucial port. The Bunge du Canada remains an important part of the city's landscape and its economic strength.

its surroundings; in fact, the merchants complained that the bust took up valuable space, and so it was removed and placed at the intendant's house.

Damaged during the Seven Years' War, the square was gradually rebuilt, and by the 19th century the square was part of an urban complex that included warehouses, two markets, and a number of businesses. Up until the early 20th century many of the buildings went through major transformations; floors were added, roofs were flattened, storefront windows were built on the ground floor. It wasn't until an economic downturn in the 1960s forced the city to reconsider its purpose that the area was restored.

After restoring a few buildings (the Chevalier hotel, the Maison Fornel, and the Notre-Dame-des-Victoires church), the government decided it wanted to recreate the ambience of the early 17th century and went about completely renovating the buildings to closely resemble how they would have looked during the French regime. Following the detailed plans of the original structures, the buildings were rebuilt using Norman construction with firewalls, stone, and ladders on the roofs.

Grab a coffee at Café La Maison Smith (which has a patio on the square), do some people-watching, and imagine yourself transported back hundreds of years . . .

MAP 2: Corner of rue de la Place and rue Notre-Dame

★ QUARTIER DU PETIT-CHAMPLAIN

The charming restaurants, quaint boutiques, and tourist-packed cobblestone streets of this picturesque neighborhood often belie its rich and interesting history. The oldest street in the city, **rue du Petit-Champlain** in the 17th century was little more than a dirt path down which residents would walk to get their water. Over the next 200 years, the street would grow to become a bustling area full of houses and businesses of many working-class families and men who worked in the port.

In the mid-1800s, the area saw an influx of immigrants. The Irish Potato Famine saw the Irish fleeing the country in boatloads and consequently arriving in Québec, one of the first ports of call. Many of these immigrants stayed, settling on rue du Cul-de-Sac and la Petit rue Champlain, calling it instead Little Champlain Street. In time, the Francophones adopted the name as well, turning it into rue du Petit-Champlain. This was a poor, working-class neighborhood, and the reconstruction of the nearby Place Royale in the 1970s forced a change in Petit-Champlain as well. The low rent meant that many artists had moved into the area, and it was the artists who rejuvenated it, financing renovations themselves and doing much of their own work. Since none of the buildings were entirely destroyed, a walk through this quarter gives visitors a view of the city's architecture through the ages, with buildings from different eras lovingly preserved.

At one end of rue du Petit-Champlain you'll find **L'Escalier Casse-Cou,** a narrow, steep and picturesque set of steps that offer one popular way to get from Upper Town to Lower Town. First built in 1660, the steps are squished between two buildings and can get icy in winter. The unusual name (Breakneck Stairs) is rumored to come from American soldiers during their attempted invasion. At the other end of the street, you'll find La Fresque de Petit Champlain, which represents the life and history of the area, including the 1759 siege and the fires that came with it.

MAP 2: Between rue du Petit-Champlain and Place Royale

★ RUE SOUS-LE-CAP

La rue Sous-le-Cap, which means "street beneath the cape," is unlike any other street in the city and totally enchanting. Wedged between the cliff face and the backs of the houses that face rue St-Paul, it was the only road that pedestrians could use at the beginning of the 19th century to get from their homes in this section of Lower Town to the Côte du Palais, a winding street that would take them to Upper Town. What today are the backs of houses fronting on rue St-Paul used to be front entrances of homes along the waterfront, and during high tide, the roadway would be submerged under water.

The narrow street, which measures three meters across, was also at one time the city's red-light district, with brothels in regular operation. Characterized by the stairs and walkways crossing overhead for much of the length of the street, it's here that you'll be able to sneak a peek (and some photos) of tiny, slightly crooked houses and some of the prettiest private patios in the city.

MAP 2: Behind rue du Sault-au-Matelot, between rue de la Barricade and rue St-Paul

VIEUX-PORT DE QUÉBEC

At the base of Cap Diamant, where the waters of the St. Lawrence and St. Charles Rivers converge, the Vieux-Port de Québec (Old Port) is steeped in history. Lined with buildings that are both old and new, it maintains a connection to the past while looking to the future. The basins that once accommodated large cargo and passenger ships are now marinas docked with pleasure cruisers and sailboats, though the old locks of Louise Basin are still in use.

During its heyday in the 19th century, it was one of the world's five biggest ports, a hub of activity with commerce and transatlantic voyages. It was and still is a major contributor to the economic development of the

Top: the marina at the Vieux-Port de Québec. **Bottom:** L'Escalier du Cul-de-Sac, leading to the rue de Petit-Champlain.

region. Ships from here deal in commercial trade with over 60 countries, and the city is a popular cruise destination. On the very outskirts of Petit-Champlain, one of the areas that border the Vieux-Port, are some of the city's oldest defenses. Low walls, cannons, and a moat are the only remnants of what was once part of the Lower Town's fortifications. To celebrate the city's 400th anniversary in 2008, the waterfront was rejuvenated with bike paths that follow the water's edge and take cyclists right into the Old Port. Along the quays and among the docked boats, people stop for an ice cream or a cold drink in the summer and look back at the city that stands, perfectly lit, on the hill. In summer, check out **La Cour Arrière du Festibière** (418/802-8233, www.infofestibiere.com, 11am-11pm daily), where you can grab a beer and dip your feet into the wading pool on their popular *terrasse*.
MAP 2: East of rue Dalhousie, along the water; 24 hours daily; free

Parliament Hill and the Plains

Map 3

FONTAINE DE TOURNY

Fontaine de Tourny was a gift from La Maison Simons (one of the oldest department stores in the province) to Québec City for its 400th anniversary in 2008. It came to its place in front of the Parliament by a circuitous route. Created in France in 1854, it won an award at the Universal Exposition in Paris the following year before being installed, in 1857, in the heart of Bordeaux in the Allées de Tourny. By 1960, however, the city no longer wanted the fountain, which was in a state of near disrepair. It was dismantled and stored in the Château Larivière near Bordeaux before being sold to a Parisian antiques dealer at the beginning of the 21st century.

During a trip to Paris in 2003, Peter Simons, president of the department store, discovered it in a flea market and had it shipped to Québec for restoration. Measuring seven meters high and four meters wide, it's adorned with 43 jets and decorated with statues, by sculptor Mathurin Moreau, of one man and three women symbolizing water, which matches well with the history of the port city. Five other statues were made from the same mold and can be found in cities across Europe, including Geneva in Switzerland and Porto in Portugal.
MAP 3: Ave. Honoré Mercier between La Grande-Allée and blvd. René-Lévesque

LA GRANDE-ALLÉE

Dubbed the "Champs d'Elysées of Québec," La Grande-Allée is one of the larger boulevards in the city and is the city's nightlife hot spot. It's lined with grand Victorian mansions, and the homes have been converted into cafés, restaurants, and nightclubs. Once lined with terraced houses, it was the chichi neighborhood of Québec, but many of those homes were torn down to make way for the Hôtel du Parlement, found on the south end of the *allée,* just in front of the Saint-Louis Gate.

It is the Grande-Allée that separates the rest of the city from the Plains of Abraham, which run along its back. The architecture of the strip's buildings is still stunning, with much of the stonework dating from the late 19th century.

MAP 3: Between Fontaine de Tourny and rue de l'Amérique Française

HÔTEL DU PARLEMENT

The Parliament Building, house of the National Assembly of Québec, is one of the most impressive buildings in the province's capital city. Located on one of the highest spots of Upper Town, just outside the city walls, the quadrilateral building was constructed between 1877 and 1886 by the French architect Eugène-Étienne Taché. Inspired by the Louvre in Paris, the style of building, Second Empire neo-French Renaissance, is unique in North America. The front of the building also features a pantheon representing the province's rich history.

Incensed by the Durham Report, in which the British lord said that the French-Canadians could not be civilized because they had no history, Taché included 15 statues depicting important figures in the province's history, to show that they did indeed have a strong past. Figures include Samuel de Champlain, Louis de Buade de Frontenac, James Wolfe, the Marquis de Montcalm, and, at the very top, an indigenous family. As the province's political life continues to grow, so does the number of statues; there are 26 statues featured on the building's facade and more scattered across the grounds.

Since it is still a functioning government office, the only way to see the interior of the building is to take a free guided tour. At 45 minutes long, the tour provides a great opportunity to appreciate the unique architecture of the building, as well as gain insight into Québec's history and political scene. Make sure to have a photo ID with you, however; otherwise you won't pass the security check. In the summer, outdoor tours are also given to discover the surrounding gardens, which highlight the many trees and flowers of Québec and also give an overview of the many sculptures. All tours leave from the visitors center.

MAP 3: 1045 rue des Parliamentaires, 418/643-7239, www.assnat.qc.ca; 8am-5pm Mon.-Fri. first Tues. of Sept.-June 23, 8:30am-4:30pm Mon.-Fri., 9:30am-4:30pm Sat.-Sun. June 24-first Mon. of Sept.; free

MANÈGE MILITAIRE

This iconic piece of Canadiana was destroyed by fire in 2008, and though 90 percent of the museum's artifacts were saved, only the shell of the historic drill hall remained post-fire. Built in 1887, between the Plains of Abraham and the Grande-Allée, the Manège Militaire is home to the Voltigeurs de Québec, a primary reserve regiment founded in 1862. It was designed by Eugène-Étienne Taché, who also designed the Hôtel du Parlement, and the

Clockwise from top left: a statue commemorating the historical battle that took place at the Plains of Abraham; Hôtel du Parlement; Musée National des Beaux-Arts du Québec.

architectural style is inspired by the French châteaux of the 14th and 15th centuries, with circular turrets, pointy roofs, and high dormer windows. This particular style, extremely unique in North America, is recreated in countless other important structures in the country. It is one of the most recognized Canadian military buildings in the world. Reconstruction on the building finally began in 2017 and is expected to be completed sometime in 2018.

MAP 3: 805 ave. Wilfrid-Laurier

★ MUSÉE NATIONAL DES BEAUX-ARTS DU QUÉBEC

Located in the middle of the Plains of Abraham, Musée National des Beaux-Arts du Québec holds the largest existing collection of Québec art, with works dating from the 17th century onward. The major focus is on fine art, and the exhibits rarely revolve around the work of contemporary artists, though plans for a new addition will hopefully change that.

The museum consists of three distinct structures: the Gérard-Morisset building, the Charles-Baillairgé building, and the Grand Hall. Each has its own atmosphere, and the work exhibited therein reflects that. Inaugurated in 1933, Gérard-Morisset is classical in style. It was designed by architect Wilfrid Lacroix and built in a neo-Italian Renaissance style. The first of the buildings to hold the museum's collection, it's full of white marble, wide Victorian steps, sculpted ceilings, and columns, and it holds permanent collections dedicated to Québécois artists like Emile Bourdos.

Much less conventional is the Charles-Baillairgé building, a former prison. It was incorporated into the museum in 1991 but retains a number of cells, which visitors are invited to explore. Opened in 1867, the prison was modeled after the Auburn Penitentiary in New York state and was all about rehabilitation through isolation. Overpopulated from the beginning, it sheltered not only criminals but the poor and needy. Despite its old-fashioned design, it housed inmates until 1970.

The Grand Hall joins these two structures with its pyramid-like glass facade, which adds light and airiness to the entire structure. A monument directly out front of the museum commemorates the place where General James Wolfe was shot and killed.

MAP 3: Parc des Champs-de-Bataille, 179 La Grande-Allee W., 418/644-6460, www.mnbaq.org; 10am-6pm Thurs.-Tues., 10am-9pm Wed. June-Labor Day; 10am-5pm Tues. and Thurs.-Sun., 10am-9pm Wed. Sept.-May.; $20 adults over 30, $18 seniors, $11 adults 18-30, $6 youth 13-17, children 12 and under free

OBSERVATOIRE DE LA CAPITALE

It might not look like much on the outside, but on the 31st floor of the building is one of the best views of the city. Perfect for a general overview of Québec, at 221 meters high the *observatoire* is the highest spot in Québec and offers 360-degree views of the city and its environs.

As you look out over the city at various vantage points, you will see important buildings and monuments, pointed out and explained on

Bridge over Troubled Water: Le Pont de Québec

The longest cantilever bridge in the world, the Pont de Québec (Québec Bridge) is also the easternmost bridge to cross the St. Lawrence River. Measuring 987 meters long, 29 meters wide, and 104 meters high, it has three highway lanes, one rail line, and one pedestrian walkway, and connects Québec City in the north with Lévis in the south.

Before the bridge was completed, after two disasters, the only way to get from one side of the St. Lawrence to the other was by ferry. Politicians and government officials were looking into building a bridge as early as 1852, but it wasn't until the turn of the 20th century that construction got underway, headed by the Phoenix Bridge Company out of Pennsylvania.

In the summer or 1907, with three years of work nearing completion, the bridge collapsed, killing 75 workers, the majority of which were Mohawk steelworkers from the Kahnawake reserve near Montréal. Though engineer Norman McClure had noticed abnormalities in the foundation structure, his eventual call to halt production never made it to Québec. That same afternoon the southern arm and central section collapsed into the river in 15 seconds.

After a Royal Commission of Inquiry, construction started on a second bridge. This time construction was headed by three engineers: Canadian H. E. Vautelet, Maurice Fitzmaurice from Britain (who worked on the construction of the Forth Bridge in Scotland), and Chicago's Ralph Modjeski. With the bridge nearing completion, the central span was raised into position on September 11, 1916, only to crash into the river, killing 13 workers. Because it was in the midst of World War I, rumors quickly spread that it was German sabotage. It soon became clear, however, that it was another unfortunate accident.

Reconstruction started almost immediately after the collapse and the project was granted special permission to use steel, which was in high demand because of the war effort. After nearly 20 years of construction, the bridge opened for rail traffic on December 3, 1919. Today it is still one of the most impressive engineering feats in North America. Though it's not visible from downtown Québec City, those traveling to and from Québec City by Autoroute Duplessis or heading for a stroll beside the river in Parc de la Plage Jacques-Cartier will get a stunning view of the bridge in all its glory.

the easy-to-read plaques that adorn the windows. Sights like the far-off Québec Bridge are easily seen, along with the Laurentian Mountains and the St. Lawrence River. Alongside points of interest, the Observatoire de la Capitale also gives you information on the province and its history, such as the destruction of Chinatown, which took place to make way for highways to the suburbs. Temporary exhibits, including photographs of local sights, are also on view.

MAP 3: 1037 rue de la Chevrotière, 418/644-9841, www.observatoirecapitale.org; 10am-5pm daily Feb.- late June, 10am-6pm daily late June-Labor Day, 10am-5pm daily Labor Day-Canadian Thanksgiving, 10am-5pm Tues.-Sun. Canadian Thanksgiving-Jan.; $14 adults, $11 seniors and students, children 12 and under free

★ PARC DES PLAINES D'ABRAHAM

On the Plains of Abraham on September 13, 1759, the French fell to the British, forever changing the course of North American history. After Champlain's arrival in 1608, there were skirmishes on and off with the British, who at the time were fighting for control of the North American colonies against the French, but it wasn't until 1759 that the real battle took place.

Led by General James Wolfe, the British army advanced up the St. Lawrence in the spring of 1759, setting up camp north of Québec. During that summer, they laid a near constant siege on the city, destroying houses and monuments but not breaking French general Montcalm's reserve. For all intents and purposes, life continued within the walls of the city amid the bombardments and fires. The siege lasted three long months. With winter approaching, Wolfe discovered the Canadians were awaiting a shipment of supplies from France to arrive on September 13. The supplies never arrived, but Wolfe continued with his plan regardless, maneuvering his men through the hard-to-navigate narrows in rowboats and mounting the cliff by way of a dried-up creek. By the time the Canadians arrived on the battlefield, the British army was already in formation. It was all over in 15 minutes. Wolfe was shot and killed on the spot, but Montcalm was only wounded; he was rushed back inside the city walls, where he was taken to a friend's house and died the following day. Five days later, Québec capitulated.

The peculiar name Plains of Abraham can be traced as far back as 1635, when Abraham Martin, a pilot of the St. Lawrence and a friend of Samuel de Champlain, was given 12 acres of land in the area and an additional 20 acres 10 years after. Today there is little trace of the battle on the rolling green hills of the plains that border the cliff above the river. The grandiose stone building set back from the Plains houses the park's museum and interpretation center, which offers a multimedia exhibit of its history, from the battle to its popularity with prostitutes in the 19th century and as a choice spot for duels, hangings, and the Stanley Cup playoffs. The park itself was part of the 300th anniversary celebrations and was designed by Frederick Todd. Many of the cannons that line the park were gifts from other nations to remind people that this was once a battlefield.

If you're interested in doing more than just strolling and picnicking in the park, you can head to the **Plains of Abraham Museum** ($17 adults, $12.50 seniors and students, $5.50 children; includes admission to the Martello Tower exhibit in Tour Martello 1), where you can visit the Battles 1759-1760 exhibit, which features first-hand soldiers' accounts, battle paraphernalia, and immersive video.

MAP 3: 835 ave. Wilfrid-Laurier, 418/649-6157, www.theplainsofabraham.ca; 10am-5pm daily; free

TOURS MARTELLOS

In 1807 the United States Congress closed U.S. ports to all exports and restricted imports from Britain because of British and French interference with U.S. merchant ships during the Napoleonic Wars. Dubbed the American-Anglo crisis, it prompted Sir James Craig, then governor in chief of Canada, to increase the city's fortifications. Built between 1808 and 1812, four Martello towers were constructed around Québec as defenses and were positioned at various points outside of the city walls, mostly along the Plains of Abraham.

Round in shape, with limited openings, the west sides of the towers were built stronger than the east sides, based on the idea that if an attack were to happen, it would likely come from the west. In the event that the Martellos were under siege from the east, the eastern wall could easily be battered down and the men would be able to escape and continue fighting.

The smooth sandstone was cut in such a way that the constructions are perfectly rounded. Each Martello has a single door, placed at 4.5 meters above ground, 2.5 times the height of men at that time. It was originally reached by a ladder.

The towers became obsolete in the 1860s but continue to stand as monuments of and windows onto the city's past. Exhibitions and events vary seasonally. **Tour Martello 1,** on the Plains of Abraham, usually hosts an exhibition in summer (mid-June-early Sept.), inviting visitors to discover the military history and examine the lives of the soldiers who occupied the towers via a self-guided interactive tour. **Tour Martello 2,** not far from the Plains on the corner of Taché and Wilfrid-Laurier, hosts seasonal events like haunted tower tours from mid- to late October. Visit the Plains of Abraham website for more information.

MAP 3: Parc des Champs-de-Bataille, 418/648-6157, www.ccbn-nbc.gc.ca; 9am-5:30pm daily mid-June-early Sept., plus other seasonal events; $17 adults, $12.50 seniors and students, $5.50 children (Tour Martello exhibit is included in the admission price to the Plains of Abraham Museum)

Saint-Jean-Baptiste and Saint-Roch

Map 4

ÉGLISE SAINT-JEAN-BAPTISTE

Built in 1882, this parish church is one of the most stunning in Québec City. Situated outside of the walls in Saint-Jean-Baptiste, a neighborhood that at the time was home to blue-collar workers of both French-Canadian and Irish origin, it's now surrounded by shops, restaurants, and residential homes.

A fire destroyed the previous church and much of the neighborhood in 1881, and the job of rebuilding the church was passed on to Joseph-Ferdinand Peachy. Of mixed Québécois (his mother) and Irish (his father)

Clockwise from top left: Église Saint-Jean-Baptiste; rue St-Jean; Jardin Saint-Roch.

descent, Peachy was an ideal choice for an architect in this region. Inspired by both a 12th-century church and Église-de-la-Sainte-Trinité in Paris (which was built a mere 10 years earlier), Église Saint-Jean-Baptiste is a combination of very distinct styles: neo-Renaissance, neo-Roman, and Second Empire. The facade is unmistakably Second Empire and almost a direct copy of the Sainte-Trinité.

The church opened to the public in 1884, but it wasn't completely finished until 1896. Many of the church's embellishments, from the pews to the baldaquin, were made in Québec City, by members of the parish. Currently closed to the public—the parish shuttered its doors after not being able to afford $10 million in necessary renovations—the church's photo-worthy exterior, boasting a 240-foot spire as well as a gilded statue of its namesake saint, is still worth visiting. The west side of the church acts as a bit of a public square, offering good people-watching, and contains stairs that help to connect the Saint-Jean-Baptiste and Saint-Roch neighborhoods.

MAP 4: 400 rue St-Jean

JARDIN SAINT-ROCH

Once an empty dirt lot, the Jardin Saint-Roch has become a symbol for the ongoing revitalization of the Saint-Roch (pronounced "ROCK") area in the city's Lower Town. Inaugurated in 1992, it was one of the first places to get a much-needed facelift. With the opening of the park, the centerpiece of which is a waterfall featuring local stone, other businesses came to the area, taking up residence in old warehouses and factories and transforming them into workable, creative environments.

Displayed in the park are busts of René Richard, Alfred Pellan, and Horatio Walker, three important Québécois painters. Though their styles differed wildly, they represent the diversity and the richness of art and culture in Québec. The park is now surrounded by gaming companies, art studios, galleries, and theaters.

MAP 4: Between Côte d'Abraham and blvd. Charest at rue du Parvis and rue de la Couronne; 24 hours daily; free

★ RUE ST-JEAN

This section of rue St-Jean, part of the area known as Faubourg Saint-Jean-Baptiste, is a continuation of the St-Jean found within the city's historic walls. And though these two sides of the street—within and without the walls—are linked by a shared past, their appearance and history are markedly different. The word *faubourg* means "suburb" or "city outskirts" in English, and during the early days of the city, when its gates were opened in the morning and closed in the evening, that's exactly what Faubourg Saint-Jean-Baptiste was, an outskirt with no services or protection available from the city center once the gates were locked.

In the beginning of the 18th century, craftspeople built their workshops and homes along the inside walls of the fortifications. In 1745, however, the defenses were expanded, forcing many to move. This construction pushed

Up-and-Coming Limoilou

Like its neighbor Saint-Roch, Limoilou is fast becoming one of the coolest neighborhoods in the city. Full of cozy bars and cafés, artist boutiques, kid-friendly restaurants, and some of the best food shops in Québec City, it's an ideal place to spend the day wandering and scouring for antiques.

Situated across the St. Charles River, it is one of the oldest boroughs in the city. The first thoroughfare, now called 1e avenue (1st Avenue), was built in 1665. The area was entirely rural up until the end of the 19th century. Its proximity to downtown and placement alongside the river allow for an exceptional view of the city. It's a predominantly residential neighborhood, and the majority of shops and cafés are found in Vieux-Limoilou, easily reached by crossing the rue du Pont in Saint-Roch. Inspired by the grid system used in New York, the streets and avenues are numbered. The majority of cafés and shops are concentrated on 3e avenue, a continuation of rue du Pont on the other side of the St. Charles River. Cafés and neighborhood shops are on 1e avenue, while 2e avenue is perfect for taking in the old Victorian architecture and apartment blocks with spiral staircases.

Open and bright with a modern, minimalist decor, **Le Fun en Bouche** (1073 3e ave., 418/524-7272, www.lefunenbouche.com; 8am-2pm and 5pm-10pm Wed.-Fri., 8:30am-2pm and 5pm-10pm Sat., 8:30am-2pm Sun.; $15) is a neighborhood bistro in the heart of Vieux-Limoilou. Head here for the daily brunch and try the eggs Benedicts or French toast. The lunch selections include sweet and savory crêpes, panini, and homemade soups. If you're in the mood for something to warm you up, **Soupe et Cie** (522 3e ave., 418/948-8996, www.soupecie.com; 11am-9pm daily; $15) has hearty soups and combos, everything from won ton to pho to bouillabaisse, on the menu. Closer to the bridge but still in the center of the community, this long restaurant with brick walls, old chandeliers, and tons of bright cushions is a cozy place to grab a bite. Despite its chic decor, it's kid-friendly—in fact, kids rule here and their exuberance and chitchat make up most of the ambience.

Just down the block is **Hosaka-Ya** (491 3e ave., 418/529-9993; 11:30am-2pm and 4:30pm-9pm Tues.-Fri., 4:30pm-9pm Sat.-Sun.; $10), a relaxed Japanese restaurant inspired by the traditional *izakaya* (Japanese pub). The menu offers mostly sushi but includes *izakaya*-like appetizers and share plates as well. If you're looking for a drink, stop into **Le Bal du Lézard** (1049 3e ave., 418/529-3829, www.lebaldulezard.com; 2pm-3am daily), a friendly little neighborhood bar that's been a staple here since 1985. It has a laid-back feel and features a foosball table and nice sidewalk *terrasse* come summer. For a cozy, rustic bar, you can't do much better than **La Souche** (801 Chemin de la Canardière, 418/742-1144, www.lasouche.ca; 11am-1am Sun.-Wed., 11am-3am Thurs.-Sat.; $7), or "The Stump" in English. This local

them outside of the walls, and they quickly established themselves and took their trades to the *faubourg*, bringing commerce to the area for the first time. In 1845, however, the first of two fires would decimate the area. Two churches, three schools, and 1,300 homes were burned to the ground during the 1845 fire, which subsequently led to the widening of the street. This and other fire prevention measures, such as restrictions on the layout of foyers in homes, were soon put into practice. In 1881 the area was hit

bar offers local brews in a relaxed, stump-strewn setup. They also have a patio come summer.

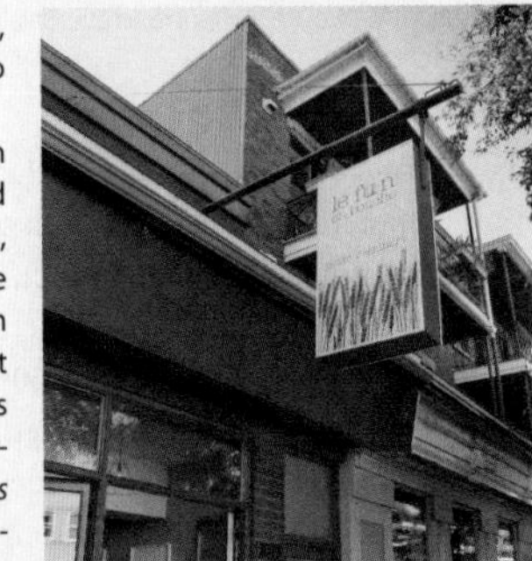

Le Fun en Bouche, a popular bistro in Limoilou

Decked out in red and green tablecloths with multicolored streamers adorning the walls, **Restaurant la Salsa** (1063 3e ave., 418/522-0032; 11:30am-10pm Mon.-Sat., $15) is one of the best Mexican-Salvadoran restaurants in the city. The interior might border on kitsch, but their *pupusas* (stuffed and fried tortillas), enchiladas, and tamales are nothing but delicious. Cheese lovers should make a stop at **Yannick Fromagerie** (901 3e ave., 418/614-2002, www.yannickfromagerie.ca; 10am-6pm Tues.-Wed., 10am-7pm Thurs.-Fri., 9am-5pm Sat., 10am-5pm Sun.), which specializes in specialty cheese from Québec, while a fresh baguette from **La Fournée Bio** (1296 3e ave., 418/522-4441; 7am-6:30pm Mon.-Wed., 7am-7pm Thurs.-Fri., 7am-5:30pm Sat.-Sun.; $10) acts as the perfect accompaniment. La Fournée Bio is an artisanal organic bakery that makes everything from croissants to sourdough and even serves a good cup of coffee.

La Planque (1027 3e ave., 418/914-8780, www.laplanquerestaurant.com; 11:30am-2pm and 5:30pm-11pm Tues.-Fri., 5:30pm-11pm Sat.; $25) is a Canadian gastropub with a young, superstar chef whose seasonal creations, like New Brunswick gravlax and horse carpaccio with marinated carrots and grilled cucumber, garnered the establishment a nomination for best new Canadian restaurant in 2013, as well as clients from across the St. Charles River.

For a bit of antiquing, head into **Objet-Mobilier** (431 3e ave., 418/266-2635, www.objet-mobilier.com, 10am-5pm Mon.-Wed. and Sat., 10am-8pm Thurs.-Fri.), an antiques store that carries an eclectic mix of antiques and collectibles as well as upcycled furniture and home decor. **Article 721** (721 3e ave., 418/742-4333, www.article71.com; 11am-6pm Tues.-Wed., 11am-7pm Thurs.-Fri., 11am-5pm Sat.-Sun.) specializes in locally made products for the home and for kids and adults. They've got everything from pineapple-printed pillows to googly-eyed baby onesies. **La Boutique du Skate** (2255 rue Fleur-de-Lys, 418/781-2030; 10am-5pm Sat.-Wed., 10am-9pm Thurs.-Fri.) has a selection of skateboarding shoes as well as a huge selection of boards—perfect if you're traveling with your teen.

with a second fire, and in just seven hours the church went up in flames and 5,000 were left without homes. This time the architectural restrictions were more drastic and wood was banned in construction.

These two disasters and the resulting architectural restrictions, coupled with a meshing of cultures that came later (the working-class Protestants and Catholics), have created the vibrant street today. The *faubourg* remains a vital part of day-to-day life as one of the busiest commercial streets in a busy residential neighborhood. As you wander along the street, the city's history is mapped out before you in the various architectural styles and businesses telling the story of each important epoch.

MAP 4: Between Autoroute Dufferin and ave. Salaberry

RUE ST-JOSEPH

From the end of the 19th century until the 1960s, this was one of the most important commercial streets in the city. Akin to Fifth Avenue in New York, it was the chichi shopping district, the home of upscale shops and historic department stores. The construction of large shopping centers on the outskirts of town in the 1950s and '60s, however, drew consumers out of the downtown core. Soon the stores left too, moving to new digs in the suburban malls, leaving the stores boarded up and the street run-down.

With hopes of luring business and shoppers back to the street, the city decided to turn it into the closest thing they could to a mall. In 1974, they covered the majority of the street with a Plexiglas arcade. Instead of drawing business, however, the new scheme attracted the marginalized and disenfranchised—the arcade was ideal shelter against the elements. Except for department store Laliberté and the Brunet pharmacy next door, both of which resisted the original exodus, most businesses consisted of cheap cafés and diners and five-and-dime stores.

It was Mayor Jean-Paul L'Allier, who governed for four terms, who would eventually bring business back to the area and the street. His first gamble was convincing Université Laval to move its art school from its campus on the fringes of the city to an old, unoccupied corset factory. The gamble paid off, and slowly but surely other businesses, drawn by incentives, returned to the strip. The Plexiglas arcade had been fully removed by the time the city celebrated its 400th anniversary in 2008, but there are still sections along this diverse and interesting street where you can see where the arcade roof once sat.

MAP 4: Between rue St-Dominique and rue Caron

ST. MATTHEW'S CHURCH AND CEMETERY

Distinctly English with its slender steeple and neo-Gothic stonework, reminiscent of medieval English parish churches, St. Matthew's Church and Cemetery stands out in an otherwise French-influenced Faubourg Saint-Jean-Baptiste. The first cemetery in the city to exclusively bury Protestants, it encircled the church and was in use from 1772 to 1860. It is the burial place of many of the earliest English settlers in Canada and is the oldest cemetery in Québec City.

The church was originally the city gravedigger's house. It was only in 1822 with the arrival of French-speaking Protestant immigrants from the Channel Isles that services started to be held in French. By 1827, the services had become so popular, with a French service in the morning and an English one in the evening, that the house was modified into a chapel. Destroyed by the great fire of 1845, it was rebuilt in 1849 and renovated and

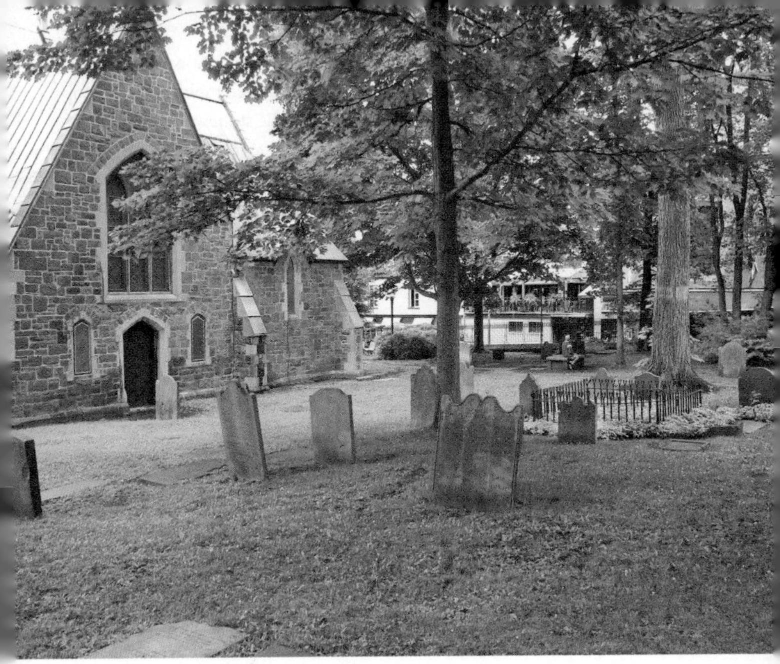

Top: St. Matthew's Church and Cemetery. **Bottom:** the Awesome Ocean, a glass tunnel at the Aquarium du Québec.

enlarged again between 1870 and 1882. The interior maintains its late-19th-century architecture with its exposed beams, rounded moldings at the top of the arcades, and delicate embellishments in the stonework.

Today it is a public library, and visitors can stroll among the bookshelves and admire the preserved interior, which has remained virtually untouched.

MAP 4: 755 rue St-Jean, 418/641-6798, www.bibliothequesdequebec.qc.ca; 10am-5pm Fri.-Tues., 1pm-8pm Wed.-Thurs.; free

Greater Québec City

Map 5

AQUARIUM DU QUÉBEC

Staying true to its roots, this aquarium specializes in boreal and arctic wildlife, though over 10,000 animals call this place their home. It's divided into eight areas, both indoor and outdoor, and the main attraction is the Awesome Ocean, a glass tunnel through a massive seawater tank that allows visitors to get up close and personal with the marine life. Species from Québec wetlands and the St. Lawrence River are also here, along with polar bears, harp seals, and walruses from both coasts in the Arctic display. The newest addition is a tropical exhibition space showcasing jellyfish, stingrays, seahorses, and other southern species.

First opened in 1956 as a marine biology laboratory and research center, it soon attracted visitors eager to see the species that occupied the two aquariums. Continuing its slow growth over the next 40 years, the sight was given a major renovation in 2002 that saw it expand with outdoor gardens and seal and polar bear viewing pools. Located just outside of the city in Sainte-Foy, this is a great attraction for families and has drawn over eight million visitors.

In summertime kids can cool off in the adjoining water park or clamber their way through the Arbre-en-Arbre pathway adventure.

MAP 5: 1675 ave. des Hôtels, Ste-Foy, 418/659-5264, www.sepaq.com/aquarium; 9am-5pm daily June-early Oct., 10am-4pm daily mid-Oct.-May; $19 adults, $17 seniors, $9.50 children 3-17

Restaurants

Look for ★ to find recommended restaurants

Highlights

★ **Best Place to Get a Taste of the North:** The menu at **Chez Boulay Bistro Boréal** is full of game and fish, with a focus on meats that are sustainable and come from the northern part of the province (page 69).

★ **Best Late-Night Eats:** Credited with popularizing poutine, **Chez Ashton** is Québec's preeminent fast-food joint and the ideal spot to refuel after a night on the town (page 77).

★ **Most Authentic Québécois Grub:** Established in 1975, **Buffet de l'Antiquaire** serves heaping portions of traditional cuisine and some great breakfasts in a tiny 1950s-style diner (page 78).

★ **Best Upscale Bistro:** Situated on a tiny street in the Vieux-Port, **L'Échaudé** has both an elegant and relaxed atmosphere with classic bistro dishes (page 78).

★ **Best People-Watching: Lapin Sauté** is right in the heart of rue du Petit-Champlain in Lower Vieux-Québec, and its *terrasse* boasts the best lunchtime people-watching spot in the city (page 82).

★ **Best Tasting Menu:** One of the best haute cuisine restaurants in the city, **Restaurant L'Initiale** features tasting menus with local food in a down-to-earth, modern interior (page 82).

★ **Most Bang for Your Buck:** Eat among savvy locals at **Le Clocher Penché,** where the bistro fare is made with fresh, regional ingredients and the bill is always a pleasant surprise (page 91).

★ **Most Likely to Surprise:** Both the wine and food menu change regularly at **Le Moine Échanson,** an unassuming restaurant that's all about getting you to discover new flavors from various corners of the globe (page 91).

★ **Most Authentic Crêpes:** Run by an expat from Brittany, **Crêperie le Billig** serves up the best crêpes in the city, which are even more delicious when you down them with cider (page 92).

★ **Best Café: Brûlerie St-Roch** is packed for a reason: The lattes are the best and the ambience is effortlessly cool (page 94).

Crêperie le Billig

PRICE KEY

$ Entrées less than CAN$15
$$ Entrées CAN$15–25
$$$ Entrées more than CAN$25

With the most restaurants per capita in the country, Québec City has no shortage of choice when it comes to dining. The challenge isn't finding a decent place to eat, it's deciding which ones you have time for. The number of noteworthy, award-winning chefs and restaurants in Québec, which is well respected for its gastronomy, can be both tiring and exhilarating. Whether serving up a simple breakfast or an intricate haute cuisine meal, chefs tend toward *terroir,* cooking that uses local produce and ingredients. In this region of the province those ingredients include wild game, such as elk, red deer, and bison, and seafood like scallops and cod.

Whereas the big trend at Montréal restaurants is market-fresh cuisine cooked by up-and-coming chefs in a boisterous atmosphere, the trend in Québec is more traditional, with a focus on details and inventive preparation, though a few young, breakout stars can be found, mostly in the Saint-Roch section of town. Even the decor of some of the city's best restaurants can feel a little staid and reserved—few, if any, of the city's restaurants turn into nightclubs once the tables have been cleared. The ones that do, however, can be found on La Grande-Allée, just outside the old walls.

Since so many of the restaurants offer top-quality ingredients and service, the price tag can also be high, though it's often worth it. One way to circumvent the cost without sacrificing the experience is to order the table d'hôte, which gives you the option of a three-course meal, usually appetizer, main, and dessert, for a set price. Another option is to go to one of the more expensive restaurants for lunch. Following the French tradition, restaurants here serve lunch well into the afternoon (service ends around

---

Previous: Lapin Sauté; Chez Boulay Bistro Boréal.

2pm), often with a specific lunchtime menu. Also in the French tradition is the city's love affair with cafés and bakeries; they're abundant, delicious, and much cheaper than a sit-down restaurant.

Barely a street goes by that doesn't feature a cute, independent café or two, most of which serve delectable pastries, light lunches, and choice coffee. Though you can always get your coffee to go, it's rare to see resident Quebeckers striding along with their lattes; in fact, there are only four Starbucks shops in the city, and other chain coffee shops are just as rare. Bakeries, too, can be found in every neighborhood, each offering its own take on freshly baked bread and pastries.

If you're vegetarian, it's best to plan ahead when it comes to meals. Though some restaurants offer a vegetarian option, many do not, and vegans will be flat out of luck for most table d'hôte options. Pescatarians will find abundant choices—fresh fish is widely available—but vegetarians may need to rely on salad, and plan to seek out specialty spots that cater to those who'd prefer to avoid foie gras and game meat.

Québec is generally pretty tourist-friendly, and menus are often available in English. Even when they're not, most servers are happy to translate for you if they're able. A lot of fuss can be made about the dangers of falling into a "tourist trap" when you're visiting a city like Québec, but the reality is, most restaurants, regardless of the number of tourists at their tables, are adept at making some seriously good meals. Whether you're enjoying a tasting menu by one of the top chefs or eating meat pie by candlelight in a laid-back bistro, you'll always find a lively and welcoming atmosphere—the city's most charming and infectious trait.

Vieux-Québec's Upper Town Map 1

QUÉBÉCOIS

AUX ANCIENS CANADIENS $$

Located in the oldest house in the city (built in 1675), Les Anciens Canadiens is firmly planted in Québécois tradition. It's not hard to fall for its charm, with its white-washed walls, red roof, and miniature stature. It's a huge tourist destination. Servers are dressed in slightly unconvincing old-timey costumes, and the food on the menu is traditional Québécois—that is to say, plentiful and heavy. Despite the kitschy costumes and themed dining rooms, the food is excellent. If you want to discover everything about traditional regional cooking, try the Trapper's Treat (meat pie with a pheasant and bison casserole) or the Québec Tasting Platter (meat pie with meatball and pig's knuckle ragout and baked beans). As for dessert—well, you'd better like maple syrup.

MAP 1: 34 rue St-Louis, 418/692-1627, www.auxancienscanadiens.qc.ca; noon-9pm daily

TOURNEBROCHE BISTRO GOURMET $$

Like many great restaurants in the city, the modern, airy Tournebroche Bistro Gourmet puts a heavy focus on honoring locally sourced ingredients in fresh, unpretentious cuisine. Emphasizing fish and seafood, Ocean Wise seals (indicating sustainable seafood) and gluten-free items are marked on the menu, allowing diners to make choices to suit their specific needs. Try the smoked salmon *tataki* (smoked salmon that has been quickly seared) or the house-fried fish with black currant mayo. Bonus: Dessert and coffee are included with the price of an entrée.

MAP 1: 1190 rue St-Jean, 418/692-5524, www.tournebroche.com; 11am-11pm Mon.-Sat., 5pm-11pm Sun.

FRENCH

LE CHAMPLAIN $$$

Located in the historic Château Frontenac, Le Champlain has gorgeous views of the river and boasts a glass-roofed sun lounge. With patterned carpets, luxurious chandeliers, and rich wood paneling, the decor is traditionally elegant. Though new flavors have been added to the menu, it retains much of its original charm, including the century-old tradition of afternoon tea, which is served on Saturday afternoons. Chef Stéphane Modat, originally from southern France, rose to prominence in Québec as the cofounder of beloved restaurant l'Utopie (now closed) and star of the French cooking show *Papilles*. Reservations and smart casual attire are a must.

MAP 1: 1 rue des Carrières, 418/692-3861, www.restaurantchamplain.com; 24 hours daily

★ CHEZ BOULAY BISTRO BORÉAL $$$

This spot on rue St-Jean is unlike any other dining experience in the city. Jean-Luc Boulay, chef and owner of Le Saint-Amour, teamed up with up-and-comer Arnaud Marchand to create a restaurant that's centered on cooking and delicacies from the northern, or boreal, region of the province. The menu is chock-full of game and fish, with a focus on meats that are sustainable. Standout dishes include confit bison cheeks, confit goose legs, and seared black cod with shellfish mousse. The decor is sleek and black with lots of banquette seating and chic white walls in the open-concept dining room. Weather permitting, there's also an outdoor patio. Stop in for a three-course lunch if you fancy experiencing the boreal flavors with a smaller price tag.

MAP 1: 1110 rue St-Jean, 418/380-8166, www.chezboulay.com; 11:30am-10pm Mon.-Fri., 10am-10pm Sat.-Sun.

LES FRÈRES DE LA CÔTE $$

A cheerful and festive ambience oozes from this restaurant full of bon vivants. Located on a busy stretch of Old Québec, the casual dining room, decorated with checkered tablecloths and banquette seating, can be a bit cramped at times, with neighboring diners squished in beside each other. This is all part of the lively atmosphere, which in summer extends to a tiny

A Quick Guide to Québécois Food

Québec has its own distinct, well-developed cuisine; some foods are variations on old French recipes and some are creations that are uniquely their own. In the early days of the colony much of Québec society relied on hunting and fishing for sustenance, and wild game is still a big part of cooking in the region. Here's a quick guide to some of the more common but obscure foods you may come across.

- **Caribou:** This is one of the more popular meats, and you'll find it on menus across the city. It's an especially popular ingredient in meat pies.
- **Caribou (beverage):** During the city's world-famous annual Winter Carnival this stuff is available in all the SAQs (liquor stores). This mixture of port or red wine, hard liquor (usually whiskey or vodka), and maple syrup with the optional addition of black-currant liqueur might be tough to get down but it will keep you warm and give you enough courage to tackle *les glissades*—the enormous toboggan run on Terrasse Dufferin.
- **Cheese Curds:** This is the special cheese they put on top of poutine, but it is also eaten on its own as a snack and can be found at most corner stores. Made from fresh cheddar, it has a rubbery texture and, if fresh, squeaks when it's chewed.
- ***Cheval:*** Though it's not as common a meat here as in Belgium, horse can still be found on menus across the city, mostly likely listed as *bavette de cheval,* horse steak. Similar to beef in consistency, it is both sweeter and more tender.
- ***Cretons:*** If you order a traditional Québécois breakfast, there's a good chance you'll find a serving of this on your plate. A salty pork product, it's made by boiling the pork in milk with onions and spices until its consistency is halfway between a spread and a pâté. It's best eaten on toast.
- **Foie Gras:** Made from duck and goose liver (the name literally means "fatty liver"), this typical French dish has turned into an industry in Québec. Locally produced foie gras is now a staple in most bistros and restaurants serving haute cuisine.

sidewalk *terrasse.* Cuisine runs the gamut from *bavette de cheval* (horse flank) and osso bucco to thin-crust pizzas and mussels with fries.
MAP 1: 1129 rue St-Jean, 418/692-5445, http://restaurantlesfreresdelacote.com; 11:30am-10pm Mon.-Fri., 10:30am-10pm Sat.-Sun.

LE SAINT-AMOUR $$$

At one of the most renowned restaurants in Québec, award-winning chef Jean-Luc Boulay offers creative French-inspired dishes. Try the homemade terrine cooked sous vide, stuffed and roasted scallops from the Îles de la Madeleine, or the red deer seared and served with wild mustard seeds. Art nouveau touches can be found throughout the restaurant, framing the

- ***Galvaude:*** A variation on poutine, this dish adds chicken and peas to the fries, gravy, and cheese for a more "rounded" meal.
- ***Grand-père dans le Sirop:*** A popular dessert during the Great Depression, this is essentially a sweet dumpling made by boiling batter in sugar water, then serving it doused with maple syrup. Translated it means "Grandpa in the syrup."
- ***Guedille:*** Found mostly in *casse-croûtes* (snack shacks), *guedilles* are hot dog buns stuffed with lettuce, mayonnaise, and just about anything else, including egg, chicken, and fries. Commonly found outside of the cities, it's one version of Québec's take on fast food.
- ***Oreilles de Crisse:*** Translated this means "Christ's ears." Made from fried salted pork, they've been a snack since the time of Nouvelle France. Variations on this can be found in upscale restaurants across the province, especially those that specialize in *terroir* cooking.
- **Poutine:** Fries, gravy, cheese curds—this is the unofficial national dish of Québec.
- ***Ragoût de Pattes de Cochon:*** This stew made with pig's feet is part of the *réveillon,* or Christmas meal. A variation on this includes *ragoût de boulettes,* which means meatballs, though likely made with pork and not beef.
- ***Tarte au sucre:*** Also known as sugar pie, this dessert is kind of like a large, simple butter tart, or a pecan pie without the pecans—just the delicious butter, flour, sugar, and cream mixture.
- ***Tourtière:*** Otherwise known as meat pie, this is likely the most common of all the dishes as well as the oldest. Records show that it was first being made in Québec as early as 1611. It's usually made with beef or pork, but different regions in the province have different versions. In Montréal, it's a shallow pie filled with ground pork, while in the Lac-Saint-Jean region, north of Québec City, the pie is deeper and made with wild game like moose, caribou, elk, and hare. It's called *cipaille* in most restaurants.

mirrors and illuminating the bar with a beautiful stained-glass mosaic. Watch the kitchen magic happen through the open kitchen design and sip a glass of red from their exquisite wine list, reputed to be one of the best in the country.

MAP 1: 48 rue Ste-Ursule, 418/694-0667, www.saint-amour.com; 5:30pm-10pm daily, 11:30am-1:30pm Mon.-Fri.

CRÊPERIES

CASSE-CRÊPE BRETON $

No matter the time of day, the line at this bustling crêperie is usually out the door. Luckily, it moves pretty fast and customers are soon seated in the banquettes that line the restaurant's walls or at the bar with a full view of the action. Open since 1983, it can sometimes feel like an upper-class fast-food joint, in the swiftness of service and the way they churn out the crêpes. Choose from a list of suggestions—egg, bacon, mozzarella—or build your own with fillings like berries, chocolate, asparagus, and swiss cheese. While it's not the best crêperie in the city (that honor probably goes to Café Bistro du Cap), it's a good choice for a quick and inexpensive meal.

MAP 1: 1136 rue St-Jean, 418/692-0438, www.cassecrepebreton.com; 7am-10pm daily

AMERICAN

CAFÉ BUADE $

Established in 1919, Café Buade is the oldest restaurant in the city. Not far from Château Frontenac and facing the Basilique-Cathédrale Notre-Dame-de-Québec, it's a popular place with both tourists and long-time regulars. Serving basic family restaurant fare like pasta, pizza, and prime rib, it may not be the best meal you'll eat in the city but it won't break the bank either. If you do find yourself intrigued by the homey and warm atmosphere, opt for a classic club sandwich or one of their generous breakfasts, available daily until noon.

MAP 1: 31 rue de Buade, 418/692-3909, www.cafebuade.ca; 7am-10pm daily May-Sept., 7am-9pm daily Oct.-Apr.

ASIAN

APSARA $$

Located directly across from Place d'Youville, Apsara is a conveniently situated pan-Asian restaurant, the perfect spot to take a break from *steak frites*. Opened decades ago by Beng An Khuong and Kim Phean Tan after they left Cambodia during the Khmer Rouge era, this restaurant continues to be a family affair. The ambience is quiet and calm with impeccable service and traditional music playing in the background. Apsara specializes in Cambodian, Thai, and Vietnamese cuisine, and with five or six mains available from each region, deciding on a single dish can be tough. Those facing a bout of indecision should go for the one of the shared plates, featuring dishes from each country, including Khemara beef (flavored with Cambodian spices and peanuts) and shrimp d'Anam (breaded shrimp with Vietnamese sauce).

MAP 1: 71 rue d'Auteuil, 418/694-0232, www.restaurantapsara.com; 11:30am-2pm and 5:30pm-11pm Mon.-Fri., 5:30pm-11pm Sat.-Sun.

ITALIAN

BELLO RISTORANTE $$$

Bello Ristorante serves up fresh, handmade Italian food—everything from risotto and pasta to pizza, tartare, and fish—in a comfortable, professional atmosphere. The menu has something to suit most tastes, including vegetarian and gluten-free. They've also got a covered terrace with views of

Top: Aux Anciens Canadiens. **Bottom:** Casse-Crêpe Breton.

Vieux-Québec, so you can catch a summer breeze even if the weather isn't quite pitch-perfect. Check them out at lunchtime to beat the crowds.

MAP 1: 73 rue St-Louis, 418/694-0030, www.belloristorante.com; 11:30am-11:30pm daily

CONTI CAFFE $$$

The resolutely modern decor of this Italian-style restaurant is a breath of fresh air compared to many restaurants in Old Québec that stick to a more traditional look. The little brother of Le Continental, from which it took its name, Conti Caffe has an atmosphere that is younger, more relaxed, and more fun than that of its older counterpart. It serves Italian dishes like veal parmigiana and spaghetti carbonara, and specialties include lamb chops, filet mignon, and pan-fried sea scallops. Of course, the classic brick and stone walls still add an air of charm and romance, but the rich blue walls and contemporary furnishings are a vibrant touch.

MAP 1: 32 rue St-Louis, 418/692-4191, www.conticaffe.com; 11:30am-11pm daily

LE CONTINENTAL $$$

Waiters in white dinner jackets prepare mains tableside, making Le Continental the pinnacle of fine dining. Set in an elegant Victorian house, Le Continental is a traditional, rather formal restaurant known for impeccable service and unmatched cuisine. Blending Italian and French traditions, the restaurant is known for its flambé dishes, which include shrimp with whiskey, orange duckling, and flambé sirloin. Other classic dishes include braised veal sweetbreads and steamed snow crabs. Though there is no formal dress code, this is the time to break out your dinner jacket and dress shoes.

MAP 1: 26 rue St-Louis, 418/694-9995, www.restaurantlecontinental.com; 11:30am-10:30pm Mon.-Wed., 11:30am-11pm Thurs.-Fri., 5pm-11pm Sat., 5pm-10:30pm Sun.

IL TEATRO $$

With one of the most eye-catching terraces in the city—think overflowing flower pots and a view of Saint-Jean Gate—Il Teatro is a no-brainer when it comes to dining alfresco. It's in the magnificent Le Capitole theater (hence the name), and the interior is modern and welcoming with brick walls, simple decoration, and huge windows that look onto Place d'Youville. Chef Serge Gagné, despite his not-too-Italian name, has been cooking some of the best Italian food in the city for the past two decades. The risotto *al mascarpone* and scaloppini *del capo* are among the best dishes. Cap the night off with a cappuccino, a slice of panforte, and a stroll around the city's walls.

MAP 1: 972 rue St-Jean, 418/694-9996, www.lecapitole.com; 7am-11:30pm Mon.-Fri., 7am-2am Sat.-Sun.

JAPANESE

MASARU SUSHI $$

Working with one fresh fish brought in daily, Masaru's menu is unique. The chef uses that one fish to create three or more different dishes that are served to diners as a set. Not great for picky diners, Masaru—with its calm, white-washed interior—is nonetheless worth the dice roll for most. Reservations are recommended.

MAP 1: 46 rue Garneau, 581/741-3600, www.masarusushi.com; 11am-8pm Tues.-Fri.

CAFÉS AND CHEAP EATS

CAFÉ-BOULANGERIE PAILLARD $

Modern and open, the long communal tables of this pastry shop, bakery, and *sandwicherie* are cafeteria-like in style, but the tall ceilings and lots of light make it feel effortlessly spacious. In traditional New York style, you must line up to order, be it a fresh Paillard salad with walnuts, blue cheese, and pears or a frothy cappuccino and almond croissant. They're known for their macarons, those sweet, one-bite-and-you're-done cookies; they come in a rainbow of colors and flavors and rival any that you'd find in the tiny back lanes of Paris.

MAP 1: 1097 rue St-Jean, 418/692-1221, www.paillard.ca; 6:30am-10pm Mon.-Wed., 6:30am-11pm Thurs.-Fri., 7am-11pm Sat., 7am-10pm Sun.

CHEZ TEMPOREL $

Established in 1974, this two-story café on rue Couillard, a quaint and winding side street, has become an institution. A favorite with students and artists, it is frequented by locals who come here to grab a quiet coffee or light lunch, offering a nice alternative in the otherwise touristy and busy part of Old Québec. It's simply decorated, with wood tables, brick walls, and work by local artists on the wall, and the food follows suit with homemade croissants, muffins, soups, salads, and quiches.

MAP 1: 25 rue Couillard, 418/694-1813; 11am-9:30pm daily

LE PETIT COIN LATIN $

Just inside the city walls on a steep side street you'll find Le Petit Coin Latin, one of the oldest cafés in Québec. Stone walls, a fireplace, and burgundy banquettes give it an intimate, homey atmosphere. Like its surroundings, the food is unpretentious and includes Québécois classics like *tourtière au caribou* (caribou pie) and *tarte au sucre* (sugar pie). It's a popular place for breakfast and brunch, especially in the summer when the garden terrace is open out back; their plentiful omelets and *pain doré* (French toast) will leave you stuffed. In winter, order the hearty and warming raclette.

MAP 1: 8½ rue Ste-Ursule, 418/692-2022; 8am-11pm Mon.-Fri., 7:30am-11pm Sat.-Sun.

LES TROIS GARÇONS $$

Started by three friends (hence the name, which means "Three Guys") who wanted to create an eatery somewhere between Parisian bistro and New

Clockwise from top left: Café-Boulangerie Paillard; Chez Ashton; Le Petit Coin Latin.

York diner, Les Trois Garçons serves gourmet burgers and the like. Located on a bustling strip of rue St-Jean, the restaurant has a pleasant sidewalk patio in the summer that's almost always packed. Outfitted in red, white, and black, it has a slight 1950s diner feel thanks to the art deco metal railing on the second floor that lets you oversee the diners below. The crowd is in the know when it comes to food trends, and you'll often see diners chowing down on a trio of mini burgers—the best way to taste them all.

MAP 1: 1084 rue St-Jean, 418/692-3900, www.bistro3garcons.com; 7am-10pm Mon.-Wed., 7am-11pm Thurs.-Fri., 8am-11pm Sat., 8am-10pm Sun.

BREAKFAST

CAFÉ BISTRO L'OMELETTE $

Sometimes you just need a simple breakfast at a place where you'll be seated immediately. Café Bistro l'Omelette fills that need—unpretentious standard breakfast options at reasonable prices for the Upper Town. With its cluttered, haphazardly decorated dining room, it's nothing to write home about—but the coffee's half decent and the omelets will fuel a long morning of sightseeing.

MAP 1: 66 rue St-Louis, 418/694-9626; 7am-10pm daily

LATE-NIGHT EATS

★ CHEZ ASHTON $

Founded in 1969 by Ashton Leblond, Chez Ashton is fast food *à la québécoise.* Sure you can get your burgers and fries, but Ashton prides itself on its poutine. It's the single culinary achievement of the region (origins remain obscure and hotly debated), and Mr. Leblond helped popularize the combination of French fries, cheese curds, and brown gravy that has since gone on to conquer the rest of the province. Add shredded turkey and green peas onto the rest and you have a *galvaude,* a popular selection here. The decor is typical of fast-food chains—neon lights, vinyl banquettes, and a crowd of starving late-night revelers. You can find many Chez Ashton locations in the city, including one in Saint-Roch (830 blvd. Charest, 418/648-0891) and one near the Parliament (640 La Grande-Allée, 418/522-3449).

MAP 1: 54 Côte du Palais, 418/692-3055, www.chez-ashton.com; 11am-11:30pm Sun.-Thurs., 11am-4am Fri.-Sat.

VEGETARIAN

RESTAURANT MONASTÈRE DES AUGUSTINES $$

Le Monastère des Augustines is a nonprofit hotel converted from a monastery dating to the 18th century. Focused on wellness, its bright, open, modern restaurant is open to guests and the general public. Breakfast is healthy and hearty and eaten in silence, carrying on the tradition of the nuns, some of whom still reside in the building—though they take their meals elsewhere. Breakfast, lunch, and dinner are served buffet style with a serious emphasis on vegetarian and vegan fare, high in fiber and nutrients. Wine and beer are available at dinner, and teas and infusions are on the menu at every meal. If the restaurant schedule doesn't work for you, stop by the hotel's snack counter for a salad, rice bowl, or high-fiber muffin or granola bar.

MAP 1: 77 rue des Remparts, 418/694-8565, ext. 3333, www.monastere.ca/en/pages/restaurant; 7am-9:30am, noon-2pm, and 5:30pm-8pm daily; reservations necessary for dinner

Vieux-Québec's Lower Town Map 2

QUÉBÉCOIS

★ BUFFET DE L'ANTIQUAIRE $

Set among the chichi bistros and idyllic antiques stores of rue St-Paul, the Buffet de l'Antiquaire is a no-frills diner. Established in 1975, it serves up breakfasts and traditional Québécois grub like *ragoût de boulettes* (meatballs, potatoes, and gravy), *pâté à la viande* (meat pie), and *cipaille* (game meat pie). Usually the busiest place on the block, it's adored by locals and tourists alike for its old-time charm—diner stools, vinyl banquettes, and line cooks in full view. The all-day-long breakfast is served in heaping amounts and with their unforgettable homemade jam. In summer, tables and chairs are set up on the sidewalk outside for a makeshift patio.

MAP 2: 95 rue St-Paul, 418/692-2661, https://lebuffetdelantiquaire.com; 6am-11pm daily

CHEZ MUFFY $$$

Situated in the Auberge Saint-Antoine, this former 19th-century warehouse has been transformed into one of the most inviting dining rooms in the city, with exposed wood beams, stone walls, and original wood flooring. A wrought-iron staircase leads to a second dining level, with tables tucked away under the eaves for an intimate and romantic setting. Using local ingredients and taking much of his inspiration from the fresh produce available, chef Julien Ouellet creates farm-to-table dishes that cater to the season and the palate. Gaspésie lobster, veal sweetbreads, and local Québec cheese, however, can always be found on the menu. Reservations are recommended.

MAP 2: 10 rue St-Antoine, 418/692-1022, www.restaurantpanache.com; 6:30am-10:30am, noon-2pm, and 6pm-10pm Mon.-Fri., 7am-11am, 11:30am-2pm, and 6pm-10pm Sat.-Sun.

★ L'ÉCHAUDÉ $$

With a stainless-steel bar and tables covered with butcher paper, this Vieux-Québec bistro strikes the perfect balance of relaxed elegance. The focus is on organic and locally sourced food treated with different flavor profiles—think salmon tartare with ginger and curry, or grilled lamb with mint and red pepper purée—while the wine list is selected from a sustainable vineyard. The French bistro cuisine mixed with fusion flavors is perfect if

Clockwise from top left: Lapin Sauté's leafy patio; sidewalk dining at Buffet de l'Antiquaire; farm-to-table fare at Chez Muffy.

you're seeking something just off the beaten path—and the dessert menu is spot-on, so make sure to leave some room.

MAP 2: 73 rue du Sault-au-Matelot, 418/692-1299, www.echaude.com; 11:30am-2:30pm and 5:30pm-10pm Mon.-Fri., 10am-2pm and 5:30pm-10pm Sat.-Sun.

LAURIE RAPHAËL $$$

At Laurie Raphaël it's all about infusing the flavors and aromas of the region into the cuisine. The menu changes by season and is offered as a three-"theme" or five-"theme" table d'hôte. Example dishes include halibut ceviche, deer *tataki*, and ash-coated local cheese. The interior is luxurious and inviting thanks to the subtle color palette, with tones of grays and sand; floor-to-ceiling windows open onto the dining room, but gauzy, sheer curtains afford the perfect balance of privacy and light. Reservations are a must. (If you're heading to Montréal, visit their sister location!)

MAP 2: 117 rue Dalhousie, 418/692-4555, www.laurieraphael.com; 5:30pm-9pm Wed.-Sat., 11:30am-2pm Thurs.-Fri.

LÉGENDE $$$

Named one of Canada's best new restaurants in 2014, Légende promises cuisine that will "stimulate all of your senses" in a high-ceiling, cozy yet contemporary atmosphere. Following culinary trends, dishes are meant to draw from history and terroir to weave a story. Small plates are tailored for tasting and experimentation, and a tasting menu will set you back $79. The menu changes based on seasonal availability, but staple proteins include scallops, duck, and foie gras.

MAP 2: 255 rue St-Paul, 418/614-2555, www.restaurantlegende.com; 5:30pm-10pm Wed.-Sun.

SSS $$

From the people who brought you Toast!, SSS (Simple, Snack, Sympathique) is more relaxed and hipper (not counting the name) than its progenitor. Drawing a young, fashionable crowd, it has two different rooms: a small bar lounge with high tables, red accents, and lips on the wallpaper, and an adult dining room with stone walls, black-lacquered floors, and crisp white tablecloths. The main menu is French-influenced and heavy on the meat, with dishes like ribs, crab, and Cornish hen. The relaxed atmosphere, along with good veggie and gluten-free options, makes it a great choice for an evening cocktail or late dinner.

MAP 2: 71 rue St-Paul, 418/692-1991, www.restaurantsss.com; 11:30am-2:30pm and 5pm-10:30pm Mon.-Fri., 5pm-10:30pm Sat.-Sun.

TOAST! $$$

Located in the heart of the Vieux-Port in the Priori hotel, Toast! offers modern cuisine in a picturesque setting. The atmosphere is hip, with warm, orange-hued lighting illuminating the 200-year-old stone walls. Using French and Italian influences, dishes include Jerusalem artichoke vichyssoise, surf and turf, and homemade ravioli. For dessert, they offer a selection of cheeses, including Québec cheese plates, black forest parfait, and citrus sorbet made with in-season fruits. In the summer, a large terrace is open out back, drawing everyone from young families to passing tourists and young professionals.

MAP 2: 17 rue du Sault-au-Matelot, 418/692-1334, www.restauranttoast.com; 6pm-10:30pm Sun.-Thurs., 6pm-11pm Fri.-Sat.

FRENCH

CAFÉ DU MONDE $$

Café du Monde is in the Vieux-Port on a quay that juts out into the river. Aiming to bring a little Parisian Rive-Gauche to Québec, the interior is precisely decorated with black and white checkered tiles, walls of wine, and even black-apron-clad servers to really give diners that Parisian feel. Though the atmosphere isn't entirely convincing—since when is the Rive-Gauche surrounded by grain silos and shipping relics?—the food, with options like mussels, salmon tartare, and duck legs confit, transports you across the Atlantic in no time.

MAP 2: 84 rue Dalhousie, 418/692-4448, www.lecafedumonde.com; 11:30am-10pm Mon.-Fri., 9am-10pm Sat.

CAFÉ ST-MALO $$

Charming and perfectly French, this café, run by two chefs—one Québécois, one from France—offers bistro classics like *steak frites*, homemade duck confit, and mussels, all perfectly seasoned and cooked. Create your own table d'hôte by adding soup, coffee, and dessert to a main dish for an additional $12. The ambience is cozy in the winter—there's a fireplace—and airy in the summer. Pull up a seat on the small *terrasse* if you'd like some sun and people-watching.

MAP 2: 75 rue St-Paul, 418/692-2004, www.lecafesaintmalo.com; 11:30am-2pm and 5:30pm-10pm daily

CHEZ RIOUX ET PETTIGREW $$

A new iteration of old favorite le Quai 19, Chex Rioux et Pettigrew is in a rustic location meant to recall a turn-of-the-20th-century general store: exposed brick walls, fireplace, wooden boxes, old bottles, rice sacks. Chef Dominic Jacques comes to the restaurant with more than 10 years of experience in high-end Québec cuisine, aiming to provide both technical rigor and creativity in his dishes, which run the gamut from house-smoked gravlax to pot-au-feu made with braised Prince Edward Island beef.

MAP 2: 160 rue St-Paul, 418/694-4448, www.chezriouxetpettigrew.com; 11:30am-3pm and 5:30pm-10pm Mon.-Fri., 9:30am-3pm and 5:30pm-10pm Sat.-Sun.

LE COCHON DINGUE $$

Started in 1979, French bistro Le Cochon Dingue (The Crazy Pig) has become one of the most popular restaurants in the city. Famous for mussels, *steak frites*, and pork filet mignon, they also serve breakfast and lunch, with daily specials. Though they've since opened other outlets, including one near rue Cartier (46 blvd. René-Lévesque, 418/523-2013), the original establishment is still the most charming, with brick walls, sharp white tablecloths, and bistro chairs. It's both elegant and relaxed. In summer, their sidewalk *terrasse* takes up almost the entire street, with Le Petit Cochon Dingue at number 24, serving coffees and sweets.

MAP 2: 46 blvd. Champlain, 418/694-0303, www.cochondingue.com; 7am-10pm Mon.-Thurs., 7am-11pm Fri., 8am-11pm Sat., 8am-10pm Sun.

★ LAPIN SAUTÉ $$$

Run by the same people who own Le Cochon Dingue, Lapin Sauté (Jumping Rabbit) is more laid-back and romantic than its bustling neighbor. Located in a turn-of-the-20th-century home, the small dining room—it seats 32—has a rustic feel with a low wood ceiling and a stone fireplace. The food is rustic as well, specializing in country-style cuisine. Their specialty is rabbit, served in a pie, a cassoulet, or roasted with maple and raspberry sauce. They also have (limited) vegetarian options, an affordable lunch menu, and a leafy *terrasse* perfect for people-watching.

MAP 2: 52 rue du Petit-Champlain, 418/692-5325, www.lapinsaute.com; 11am-10pm Mon.-Thurs., 11am-10:30pm Fri., 9am-10:30pm Sat., 9am-10pm Sun.

★ RESTAURANT L'INITIALE $$$

One of the most renowned restaurants in the city, this is a must for those who enjoy haute cuisine and is frequented by foodies from the world over. There is no set menu but various tasting menus that change with the seasons and the local products available. Known for his innovative dishes, head chef Yvan Lebrun marries unlikely flavors, such as suckling pig with squash, and crispy sweetbreads with mustard kidneys. Housed in a century-old building, the interior of l'Initiale is distinctly modern with a sleek comfortable design. The entire restaurant follows a beige and cream color scheme and this subtly works in achieving a rich atmosphere.

MAP 2: 54 rue St-Pierre, 418/694-1818, www.restaurantinitiale.com; 11:30am-1:30pm and 5:30pm-9pm Tues.-Fri., 5:30pm-9pm Sat.

CRÊPERIES

CAFÉ BISTRO DU CAP $$

On a narrow cobblestone street backing onto the sheer cliff face, Café Bistro du Cap is in a gem of a spot, with a small *terrasse* out front and a modest, no-frills interior. The entire atmosphere is unpretentious and intimate. This is a small operation run by a couple; he runs the kitchen while she runs the front of the house, so selection isn't huge and is often determined by availability. Praised by both locals and tourists, their menu includes items like pan-fried salmon, lamb shank, and chowder. They are especially known for their crêpes. Savory or sweet, the crêpes are some of the best in the city, perfect for a midafternoon snack.

MAP 2: 67 rue du Sault-au-Matelot, 418/692-1326; 11:30am-2:30pm and 5:30pm-9:30pm Tues.-Sun.

ITALIAN

LA PIZZ $$

The delicious thin and crispy crust may be the trademark of this pizza joint, but the secret of their success is their ingredients. Fresh vegetables from the Marché du Vieux-Port and imported French cheese are mixed to produce unique flavor combinations, like tomato, bacon, egg, and Emmenthal or tomato, crème fraîche, leeks, scallops, and Emmenthal. The restaurant has a homey feel with bistro chairs and red banquettes; its location makes it a default tourist destination.

MAP 2: 3 Place Royale, 418/692-3003, www.la-pizz.com; 11am-11pm daily

CAFÉS AND CHEAP EATS

CAFÉ LA MAISON SMITH $

Located in the heart of Place Royale, Café La Maison Smith serves up coffee, baked goods, and sandwiches in what they rightly describe as a "poetic" atmosphere—warm lighting, the smell of freshly baked bread, a patio that recalls Paris at the height of the Belle Époque. The café is bustling in the summertime; you may need to jostle for an outdoor spot, but the effort is worth it to enjoy a light breakfast or lunch at the site of the founding of the city.

MAP 2: 23 rue Notre-Dame, 581/742-6777, www.lamaisonsmith.com; 7am-9pm daily

LES CAFÉS DU SOLEIL $

Over 40 kinds of coffee, some from as far as India and Japan, line the walls of this Vieux-Port café. Dedicated to the art of coffee and coffee-making, this popular neighborhood café, full of locals and browsing tourists, was originally a store selling espresso makers and other coffee accessories and making some *allongée* (long espresso) on the side. It only became a full-fledged café when they decided to make sandwiches and snacks for the customers who were spending more and more time hanging out and sampling their coffee. A small but lively place, it's usually packed with regulars. Besides coffee, they offer sandwiches, salads, soups, and pastries, as well as a selection of teas.

MAP 2: 143 rue St-Paul, 418/692-1147; 6:30am-6pm Mon.-Fri., 8am-6pm Sat.-Sun.

Parliament Hill and the Plains

Map 3

QUÉBÉCOIS AND FRENCH

BISTRO B $$$

Bistro B's large picture windows overlook avenue Cartier and the sleek yet overstuffed sofas of the restaurant's outdoor lounge area come summer. Opened in 2012, it's a great place to grab a fancy cocktail—they regularly post their latest creations on a chalkboard in the window to entice passersby—or a casual yet sophisticated meal. The interior is large and spacious, with the high wooden chairs and tables populating the open-concept restaurant. Even the kitchen is open for all to see, with the stools along the chef's counter being the most sought after in the place. The menu, handwritten daily above the kitchen, features everything from veal in truffle oil to arugula risotto and Caesar salad with blood sausage and a poached egg.

MAP 3: 1144 ave. Cartier, 418/614-5444, www.bistrob.ca; 11:30am-2pm and 6pm-11pm Mon.-Fri., 6pm-11pm Sat., 10am-2pm and 6pm-11pm Sun.

CAFÉ KRIEGHOFF $$

No matter the time of day, this place is always packed with both locals and tourists. Named after a famous early-Canadian painter who lived in the area, Café Krieghoff serves everything from your basic breakfast (eggs, toast, potatoes) to bistro-style dinners (quiche lorraine, grilled salmon). Neither the food nor the coffee is out of this world, and, beyond the hustle and bustle, the ambience is lacking, but the prime real estate (on the popular avenue Cartier close to the Plains of Abraham and Musée National des Beaux-Arts) and the large front and back terraces keep customers coming back. They also have a cozy seven-room B&B, which occupies the top two stories.

MAP 3: 1091 ave. Cartier, 418/522-3711, www.cafekrieghoff.qc.ca; 7am-10pm Mon.-Fri., 8am-10pm Sat.-Sun.

GRAFFITI $$$

This chic and modern restaurant—exposed brick, soft lighting, modern furnishings—serves dishes influenced by both Italian and French traditions. Chef Robert Saulnier is known for his personal touch, which includes creations like veal sweetbread in pastry with candied apples, and roast rack of lamb with sun-dried tomato risotto. Located in the food emporium Les Halles Cartier, it's popular with neighborhood locals and especially young couples and groups of friends in their late twenties, early thirties. On Sunday, they serve a decadent brunch; pop in for the poached eggs and blintzes.

MAP 3: 1191 ave. Cartier, 418/529-4949; 11:30am-2:30pm and 5pm-11pm Mon.-Fri., 5pm-11pm Sat., 9am-2:30pm and 5pm-11pm Sun.

RESTAURANT MNBAQ $$

One of the first things you notice when you enter the Musée National des Beaux-Arts is the restaurant, just off the entrance hall. The clink of glasses and plates and wafting aromas immediately grab your attention (especially if you're hungry). Featuring regional cuisine and local, organic produce, mains include pork breast, halibut, and stuffed portobello mushrooms. The atmosphere inside is fairly subdued, with sparsely designed chairs and simple white tablecloths. During the summer, however, the *terrasse* out back has a stunning view of both the St. Lawrence and the Plains, making it a perfect spot for lunch.

MAP 3: Parc des Champs-de-Bataille, 418/644-6780, www.signemclepage.com; 10am-5pm daily

AFGHANI

LES DÉLICES D'ARIANA $$

On the second floor of an ivy-covered building on René-Lévesque, a little off the beaten path, you'll find Les Délices d'Ariana, an Afghani and Indian restaurant serving curries, freshly made naan, and tandoori chicken. Service can be slow but it's happily a bring-your-own-wine outfit; arm yourself with a bottle or two and tuck in for a good night of food and conversation with a date or friends. Great choices are available for vegans, vegetarians, and gluten-free diners.

MAP 3: 102 blvd. René-Lévesque, 418/948-8680; 5pm-11pm daily, 11am-2pm Tues.-Fri.

ITALIAN

MILANO PIZZA $$

This pizza joint's reputation as one of the best in Québec City has been cemented since its opening in 1968, thanks to the neighborhood regulars who drop in at least once a week. It's always fresh and delicious, they offer a kid-friendly menu, and the unpretentious attitude keeps bringing people back. Just off avenue Cartier, it's the perfect place for a filling, no-fuss family meal.

MAP 3: 194 rue Crémazie W., 418/529-2919, www.restomilano.ca; 11:30am-10pm Mon.-Wed., 11:30am-11pm Thurs.-Fri., 10am-11pm Sat., 10am-10pm Sun.

MORENA $

Part specialty store, part casual restaurant, Morena is your go-to place for delicious Italian staples. Whether it's a creamy latte to go, fresh homemade linguine ready to be thrown in the pot, or a can of San Marzano tomatoes, this place has you covered. There are only about six tables in the store and they're nearly always filled with neighborhood locals who pop in for a quick bite of the lasagna Bolognese or eggplant Parmesan. A great place to grab lunch or dinner, it's also a popular spot for brunch on the weekends, serving everything from two eggs the way you like them to baked eggs in tomato sauce.

MAP 3: 1040 ave. Cartier, 418/529-3668, www.morena-food.com; 8am-7pm Mon.-Wed., 8am-8pm Thurs.-Fri., 8am-6pm Sat., 9am-6pm Sun.

JAPANESE

ENZO SUSHI $$$

On the higher end of the price scale, Enzo offers sushi à la carte or as part of a tasting menu. The fish is impeccable, and they also make a range of teriyakis as well as some dishes slightly off the beaten path, like beef sashimi and sake scallops. The atmosphere is formal and calming, with lots of wooden accents—it's the perfect place for date night.

MAP 3: 150 blvd. René-Lévesque, 418/649-1688, www.sushi-enzo.com; 11am-2pm and 5pm-10pm Mon.-Thurs., 11am-2pm and 5pm-11pm Fri., 5pm-11pm Sat., 5pm-10pm Sun.

MÉTROPOLITAN EDDIE SUSHI BAR $$$

This upscale sushi spot is a bit tough to order at—more items appear on the order sheet than on the truncated menu, which prioritizes larger rolls and chef's specials—but once you figure it out the options are more than plentiful. The large dining room is split into two main areas, both painted white with dark wood accents. The service is friendly, the fish is fresh, and the chopsticks arrive in a cute folded-paper fish head.

MAP 3: 1188 ave. Cartier, 418/649-1096, www.eddiesushi.com; 4:30pm-10:30pm Mon.-Fri., 5pm-11:30pm Sat., 5pm-10:30pm Sun.

LEBANESE

BACHIR $

Affordable and delicious, Bachir serves *shish taouk* (marinated chicken kebabs), shawarma, falafel, and other hearty dishes. Vegetarians will appreciate their lightly fried, moist falafels and rich, garlicky hummus. They also have a children's menu—smaller plates for $8 for those under eight. Ambience-wise, it's down a flight of stairs and feels more like a lunch counter than a restaurant—so, good for a casual lunch or dinner, but perhaps not a pre-opera date.

MAP 3: 54 blvd. René-Lévesque, 418/523-8383, www.resto-bachir.com; 11am-3pm Mon., 11am-7pm Tues., 11am-8pm Wed.-Fri., 11am-3pm Sat.

CAFÉS

BÜGEL FABRIQUE DES BAGELS $$

Bügel Fabrique des Bagels makes the best Montréal-style bagels in Québec City—wood fired and smothered in sesame seeds. The small neighborhood staple is decorated with old church pews, and lively patrons give it a homey, comfy atmosphere. In the summer the tiny outdoor patio is the perfect place to chow down on one of their breakfast bagels, like *le poussin,* a bagel with an egg (served daily until 2pm), or dig in to one of their sandwich creations with smoked chicken and curried mayonnaise. Vegetarian meals are served, as well as soups, salads, and desserts.

MAP 3: 164 rue Crémazie W., 418/523-7666; 7am-8pm Sat.-Wed., 7am-9pm Thurs.-Fri.

LE FASTOCHE $

This great *sandwicherie,* in Les Halles Cartier on the upscale rue Cartier, has been turning sandwich making into an art since 2008. This take-away counter caters to workers on lunch or locals needing a quick bite. Creative sandwiches with a unique blend of ingredients include the baguette with duck, port, and blueberries and the prosciutto with two pestos. If you're looking for something more substantial try the *boîte-à-lunch* (lunch box), which comes with salad, dessert, and a drink. Close to the Plains of Abraham, it's a great place to pick up a last-minute picnic.

MAP 3: 1191 ave. Cartier (Halles Cartier), 418/948-3773, www.sandwicheriefastoche.com; 9am-7pm Mon.-Fri., 9am-6pm Sat.

DESSERTS

GLACIER ABERDEEN $

This ice cream shop, tucked into a nook behind avenue Cartier, is one of the best in the city, and locals flock here from all over the city just for a scoop. It has just a slim, long hallway and a walk-up window, so customers savor their treats on the sunny terrace. Across the street, a statue by a local artist also attracts some ice cream eaters. Sundaes, sorbets, frozen yogurts, and milkshakes are all made here, but the place is especially known for its soft-serve ice cream coated with Belgian chocolate and a trickle of maple syrup.

MAP 3: 90 rue Aberdeen, 418/648-6366; 10am-9pm daily mid-Apr.-mid-Sept.

TEA

SEBZ THÉS AND LOUNGE $

The calm, relaxing interior of this teahouse makes up for its plain exterior on the busy and less than picturesque boulevard René-Lévesque. The vibe is more relaxed than British afternoon tea, and the friendly atmosphere makes it popular with local residents and students. More than 150 teas from China, Japan, India, and Africa are available. Detox Tuesdays are popular with regulars, as are the infusion blends, which they roast and blend on the spot.

MAP 3: 67 blvd. René-Lévesque E., 418/523-0808, www.sebz.ca; 10am-9pm Mon.-Sat., 10am-5pm Sun.

Clockwise from top left: L'Affaire Est Ketchup; Café Krieghoff; Le Moine Échanson.

Saint-Jean-Baptiste and Saint-Roch

Map 4

QUÉBÉCOIS

BUVETTE SCOTT $$

This bar-cum-bistro has it all: great beers on tap, a super-friendly staff and ambience, and delicious food cooked well and presented professionally. The chalkboard menu is generally written only in French, but staff is more than happy to translate and recommend daily dishes. Located downstairs in a cozy spot with low ceilings, Buvette Scott is popular with locals and great for some respite from summer tourist traffic. Oh, and the music selection—they're usually spinning records—is pretty great, too.

MAP 4: 821 rue Scott, 581/741-4464, www.buvettescott.com; 4:30pm-11pm Mon.-Sat.

CHEZ VICTOR $

The ambition of this self-proclaimed burger gourmet is to make a hamburger a "piece of art." And so far, everybody in Québec—artist or not—would agree that they make the best burgers in town. The salmon burger, duck burger, and cheese curd-topped burger are interesting takes on the old standard. Vegetarians get choices as well, with tofu, nut and spinach, and legume burgers available. Every burger comes paired with an on-point beer recommendation. The success led them to open new restaurants, including one in the Vieux-Port (300 rue St-Paul, 418/781-2511), but the one on St-Jean remains the best and definitely worth the walk, with its stone walls, low ceiling, and casual atmosphere.

MAP 4: 145 rue St-Jean, 418/529-7702, www.chezvictorburger.com/st-jean; 11:30am-9pm Sun.-Tues., 11:30am-9:30pm Wed., 11:30am-10pm Thurs.-Sat.

LE COMPTOIR $

Le Comptoir (The Counter) serves up satisfying comfort food in a comfortable setting. On rue St-Jean, this cute restaurant—it's all red and white banquettes, and bar stools line the windows—offers two stories of cozy charm. Most of the clientele can be placed in three categories: locals, journalists (the offices of the Francophone version of Canada's national broadcasting network are just across the street), and families (what kid will say no to a burger?). The menu, too, aims to please. They have two specialties, the very British fish-and-chips and smoked meat. The fish is as fresh as anything you'd find on the coast of Maine, while the smoked meat is as good as any you'd find in Montréal. Their burgers and club sandwiches hit the spot too.

MAP 4: 849 rue St-Jean, 418/614-5522, www.restaurantlecomptoir.ca/home.html; 11am-8:30pm Sun.-Wed., 11am-9pm Thurs., 11am-10pm Fri.-Sat.

SNACK BAR SAINT-JEAN $

Open till at least 4am every day, this snack bar is all about being here for you when that craving for grilled cheese hits. This modern diner is nicely,

if not overly, decorated with low sturdy wooden tables and chairs that can stand up to a lot of abuse. There's even a backyard patio come summer, the perfect place to kick back with your enormous and ingenious poutine club (a club sandwich dumped on a pile of fries and covered in gravy, essentially). Everything is over the top and that's part of the charm. Come for the mac-and-cheese burger, featuring fried mac-and-cheese incorporated into a cheeseburger, and stay for the bacon *tarte au sucre* (sugar pie).
MAP 4: 780 rue St-Jean, 418/522-4727, www.snackbarsaintjean.com; 11am-4am Sun.-Thurs., 11am-5am Fri.-Sat.

FRENCH

L'AFFAIRE EST KETCHUP $$

Run by two young entrepreneurs, Olivier Lescelleur St-Cyr and François Jobin, this restaurant is fresh and contemporary and down-to-earth—no need to wear a button-down, though you can if you like. Food tends toward the French (but often includes items like dumplings or panini), favoring seasonal, local ingredients with the addition of seafood, like giant sea urchins and Alaskan crab, sourced from western and northern Canada. On the petite side, L'Affaire Est Ketchup seats about 20 diners at a time—so reservations for one of their two seatings, at 6pm or 8:30pm, are a must.
MAP 4: 46 rue St-Joseph E., 418/529-9020; 6pm-10:30pm Tues.-Sun.

AU BONNET D'ÂNE $$

Situated in what was once the local general store, this café and restaurant is a local favorite. It's not hard to imagine a shopkeeper behind the dark, heavy bar, or to think of the long bay windows, now comfortable banquettes, as filled with stuff for sale. The relaxed, sometimes boisterous atmosphere is laid-back and inviting. Artifacts line the shelves, the menu is written on the mirror behind the bar, and old photos hang on the walls. The burgers are some of the best. Their weekend brunch is always hearty, but refined. A small *terrasse* on the side is a great spot in the summer.
MAP 4: 298 rue St-Jean, 418/647-3031, www.aubonnetdane.com; 8am-10pm Sun.-Wed., 8am-11pm Thurs.-Sat.

LE CERCLE $$

Defying all conventions, Le Cercle is a restaurant, a bar, a café, and a performance venue. With its concrete floors, light wood interior, and floor-to-ceiling windows, it is one of the city's coolest restaurants. Serving both tapas-style munchies (try the fried cauliflower and rice balls) and mains (bouillabaisse and cheddar fondue), it offers classic and more experimental fare with a heavy emphasis on local, farm-fresh ingredients. It may not be surprising to learn that they serve up some of the most sought-after cocktails (at brunch you can order an entire carafe of mimosas), but one surprising twist about Le Cercle is the wine cellar. They blend in so well, you barely even notice the $1,600 bottles of Château Pètrus stacked up against the wall.

MAP 4: 228 rue St-Joseph E., 418/948-8648, www.le-cercle.ca; 4pm-11:30pm Tues.-Wed., 4pm-3am Thurs.-Sat.

★ LE CLOCHER PENCHÉ $$

If you ask Québec City residents what their favorite restaurant is, or at least which one gives you the best bang for your buck, they'll tell you Le Clocher Penché. It's set in an old bank, and the washrooms are where the big safe used to be. The ever-changing menu includes dishes like salmon tartare, seal *tataki,* and homemade black pudding—always making sure to include vegetarian options, as well. They use all local, fresh products. It's called Clocher Penché (Leaning Belfry) because the church next door has a slanted bell tower. Large windows open onto the street in summertime and give the dining room lots of light no matter the time of year. The light wood chairs and tables give the whole atmosphere a delightful airiness. Reservations are recommended.

MAP 4: 203 rue St-Joseph E., 418/640-0597, www.clocherpenche.ca; 11:30am-2pm and 5pm-10pm Tues.-Fri., 9am-2pm and 5pm-10pm Sat., 9am-2pm Sun.

LE HOBBIT $$

Open for breakfast, lunch, and dinner, Le Hobbit is a classic French spot featuring an exposed stone wall and simple decorations, modeled in the style of J. R. R. Tolkien's best-selling novella. The breakfast and weekend brunch menus are standard; lunch and dinner menus vary. For something slightly different, try the elk steak (depending on availability); you can't go wrong with the French onion soup. Though the food is French bistro, the atmosphere is a bit more casual—a great place to stop in if you find yourself peckish after a day of hoofing it around the city.

MAP 4: 700 rue St-Jean, 418/647-2677, www.hobbitbistro.com; 8am-10pm Mon.-Fri., 9am-10pm Sat.-Sun.

★ LE MOINE ÉCHANSON $$

First the translation—*échanson* means "cup-bearer," an officer whose duty was to serve the drinks at a royal table. *Moine* means "monk." The concept at this *bistro à vin* is to discover a new wine region of France every time you visit. The menu, using Québécois and French products, varies according to season and climate. For example, you'll be in Savoy and Alsace in winter, the Mediterranean in summer (including Greece, Portugal, and Spain), and Québec in fall. It's small and cozy with wood tables, a chalkboard menu, and lots of natural light; the ambience transports you to France without crossing the Atlantic. In summer, prime tables are available outside to let

Poutine!

Poutine—piping-hot, crispy French fries covered with fresh cheese curds and smothered in gravy—is the unofficial food of Québec.

It can be found on menus throughout the province, from upscale restaurants (where it's likely served with foie gras) to fast-food places. Despite the dish's popularity, its origins remain hotly debated, with a number of greasy spoon owners declaring themselves the true inventor.

Whether the first poutine was created in the town of Drummondville or Warwick, no one will ever know for sure. But one part of the origin story remains the same: The invention of poutine hinges on customers adding fresh cheese curds to their fries.

Cheese is one of the province's biggest industries, and because of this fresh cheese curds are found in greasy spoons and corner grocery stores all over the province. The curds have a slightly rubbery texture and a mild but salty taste. You can tell whether the cheese is fresh or not by the sound of the squeak it makes when chewed—the squeakier, the fresher.

Since the fries and cheese together taste a little dry, gravy is added to the mix—enough so that you taste it, but not so much that it looks like a stew. The gravy also helps melt the cheese and turn the whole thing into a glorious mess.

Poutine is popular across Québec City, especially in the winter. The fast-food joint **Chez Ashton** (page 77), credited with helping to popularize the dish, has a number of locations in the city, including one in Upper Town and one in Saint-Roch. You can find a poutine club at **Snack Bar Saint-Jean** (page 89) and an Irish version made with whiskey at **Pub Galway** (page 107). You really can't go wrong ordering poutine in Québec City—even McDonald's carries it here.

you appreciate the vibe of Faubourg Saint-Jean-Baptiste. It can get packed, so reservations are a good idea.

MAP 4: 585 rue St-Jean, 418/524-7832, www.lemoineechanson.com; 4pm-10pm Tues.-Wed. and Sun., 4pm-11pm Thurs.-Sat.

CRÊPERIES

★ CRÊPERIE LE BILLIG $

This is the most authentic crêperie in Québec City—some even say it's better than the ones found in France. It was founded by a true Breton; savory crêpes made of organic buckwheat flour and sweet crêpes made of wheat flour are both available. First-timers should try the classic crêpe Suzette, flambéed with Grand Marnier. Don't forget to wash your sweet or savory crêpe down with a cider. The lively and boisterous ambience is palpable since the place is always full of locals packed into the seven tables or taking up the one or two outside tables in the summer. Reservations are a must.

MAP 4: 526 rue St-Jean, 418/524-8341; 11am-10pm Mon.-Fri., 10am-10pm Sat.-Sun.

AMERICAN

LE BUREAU DE POSTE $

Specializing in pub grub, Le Bureau de Poste offers a flat $4.95 food menu. Chicken tenders? $4.95. Pierogies? $4.95. Poutine? $4.95. The servings are a bit on the smaller side, so if you're starving, it might be best to order some extra to share. The music is loud, the drinks are good, the crowd skews young. It's great for a night on the town or as a spot for a late-night weekday snack after hitting up an event or show. Leave room to share the donuts.

MAP 4: 296 St-Joseph E., 418/914-6161, www.lebureaudeposte.com; 11am-3am daily

JAPANESE

SUSHI TO GO $$

Part bubble tea shop, part takeout counter, part sit-down restaurant, Sushi To Go can be slightly confusing at first—but the rolls are good and the milk tea is great. The restaurant itself is light and bright, with lots of space between tables, and the staff is generally young and friendly, happy to chat during non-rush periods—you just might pick up a few tips about what to see and do while you're in town.

MAP 4: 679 rue St-Jean, 418/781-0974; 11am-8pm Mon.-Wed., 11am-9pm Thurs.-Fri., noon-8pm Sat.-Sun.

TORA-YA RAMEN $$$

Inspired by the *izakaya* (Japanese pub) concept, Tora-Ya Ramen is meant to be enjoyed with friends—small, plenteous bites, washed down with a beer or light, inventive cocktails, including a handful of better-than-usual non-alcoholic options. Hot and cold, safe and more experimental, Tora-Ya will appeal to vegetarians and picky eaters as well as those looking to experiment with more complex flavors. The space—dark wood and red walls meet diner—is usually packed with locals, so err on the early side of their lunch or dinner service to beat the crowds, or come ready to spend a bit of time in line.

MAP 4: 75 rue St-Joseph E., 418/780-1903, www.tora-yaramen.com; 11:30am-2pm and 5pm-10pm Tues.-Fri., 5pm-10pm Sat.

YUZU SUSHI BAR $$$

This sushi bar is named after a small Japanese citrus fruit whose delicate grapefruit-meets-mandarin flavor is often found in fusion cooking. There could be no better symbol for what Yuzu does: blend traditional Japanese with North American flavors. With franchise locations across the province, Yuzu's menu is expansive and has something for everyone. They're on the *poke* bandwagon, for example, but you can still find North American sushi standards like avocado and spicy tuna rolls. The interior is modern and clean, and service is friendly and quick—perfect for lunch or a quick dinner before a night on the town.

MAP 4: 795 rue St-Joseph E., 418/614-6237, www.yuzu.ca; 11am-8pm daily

MIDDLE EASTERN

SAVEURS DU MONDE $

If you're craving lamb and couscous, this Moroccan-focused resto—lovingly referred to more than once as a "hole-in-the-wall" in online reviews—is the place to go. Order a combo meal and try a bit of everything. Service is fast and friendly, and the prices are quite reasonable. Make sure to finish your meal with some digestive mint tea—you'll need it after all that lamb.

MAP 4: 847 rue St-Jean, 418/263-2977, www.saveurs-du-monde.ca; 11am-9:15pm daily

CAFÉS

★ BRÛLERIE ST-ROCH $

This is one of the best cafés in the city, and the line starts early in the morning when regulars pop in to get their usual before heading off to work. Ideally located on a corner lot, it has two walls of picture windows with bars and seats along both that are usually occupied. If it's not too packed, try to grab a seat on the tiny second-floor mezzanine that looks out over the action. Front and center when you enter is the gleaming Nuova Simonelli (the espresso machine), backed by a wall of coffee beans ready to be ground. The lattes are outstanding—it's all in the foam—and the sandwiches and pastries are mouthwatering. There are now five other locations around the city, including on rue St-Jean (881 rue St-Jean, 418/704-4420).

MAP 4: 375 rue St-Joseph E., 418/529-1559, www.brulerie-st-roch.com; 6:30am-10pm Sun.-Thurs., 6:30am-11pm Fri.-Sat.

LIBRAIRIE ST-JEAN-BAPTISTE $

A bookshop and café in one, Librairie St-Jean-Baptiste is a cultural and literary hub for the neighborhood. Situated in a building that dates from the early 1900s, the bookstore, dealing in mostly used books, has become a meeting point for local artists and students. There's also a small café, where you're invited to while away the afternoon in this inviting and relaxed atmosphere. Snacks, including sandwiches, soup, and grilled cheese, are also available.

MAP 4: 565 rue St-Jean, 581/999-0951; noon-6pm daily

NEKTAR CAFÉOLOGUE $

At Nektar, coffee is an art. Expert baristas will explain the ins and outs of a good cup of joe to you, all in a thinly veiled attempt to lure you into tasting their *grands crus,* the latest vintage of coffee. If they succeed in getting you to taste the Nektar, you'll have a hard time going back to your Starbucks Breakfast Blend. Their pastries come from well-loved Québec bakery Première Moisson and include cinnamon brioche, croissants, and date squares. In the summertime, their homemade iced tea is a must-try. In winter, Nektar's chocolate brown walls give the place a cozy feel; in summer, though, the interior feels just a bit too dark—taking your coffee outside to enjoy the sunshine might be a better bet.

MAP 4: 235 rue St-Joseph E., 418/977-9236, www.nektarcafeologue.com; 7am-11pm Mon.-Wed., 7am-midnight Thurs.-Fri., 8:30am-midnight Sat., 9:30am-9pm Sun.

BAKERIES

LA BOÎTE À PAIN $

This artisanal bakery has freshly baked bread all day long, and the smell lures in just about anyone who passes by. The pastries are also awesome, from the croissants to the *pains aux chocolates* to the brioche. They also serve sandwiches—try the tomato, mozzarella, and basil—delicious soups spiced with curry, and great salads. Though the interior is nothing fancy, it does have a few nondescript chairs and tables where locals and weary tourists recharge with a coffee and a treat. If you're slightly farther out, they also have locations in Sainte-Foy and Limoilou.

MAP 4: 289 rue St-Joseph E., 418/647-3666, www.boiteapain.com; 6:30am-8pm Mon.-Sat., 6:30am-5:30pm Sun.

LE CROQUEMBOUCHE $

Run by French master baker Patrice Soulabaille, this bakery serves melt-in-your-mouth croissants, pitch-perfect breads, and homemade soups, sandwiches, and quiches. A local favorite, it's an ideal spot for lunch (at one of their half dozen indoor tables or to go). For dessert, try the macarons or homemade ice cream.

MAP 4: 225 rue St-Joseph E., 418/523-9009, www.lecroquembouche.com; 7am-6:30pm Tues.-Sun.

LE PAINGRÜEL $

This self-proclaimed "*boulangerie artisanale et creative*" makes its breads and pastries by hand and with some of the healthiest ingredients. All breads are made using sourdough, but a variety of flours and ingredients are added according to the season. The results: multi-grain bread, cheese bread, bread with nuts. They even have a bread with chocolate and dried pears. The ambience is all business, with a simple counter and not much else. This is a take-away place, so you can feel French and eat your baguette as you stroll the street.

MAP 4: 578 rue St-Jean, 418/522-7246; 7:30am-5:30pm Tues.-Sat.

DESSERTS

TUTTO GELATO $

Opened in 1998 by Italian immigrant Giacomo Donati, this *gelateria* is the real deal. All the gelato is homemade, and there's always a different flavor to try, including green tea, mascarpone and nutella, sabayon with Marsala, pine nut, and all the classics. Modern and sleek, this slim take-away counter also has cakes, biscuits, and coffees.

MAP 4: 716 rue St-Jean, 418/522-0896, www.tuttogelato.ca; 10:30am-8pm or midnight daily (depending on the weather) late Apr.-early Oct.

TEA

CAMELLIA SINENSIS $

Québec City deserves its own branch of this great Montréal-based teahouse, and it's no surprise to find it on St-Joseph. Tea tasters travel the world to find the best and rarest of teas. More than 180 fresh teas are kept in store, and they come from as far way as Japan, India, China, and Taiwan. This small store is set up like an old sweet shop with a counter, and the soft green walls are filled with silver tea tins. The shelves in heavy dark wood give it a feel of gravitas. Tea being a serious business for them, the owners organize tea-centered activities, including tastings and workshops.

MAP 4: 624 rue St-Joseph E., 418/525-0247, www.camellia-sinensis.com; 10am-6pm Sat.-Wed., 10am-9pm Thurs.-Fri.

Nightlife

Look for ★ to find recommended nightlife

Highlights

★ **Best Place to Find Your Sea Legs:** With 50 different cocktails and an interior that makes you feel like you're drinking in the captain's cabin, **Bar Ste-Angèle** will soon have you swaying with the ship (page 100).

★ **Best Terrace:** With cocktails in mason jars, imported beer on tap, and a large patio that looks onto the old walls, **Le Sapristi** is your go-to for alfresco drinks (page 101).

★ **Best Place to Curl Up by the Fire:** Located in a corner of the Fairmont Le Château Frontenac, the **1608 Wine & Cheese Bar** is a cozy, circular spot offering perfect cocktails and great date-night vibes (page 101).

★ **Most Incomprehensible Good Time:** You might not understand the lyrics to the songs sung at **Le Pape-Georges,** but the energy at this *boîte à chansons* is infectious (page 103).

★ **Best Dance Club:** The sheer size of the dance floor and variety of music at **Le Maurice** will keep you dancing all night long (page 106).

★ **Best (and Only) Place to Smoke Indoors:** With its walk-in humidor and selection of over 200 cigars, **Société Cigare** lets smokers enjoy their stogies in dignified surroundings (page 106).

★ **Best Microbrew: La Barberie** is socially and environmentally conscious, so you can down your tasting selection of eight beers guilt free (page 107).

★ **Best Place for a Retro Night Out:** Pitchers of beer are served in watering cans at **La Cuisine,** which cooks up full-on dance parties that rage on well into the night (page 109).

★ **Most Authentic Québécois Tavern: Taverne Jos Dion** is one of the oldest bars in the city. Head here for the live accordion music and stay for the cheap beer (page 112).

★ **Best Drag Show:** Gay bar and nightclub **Le Drague** is nothing but unadulterated fun, and the dance floor is always packed with people letting loose (page 113).

Le Drague

Québec City might be known for its historic sights, but it has a distinctive nightlife scene as well. Though the rejuvenation of the Saint-Roch neighborhood has led to new venues and interesting bars, La Grande-Allée remains the epicenter of the city's nightlife, with dance clubs and bars chockablock along the strip. The late-night scene, however, still lacks a certain amount of diversity. Sure, you can always catch a band or find a place to dance the night away, but the selection can feel limited compared to most major North American cities. Nightlife here tends to stick to the neighborhood bar, where you'll find the city's true ambience.

One facet of nightlife specific to Québec is *chansonniers* (singer/songwriters). These folk singers perform in *boîtes à chansons* (intimate nightclubs; literally, "music boxes"). Deeply entrenched in Québécois identity, the *boîtes à chansons* give singers and songwriters a platform to sing about their heritage and experience—they first rose in popularity shortly after World War II. Famous *chansonniers* have included Félix Leclerc and Raymond Lévesque, who became homegrown stars in the 1950s. The "music box" format is popular today, and there are venues in the city dedicated solely to supporting emerging songwriters, who sing both old classics and new material. Those looking for a uniquely Québécois experience should make time to check out one of these performances, even if the lyrics remain something of a mystery.

Montréalers love to antagonize Quebeckers by calling their city a "town," and though it can feel small at times, that isn't always a bad thing. When the city comes alive at night, it's in the numerous small bars and taverns

---

Previous: 1608 Wine & Cheese Bar at the Fairmont Le Château Frontenac; Pub Saint-Patrick.

in neighborhoods all over the city. The clear standout neighborhood for many travelers will be Saint-Jean-Baptiste and Saint-Roch, where youngish Quebeckers have opened pubs and bars for every taste. Even in the deepest of winter the bars are packed with Quebeckers socializing over pints from local breweries. Many of the bars also feature regular live music that ranges from jazz trios to local rock acts, and if you feel like dancing, chances are you aren't alone—it doesn't take much to get the city's population out of their seats, even if there's no actual dance floor.

Those in the mood for neon lights, thumping bass, and big crowds should head to La Grande-Allée, the city's biggest boulevard, which is full of historical buildings that have been converted into bars and dance clubs. The legal drinking age is 18 throughout the province, and this is the place where teens can be found reveling in their newfound freedom. If you're in search of an LGBTQ-friendly place to cut a rug, head over to Le Drague, the city's gay club, for some guaranteed fun.

When looking for a place to pop into for a nightcap or to hear some local music, don't be afraid to wander along quiet side streets or go beyond the old city walls—it's in these places that you'll find the most authentic ambience and the most affordable beer.

Vieux-Québec's Upper Town Map 1

LIVE MUSIC

Jazz Bars

LE CHARLES BAILLAIRGÉ JAZZ BAR

Situated in the Hôtel Clarendon, the Charles Baillairgé Jazz Bar, named after an architect whose plans helped construct much of Québec City in its early days, continues the jazz tradition originally started here by L'Emprise. Found on the street level of the hotel, the large, open-concept bar with low lights, bucket chairs, and a small stage makes for an intimate atmosphere. With jazz groups playing every Friday and Saturday, the stage has hosted such legendary names as Diana Krall and John Zorn and continues to be a showcase for Québec's emerging and established jazz musicians.

MAP 1: 57 rue Ste-Anne, 418/692-2480, www.hotelclarendon.com; 8pm-11pm Fri.-Sat.; no cover

BARS

★ BAR STE-ANGÈLE

Cocktails come in a rainbow of colors and a multitude of flavors, including Red Devil, Blue Angel, and Kamikaze. With 50 cocktails to choose from, which you can get by the pitcher, they all start to become tempting after a while. They also have an extensive selection of imported beers and scotch.

The bar is designed to resemble the cabin of a ship; there's a lot of heavy woodwork, tiny windows, and mini tables. Small and often packed, it's the perfect retreat when it's super cold or rainy out. Live jazz plays Thursday, Friday, and Saturday nights.

MAP 1: 26 rue Ste-Angèle, 418/692-2171; 8pm-3am daily; no cover

★ LE SAPRISTI

Owned by the team behind burger joint Les Trois Garçons, Le Sapristi is a much-needed breath of fresh air. Located in a coveted corner spot on St-Jean just inside the old walls, Le Sapristi serves up delectable mixed drinks in old mason jars. On tap you'll find local brews alongside European staples like Newcastle Brown Ale and 1664 Blanc. The crowd is mostly full of twenty- and thirty-somethings, many of whom stop off for an after-work drink. Stone walls, rustic but nicely finished wood tables and chairs, and a newly refurbished copper ceiling pull the whole casual vibe together. If you get hungry, they also serve some mean pizzas and charcuterie plates. In summer there's not one but two *terrasses* to choose from, one out front offering a great view of the Saint-Jean Gate and a larger one around the side that's perfect for whiling away the hours with friends.

MAP 1: 1001 rue St-Jean, 418/692-2030, www.sapristi.ca; 11:30am-3am daily; no cover

★ 1608 WINE & CHEESE BAR

Featuring two fireplaces, this bar, located in the Fairmont Le Château Frontenac, is an ideal place for a romantic winter evening. They serve upscale snacks and some of the best cocktails in the city—they specialize in featuring signature cocktails from hotel bars like the Savoy (Corpse Reviver) and the eponymous Hotel Georgia, and they also nail the classics. Though the dress code is technically casual, you won't feel out of place if you spruce up a bit. Choose a seat at the bar, or find a two-chair nook if you're looking for a more intimate evening.

MAP 1: 1 rue des Carrières, 418/692-3861, www.fairmont.com/frontenac-quebec; 4pm-midnight Mon.-Fri., 2pm-1am Sat.-Sun.; no cover

DANCE CLUBS

LE BISTRO PLUS

Part sports bar, Le Bistro Plus offers free peanuts, pool tables, and a small dance floor where things get hopping if there are DJs—or if the crowd is lively enough. This spot is also a good place to catch the game—they broadcast important hockey, football, and MMA events. Bar snacks include grilled cheese and chicken wings, and though you can't go wrong with a draft beer, their spicy Caesar (a Bloody Mary variation made with Clamato juice) is also worth a try.

MAP 1: 1063 rue St-Jean, 418/694-9252; 11:30am-3am daily; no cover but some nights feature ticketed events

Clockwise from top left: Le Sapristi; Pub Saint-Patrick; Bar Ste-Angèle.

PUBS

PUB ST-ALEXANDRE

If you like beer, then you'll love Pub St-Alexandre. It's the English pub of Québec City, with mahogany paneling, big mirrors, and an "olde British pub" facade to prove it. Pub St-Alexandre has been here for more than 20 years and offers the largest selection of beer in the province. More than 250 beers are available, mostly from Ireland, Britain, Germany, and Belgium. They also carry a selection of 40 single malts. It's a hangout that attracts both locals and tourists. If you find yourself confounded by choice, the servers are all beer experts.

MAP 1: 1087 rue St-Jean, 418/694-0015, www.pubstalexandre.com; 11am-3am daily; no cover

PUB SAINT-PATRICK

Pub Saint-Patrick is hard to miss, with its ideal location and large, usually packed *terrasse* full of students, tourists, and professionals still in their suits after work. Inside this bustling pub is some fascinating architecture. The building dates back to 1749, and several rooms are made completely of stone, featuring vaulted ceilings. Once used as barracks during the French regime, they are now some of the coziest places to sip a pint of Guinness. Imported beer is a specialty, and you'll find Harp, Kilkenny, and Smithwick's on tap, as well as an outstanding scotch selection. The food is standard pub fare, made a little slowly, so it's not the best place to bring an appetite.

MAP 1: 1200 rue St-Jean, 418/694-0618, www.pubsaintpatrick.ca; 11am-3am daily; no cover

Vieux-Québec's Lower Town Map 2

LIVE MUSIC

Boîtes à Chansons

★ LE PAPE-GEORGES

It's easy to miss Le Pape-Georges, one of the best and only *boîte à chansons* bars in Vieux-Québec's Lower Town; it's hidden down a little back lane, off the popular rue du Petit-Champlain. Though it calls itself a wine bar, the crowds don't come here for the selection of wines, ports, and microbrewery beers alone. They come instead for the ambience of this welcoming bar, located in a historical house built in 1790. The patrons gather around small tables and huddle up against the stone walls to hear the songs of *chansonniers* (folk singers) and jazz bands. While you listen, snack on some Québec cheese and charcuterie, or a pot-au-feu in the winter.

MAP 2: 8 rue du Cul-de-Sac, 418/692-1320; 11:30am-3am daily summer, 4pm-3am Mon.-Wed., noon-3am Thurs.-Sun. winter; no cover

L'ONCLE ANTOINE

Right next to Place Royale, L'Oncle Antoine is one of the best-looking bars in Vieux-Québec. Located in the cellar of one of the oldest buildings in the city, it dates back to 1754, and the vaulted brick ceilings and walls make you feel like you're hanging out in an old bunker. In wintertime, a raging fireplace gives a unique ambience and keeps things cozy. Fifty different beers are on tap, including local specialties like Fin-du-Monde, and bar snacks like hot dogs, nachos, and hearty French onion soup are also available.

MAP 2: 29 rue St-Pierre, 418/694-9176; 11am-1am daily; no cover

TAVERNE BELLEY

Located in Hôtel Belley, Taverne Belley looks out over the marina and the farmers market. In the summer, the outdoor *terrasse* attracts everyone from office workers to cyclists looking for a refreshing drink and a rest. Opened in 1933, it has daily specials, including free billiards on Saturday nights. True to its name, the Belley is really all about the beer, and there are a number of imported and local microbrews available. There's also a large selection of wines and port to sip next to the fireplace as you take in the warm wintertime ambience.

MAP 2: 249 rue St-Paul, 418/692-4595; 7:30am-midnight daily; no cover

Parliament Hill and the Plains

Map 3

LIVE MUSIC

Boîtes à Chansons

RIDEAU ROUGE

This former lounge has transformed itself into a *boîte à chansons*, complete with stage and stage lights bright enough to make even the most amateur of open mic performers feel like a burgeoning star. It's a few steps down into this club; luckily, there's usually a hostess waiting to usher you down from the street. Once in the club, it's all red lights and, as the name suggests, red curtains. There's ample floor space for spectators to stand and watch the show, or you can take a seat at one of the many tables that line the walls. If live music makes you hungry, you're in luck; they also have a burger menu.

MAP 3: 1147 ave. Cartier, 418/977-6843, www.rideaurouge.ca; 4pm-3am Mon.-Fri., 5pm-3am Sat.-Sun.; free-$20 cover

LES VOÛTES NAPOLÉON

With its stone arches and low ceiling, this *boîte à chansons* has a cozy albeit cave-like feel. Located in the basement of what used to be Restaurant Bonaparte (and is now the Savini), it's a great place to listen to some traditional Québécois music. The stage is so tiny, there's little room for a backup band for the singers who pass through here, so instead they're backed by a modest-sized sound system. It's busy from the moment it opens to the moment it closes, so don't be surprised if the crowd ends up singing louder than the musician. Shows usually start around 10pm.

MAP 3: 680 La Grande-Allée E., 418/640-9388, www.voutesdenapoleon.com; 9pm-3am daily; no cover

BARS

BRASSERIE INOX

Founded in 1987, Inox is the beer institution of Québec. Located in the nightlife mecca of La Grande-Allée, its interior is modern, with high ceilings and basic bar seating. In respect to the forefathers of New France, Brasserie Inox tries to hold up the long tradition of brewing and drinking beer, which has existed in Québec since the early days of the colony. The bar's name itself refers to a type of steel alloy used for beer tanks and echoed in its design and decor. Come and savor a Double IPA or a Trouble-Fête (with coriander and citrus flavors), brewed on the spot, and enjoy it with one of their famous European hot dogs.

MAP 3: 655 La Grande-Allée E., 418/692-2877, www.brasserieinox.com; 11am-3am daily Apr.-Oct., 3pm-3am daily Nov.-Mar.; no cover

LE JULES ET JIM

Just like the famous François Truffaut film from which it took its name, this little *bar de quartier* has become a classic. Since it's a popular neighborhood bar, the patrons are mostly locals, and there's no better place to soak up the city's authentic atmosphere. Clearly stuck on the notion of French classics, music tends toward Edith Piaf, Jacques Brel, Georges Brassens, and the like. The low wooden tables and deep red velvet banquettes give it an old-world charm.

MAP 3: 1060 ave. Cartier, 418/524-9570; 1pm-1am Sun.-Mon., 1pm-3am Tues.-Sat.; no cover

DANCE CLUBS

LE CHARLOTTE ULTRA LOUNGE

This club is in what used to be the attic of this grand old house, which is now a nightlife complex (Le Maurice). It's named after former premier Maurice Duplessis's secretary, Charlotte, with whom he is suspected of having an affair—in this very attic! Québec political scandal aside, the ambience tends toward chill, compared to the dance floor action in the main bar. Retro and pop nights are popular. Appealing to a mid-twenties to late-thirties crowd, the interior is refined and rich with padded walls, velvet couches, and fur throws.

MAP 3: 575 La Grande-Allée, 418/647-2000, www.mauricenightclub.com; 10:30pm-3am Thurs.-Sat.; no cover but some nights feature ticketed events

LE DAGOBERT

Set in a huge castle-like house on the Grande-Allée, the Dag has been an institution since 1977. Inside there are two distinct sounds: The first floor has a rock vibe with regular live shows by cover bands, while the second floor is a full-blown club with a huge dance floor, neon lights, and a mezzanine running along its edges. You'll catch sets by some of the world's best DJs. The crowd is younger than at Maurice, with many barely over the drinking age. During the summer, a line forms quickly for entrance onto the *terrasse,* so get here early to avoid it.

MAP 3: 600 La Grande-Allée E., 418/522-0393, www.dagobert.ca; 10pm-3am Wed.-Sun.; no cover

★ LE MAURICE

Le Maurice is housed in the former headquarters of the Union Nationale, a conservative political party headed by Maurice Duplessis (hence the name), which governed the province throughout the 1940s and '50s. While the interior is pretty typical for a nightclub, the red-brick and gray-stone exterior, featuring gabled windows and a copper roof, offers a historical and aesthetically pleasing view while you wait in line. A large and popular club, Le Maurice draws crowds in their twenties and thirties. It features an immense dance floor and eclectic music, everything from electro to salsa and rock to R&B; Thursdays are old-school nights, and Sundays are Afro Vibe. Le Maurice is a great place to lose yourself in the beat. Come winter don't miss the famous Iceothèque, the ice disco that takes up the entire front *terrasse.*

MAP 3: 575 La Grande-Allée E., 418/647-2000, www.mauricenightclub.com; 10:30pm-3am Thurs.-Sat.; no cover but some nights feature ticketed events

LOUNGES

★ SOCIÉTÉ CIGARE

If you're nostalgic for the days when you used to be able to light up as you sipped your vintage cognac, then Société Cigare is sure to put a smile on your face. The only place in Québec City where you're allowed to smoke indoors, Société Cigare is part of the huge nightlife complex on La Grande-Allée that includes Le Maurice and Le Charlotte Ultra Lounge. Customers can choose from a selection of over 200 brands of cigars, including Cuban Cohibas and Dominican Ashtons, from the Société's walk-in humidor. The soft lighting, all-wood bar, and leather club chairs give the bar a distinctly private club feel. Smokers can choose from a range of scotch, port, and cognac to go with their cigars, and those with their own stogies are free to cut and light them here, as long as they get a drink to go with them.

MAP 3: 575 La Grande-Allée E., 418/647-2000, www.societecigare.com; 1pm-3am daily; no cover

PUBS

BLAXTON PUB AND GRILL

A former sports bar, Blaxton has reinterpreted itself as a classy neighborhood joint with the logo to prove it. If you want to see the game, however, this is still your best bet. Big-screen TVs are scattered throughout the wood and brick bar, which is populated with high stools and tables. Always a lively place, things get especially busy during weekday happy hours; this is an ideal spot to catch the game. The crowd tends to be younger, with most clients in their twenties or thirties. Shunning pub fare for more standard American food, they serve pizza, burgers, chicken wings, New York-style steaks, and mac-and-cheese.

MAP 3: 1179 ave. Cartier, 418/522-9955, www.blaxton.com; 11:30am-midnight Mon.-Wed., 11:30am-2am Thurs., 11:30am-3am Fri., 3pm-3am Sat., 3pm-midnight Sun.; no cover

PUB GALWAY

This charming Irish pub in what was traditionally the English-speaking part of town is a little slice of Ireland, full of wood paneling, stained-glass windows, and smaller tables and chairs. It's not hard to imagine yourself in a country pub some 3,000 miles away. With a selection of 40 different whiskeys and over 20 kinds of (mostly imported) beer, they also serve up pub classics like Irish poutine (it involves whiskey), fish-and-chips, and Irish stew with Guinness. The staff knows the regulars by name but still gives newcomers the same warm welcome.

MAP 3: 1112 ave. Cartier, 418/522-5282, www.pubgalway.com; 4pm-12:30am Mon., 11:30am-12:30am Tues., 11:30am-1am Wed., 11:30am-3am Thurs.-Fri., 10am-3am Sat., 10am-1am Sun.; no cover

Saint-Jean-Baptiste and Saint-Roch

Map 4

BARS

★ LA BARBERIE

This artisanal microbrewery started out as a small co-op in 1996 and now exports its beer to bars throughout the province. Situated in the heart of Saint-Roch, the brewery and bar—technically their tasting salon—are right next door to each other, so you know exactly where your pint is coming from. The owners, who are passionate about their beer but also dedicated and involved in the local community, made just about every inch of the bar and the rustic interior—wood tables, lots of light—to feel welcoming. First-time visitors should try the tasting carousel featuring eight draft beers. And if the weather is nice, drink them out on the sidewalk *terrasse*.

MAP 4: 310 rue St-Roch, 418/522-4373, www.labarberie.com; noon-1am daily; no cover

Clockwise from top left: Blaxton Pub and Grill; La Korrigane; Le Pape-Georges.

Local Brews

When you order a beer in Québec, there's a decent chance the beer you're ordering hasn't traveled more than 300 kilometers—the distance between Québec City and Montréal. Even brands that after a while start to feel as commonplace as Labatt and Budweiser come from some local, Québec-owned and -run brewery. There's a proud history of beer in the province, and the more time you spend in bars, the more you notice it.

Beer has been a part of Québécois culture for as long as Québécois culture has existed. When the first colonists arrived in Québec City from France at the beginning of the 17th century, they brought with them the tradition of brewing and were soon replicating century-old production techniques in the new world. In Québec though, they replaced hops with spruce, which made the particularly tangy spruce beer. An integral part of their diet, beer was full of important vitamins and nutrients that helped the colonists fend off scurvy. By the late 1640s, the Jesuit priests, headed by brother Ambroise, were brewing their own for themselves and the community.

People carried on brewing their own throughout the colony, and in 1671 Intendant Jean Talon opened the Brasserie du Roi, the first brewery in Québec City. Made entirely of Québec products, the beer was shipped as far away as the Caribbean and Europe. After that, home brewing started to die out in the French regime for one reason or another and only started to resurface again in the late 1700s with the arrival of British rule. With the Brits came true life-long brewers who were making beer here as early as 1791.

It's this mix of British and French (as well as some Belgian) brewing techniques that makes Québec beer so unique. Each micro- and independent brewery has its own distinct flavors and blends that can be traced back to brewing practices from one tradition or another. Some well-known local breweries include La Barberie and Brasserie Inox.

★ LA CUISINE

Started in 2006, this brightly decorated spot with a retro feel is a daytime restaurant and nighttime hot spot. The restaurant formula goes like this: seven simple meals, all at the same price and all home-cooked. Québécois classics like *pâté chinois* (shepherd's pie) join cabbage rolls and Thai chicken salad on the menu, which is all made to reproduce home-cooked comfort food. Truth be told, however, most people who go to La Cuisine (The Kitchen) have likely never eaten here. It's a place to drink and dance the night away, especially among *branchée* (hip) twenty- and thirty-somethings. Music tends toward popular indie hits and classic '80s (we're talking Blondie, Elvis Costello, the Jesus and Mary Chain) with a few Top 40 tunes thrown in for good measure; they also host live bands from time to time.

MAP 4: 205 rue St-Vallier E., 418/523-3387, www.barlacuisine.com; 11am-1am Mon.-Wed., 11am-3am Thurs.-Fri., 2pm-3am Sat., 2pm-1am Sun.; no cover

LE DEUX 22

A new arrival to the neighborhood, Le Deux 22 is one of Saint-Roch's branchée bars—popular with hip younger folks—but the atmosphere is warm and welcoming, no matter your age or the relative trendiness of your attire (though, if you're looking for some fancy duds, this place is also, somewhat inexplicably, a clothing store). Specializing in margaritas, this is also one of the better places in town to enjoy a taco or four.

MAP 4: 222 rue St-Joseph E., 581/742-5222, www.deux22.com; 11am-3am daily; no cover

FOU-BAR

Open since 1984, Fou-Bar is an institution in the Faubourg Saint-Jean-Baptiste area, hosting everything from art exhibitions to comedy nights, musical improv events, and concerts. People of all ages meet up here. Many musicians have regular nights, and the beer on tap is almost all from local breweries. Like all bars worth their weight, it also has a foosball table at the back.

MAP 4: 525 rue St-Jean, 418/522-1987, www.foubar.ca; 2:30pm-3am daily; no cover

LA KORRIGANE

Calling all beer lovers: La Korrigane, a spacious, high-ceilinged bar with summertime *terrasse,* brews small-batch artisanal beers made from local ingredients. This ethos extends to the food they serve, which is sourced with care and cooked well. The Kraken is a must-try if you're an IPA fan; if you'd like to get a sense of Québécois terroir through beer offerings, try a taster flight. Check their events calendar in advance—they often host art shows, video game tournaments, and beer conferences.

MAP 4: 388 rue Dorchester, 418/614-0932, www.korrigane.ca; 11:30am-1am Sun.-Thurs., 11:30am-3am Fri.-Sat.; no cover, though some events are ticketed

MACFLY

MacFly is a no-cover arcade bar where the beer is decently priced and the pinball games are free. That's right, free. They've got all the classics, from Space Invaders and Donkey Kong to Ms. PacMan and Centipede. The ambience is laid-back and things get a little loud as the night goes on, but it's a super-fun place to spend an energetic evening with friends. The bar staff is pretty knowledgeable about all things fun and nerdy in the city.

MAP 4: 422 rue Caron, 418/528-7000, www.macflybararcade.com; 3pm-3am daily; no cover

MÆLSTRØM SAINT-ROCH

Half coffee shop, half bar, Mælstrøm Saint-Roch is a great place to spend some public downtime. Bring a magazine or a crossword and settle in with your brew of choice; if someone in your party is looking for a cold brew and another is ready for an afternoon pale ale, Mælstrøm accommodates both with aplomb. The atmosphere is light and airy, with red-brick walls punctuated by lots of windows. Grab a soup and half-sandwich if you're peckish.

MAP 4: 181 rue St-Vallier E., 418/523-0700, http://maelstromcafe.com; 7am-1am Mon.-Fri., 9am-1am Sat.-Sun.; no cover

MO

Mo, in the hip Saint-Roch region, is part of a new breed of urban tavern that mixes a minimalist design aesthetic—cream leather couches, geometric light fixtures—with classic cheap beers. It attracts hip young professionals and beer lovers, especially those who prefer their beer-accompanying snacks to be as palatable as their IPAs and stouts. Local Québec brew Belle Gueule is available from the taps, and Mo stays true to its tavern roots and offers big 325-milliliter bottles of Tremblay and Labatt 50, a particularly Québec phenomenon. A large sidewalk *terrasse* is an inviting place in the summer.

MAP 4: 810 blvd. Charest E., 418/266-0221, www.moresto.ca; 11:30am-midnight Mon.-Fri., 10am-midnight Sat., 10am-4pm Sun.; no cover

LA NINKASI

This two-floor bar in the middle of the action on St-Jean has a nice terrace out back with a view of the Saint-Matthew cemetery next door. A popular student hangout, with a boisterous vibrant atmosphere, it's dedicated to promoting Québec music and local beer, making it one of the best spots to catch emerging bands in the city. It also features pub nights and karaoke—participatory fun—and there's always a new art installation up on the walls. With big-screen TVs, foosball, and pool tables, it's also a great place to watch hockey or any other big-time sports game.

MAP 4: 811 rue St-Jean, 418/529-8538, www.laninkasi.ca; noon-3am daily; no cover

LA REVANCHE

La Revanche is a board-game bar that runs trivia nights (mostly in French!). A bare-bones spot (think "revamped warehouse") with shelves full of games lining the walls, it's a super-fun place to spend an evening if you're looking for something to *do* while you enjoy a pint. Speaking of pints, the beer is only okay, and same goes for the food—though you can't go wrong with the poutine. The real draw is the games, whether you have a specific one in mind or you're looking for a suggestion from your server—they have literally hundreds to choose from.

MAP 4: 585 rue Charest E., 418/263-5389; 11am-midnight Mon., 11am-1am Tues.-Thurs., 11am-2am Fri., noon-2am Sat., noon-midnight Sun.; no cover

LE SACRILÈGE

This popular bar on St-Jean draws a range of clients, from *fonctionnaires* (civil servants) and drunkards in the afternoon to university students at night. Everybody mixes here for the famous 5 à 7—Québec's version of happy hour. They have a good choice of microbrewery beers on tap. Thanks to stone walls, long, almost pew-like seats, small round tables, and hanging plants, the entire atmosphere is warm, welcoming, and unpretentious. Out back you'll find one of the biggest and best terraces in the city. Music tends toward rock and indie with particular DJs taking over the decks and switching things up.

MAP 4: 447 rue St-Jean, 418/649-1985, www.lesacrilege.com; noon-3am daily; no cover

LES SALONS D'EDGAR

Part billiard room, part bistro, part tango club, Les Salons d'Edgar wears a number of different hats. Once a theater, it has since been converted into one of the most diverse bars in the city, though it's still the hangout of choice for Québécois actors. In the front of the house, the bistro is fairly typical, with heavy velvet curtains adorning the windows and candles on each table. In the second room, however, it's a whole different story. The electric blue walls of the billiard room are in striking contrast to the restaurant, but somehow it works. The five pool tables are never free for long, so grab a drink while you wait your turn. On Sundays, from 6pm onward, it turns into a tango club for amateurs and old pros alike.

MAP 4: 263 rue St-Vallier E., 418/523-7811, www.lessalonsdedgar.com; 4:30pm-1am Wed.-Thurs., 4:30pm-3am Fri.-Sat., 6pm-1am Sun.; no cover

SCANNER BISTRO

This punk-edged alternative bar is quiet in the afternoon but gets wilder at night, when an assorted mélange of metal-heads, punks, and rockabillies come to hang out. It's a no-nonsense bar with screens projecting videos and artwork, loud music on the stereo, arcade games, pool tables, and two different kinds of foosball—European and North American. They have some of the best-priced microbrewery beer in the city and typical Québécois snack foods like nachos and hot dogs to go with it. Bands play most weekends—think metal, punk, country—so check the site. They also have free Wi-Fi, if you're looking for an afternoon beer but still need to get some work done.

MAP 4: 291 rue St-Vallier E., 418/523-1916, www.scannerbistro.com; 8am-3pm Sat.-Mon., 4pm-3am Tues.-Fri.; no cover

★ TAVERNE JOS DION

Set in the heart of the working-class district of Saint-Sauveur, Taverne Jos Dion stands as a testament to taverns of a bygone era. Opened in 1933, it is the oldest tavern in Québec and, according to some, in North America. In fact, women have only been allowed since 1986, when the government forced the bar's hand, telling them to either accept women or close. Wanting to be democratic, they put it to a vote and *les habitués* (the regulars) voted to keep the bar open, and subsequently let the women in. It remains, however, decidedly masculine and is a good place to watch sports games as well as drink your weight in beer, which is ridiculously cheap. Live accordion music is featured on Thursdays and Fridays to give it an even more authentic touch.

MAP 4: 65 rue St-Joseph W., 418/525-0710; 9am-3am Mon.-Sat.; no cover

GAY AND LESBIAN

BAR LE ST-MATTHEW

Two former gay bars, Taverne 321 and the 889, came together to create the Bar Le St-Matthew, a small, welcoming bar in Upper Town. Located on a small side street, the bar is popular with both gay and straight locals who pop in for affordable drinks and drag shows. The atmosphere is laid-back with simple decor, pool tables, and a friendly staff. During the summer, the *terrasse* is open for cocktails alfresco.

MAP 4: 889 Côte Ste-Geneviève, 418/524-5000; 11am-3pm daily; no cover

★ LE DRAGUE

Le Drague takes up most of the real estate on the small cobblestone street that constitutes the city's Village Gai (gay district). It's divided into four different sections, and each area of the club has its own vibe, from the quiet bar Verrière to the dance floor intensity of the main room, from the men-only vibe of Zone3 to the Cabaret with almost nightly drag performances. The events calendar is packed and includes weekly drag acts, karaoke, quiz games, and country dancing. Most people, though—whether LGBTQ or straight—come to dance like fools to the house and Top 40 hits that blare out over the crowded dance floor.

MAP 4: 815 rue St-Augustin, 418/649-7212, www.ledrague.com; 10am-3am daily; no cover

PUBS

PUB NELLIGAN'S

A little known fact about Québec: It has quite a bit of Irish heritage. In fact, an estimated 40 percent of French-speaking Quebeckers have Irish ancestry, and Nelligan's is here to help celebrate that ancestry. Located on an unassuming side street, it's easy to miss the 200-year-old building that houses this cozy local. As at all Irish pubs, the atmosphere is inviting, with the bar stools taken up by pub regulars. The decoration is fairly bare-bones, but there's no lack of wood or handwritten Jameson signs. Take a seat near the window and down pints of Irish beer to your heart's content. Irish brews on tap include Guinness, Kilkenny, Smithwick's, and Harp.

MAP 4: 789 Côte Ste-Geneviève, 418/704-7817, www.pubnelligans.ca; 4pm-3am daily; no cover

BARS

PUB UNIVERSITAIRE

If you're a student looking for a place to party, hop the bus out to Université Laval to find your kindred spirits. Barely 15 minutes by bus, Pub Universitaire is the campus hot spot. Located in the Pavillon Alphonse-Desjardins, it has the usual student bar vibe, nondescript tables and chairs, and TVs mounted on the walls. What it lacks in ambience, however, it makes up for in cheap beer. Drink specials are available throughout the week, including weekends, when the entire bar turns into one gigantic dance floor.

MAP 5: 1312 Pavillon Alphonse-Desjardins, Cité Universitaire, Ste-Foy, 418/656-7075, www.pubuniversitaire.com; 11am-midnight Mon.-Tues., 11am-3am Wed.-Fri., 5pm-midnight Sat.; no cover

Arts and Culture

Look for ★ to find recommended arts and culture

Highlights

★ **Best Place to Get Bookish:** The library at the **Morrin Centre** is well stocked and cozy (page 118).

★ **Best Contemporary Gallery: Galerie Michel Guimont** showcases the best in contemporary Québec art (page 121).

★ **Most Intimate Venue:** Catching a show at **Théâtre Petit Champlain,** with its 140-seat capacity, means you're practically in on the act (page 123).

★ **Best Art Complex:** Home of the opera, the orchestra, the ballet, and theater company Théâtre du Trident, **Grand Théâtre de Québec** is the center of all things high culture in Québec City (page 125).

★ **Best Mix of Art and Culture: Méduse** is a hub for all things cultural, from photography galleries to multidisciplinary acts (page 126).

Grand Théâtre de Québec

Nowhere is the spirit of Québec more evident than in its arts. Though the province counts for just over 23 percent of the entire Canadian population, the cultural community is diverse and thriving. Québec City is the center for Francophone arts in the country, and the latest in theater and performing arts can be found here, as well as a strong visual arts community. There is an emphasis on homegrown talent, and though you'll often find European influences and artists, the Québec artist is championed. And why not? The culture here is so rich and unique, it doesn't need to depend on outside sources.

Since Québec is a predominantly Francophone city, English productions are rarely mounted, and it's in music, visual art, and dance that the language barriers come tumbling down. And with many of the most cutting-edge producers creating and exhibiting in Saint Roch-based cultural hot spot Méduse, you barely have to leave the building to catch it all. Once almost exclusively defined by traditional and artisanal work, the contemporary art scene has grown over the past decade. Cool, boundary-pushing galleries feature the more experimental works by local and international visual artists.

Traditional arts and crafts still play a major role in the city's visual arts scene. Take the opportunity to explore the many galleries that showcase traditional Québécois and indigenous artwork, as it's some of the finest in the province.

Previous: Morrin Centre; Place d'Youville, one of the venues for the Festival d'Été de Québec.

GALLERIES

GALERIE D'ART BROUSSEAU AND BROUSSEAU

Founder Raymond Brousseau first started collecting Inuit art in 1956 after receiving a sculpture as a present. In 1974 he opened his first gallery, and it has since become one of the most respected commercial galleries dealing in Inuit art. The large, open space with carpeted floors is a blend between store and gallery, but the aim is to display the works in the best light possible. Works from four specific regions (Kitikmeot, Kivalliq, Nunavik, and Baffin) are available, each with their own style and materials. The staff is expertly qualified in specific fields.

MAP 1: 35 rue St-Louis, 418/694-1828, www.artinuitbrousseau.ca; 9:30am-5:20pm daily; free

MUSEUMS

LE MONASTÈRE DES AUGUSTINES MUSEUM

The Monastère des Augustines Museum is located in a renovated 17th-century building that perfectly blends historical Québec gray stone with bright contemporary glass and steel features. The Augustinian Sisters first arrived in Québec in 1639. Practicing nurses, they opened hospitals to heal the sick and encourage First Nations peoples to convert to Christianity. Cloistered until the 20th century, these sisters' numbers have dwindled since their heyday—though several nuns still live on-site at the *monastère*. The museum shows select objects from the order's 40,000 artifacts, including a full historical nun's habit as well as centuries-old medical devices, to delve into their complex history in Québec. Guided tours take place 11:30am-2pm in summer and cost an extra $5.

MAP 1: 77 rue des Remparts, 418/694-8565, www.monastere.ca; 10am-6pm Mon.-Sat. late June-early Sept., 10am-5pm Tues.-Fri. early Sept.-late Dec.; $10 adult, $8 senior and student, $4 children 12-16, free under 12

★ MORRIN CENTRE

Military barracks, a city jail, and an English college make up the past lives of this cultural center dedicated to preserving and sharing the history of Anglophone culture in Québec. Built during the French regime in 1712, the original structure was used to house French troops and eventually prisoners of war. The current neoclassical structure was built in 1808 and was the first jail in Canada based on the ideas of prison reformer John Howard. Converted in 1868, it became the first English college in the city. Today, visitors can see remnants of these histories as they tour the Victorian library

Open-Air Gallery Rue du Trésor

Back in the 1960s, a group of art students looking for a place to show their work got together and started hanging their pieces on the walls of a narrow alleyway not far from Château Frontenac.

rue du Trésor, home to dozens of artists hawking their wares

Called **rue du Trésor** (Treasure Street, www.ruedutresor.qc.ca), it is one of the oldest streets in the city and has been around for three centuries. At the time of the French regime it was along this street that the colonists would pass in order to reach the Royal Treasury, where they paid their taxes. After the British conquest, the street was no longer so important and instead served its purpose as a service alley.

In fact, when the students started using it as an open-air art gallery, it was little more than a shortcut. Today, 35 artists exhibit their work, and some of those original students are still here, selling their picturesque watercolors of Québec City scenes or abstract etchings of something completely indefinable. What started out as a ballsy venture has turned into a popular spot for emerging and established artists to show off and sell their work. Locals and tourists alike come here looking for a little piece of the city to take home with them.

and head down to the old jail cells. Tea time is available in the summer on Sundays; check the website for details.

MAP 1: 44 Chaussée des Écossais, 418/694-9147, www.morrin.org; noon-8pm Tues. and Thurs., noon-4pm Wed. and Fri., 10am-4pm Sat., noon-4pm Sun.; tours $11 adult, $10 senior, $9 student, children under 8 free

MUSÉE DU FORT

Situated in a historic house in the shadow of the Château Frontenac, the Musée du Fort features a 30-minute multimedia show that recreates the six sieges of Québec City and the Battle of the Plains of Abraham. Other highlights include a model of the city as it was in 1759 at the time of British conquest, as well as a small exhibit of weapons, uniforms, and military badges.

MAP 1: 10 rue Ste-Anne, 418/692-2175, www.museedufort.com; 10am-5pm daily early Apr.-late Oct.; 11am-4pm daily late Jan.-early Apr., late Oct-early Nov., and late Dec.-early Jan.; closed late Nov.-late Dec. and early-late Jan.; $8 adult, $6 senior, $6 student

Clockwise from top left: Musée du Fort; Le Capitole, mostly a venue for movie screenings and concerts; Le Monastère des Augustines Museum.

CONCERT VENUES

LE CAPITOLE

Opened in 1903, this playhouse retains many of the architectural charms that made it so illustrious back then: a sweeping marble staircase, gold trimmings, and balustrades. Originally the place to see the biggest music hall and vaudeville acts, Le Capitole is mainly a venue for movie screenings and concerts. Tributes to bands like Emerson, Lake, and Palmer and Queen are popular, as are classic French singers like Charles Aznavour. You'll often find more popular shows performed with English subtitles (call ahead and check the calendar for details).

MAP 1: 972 rue St-Jean, 800/261-9903, www.lecapitole.com; $30-120

PALAIS MONTCALM

Built in 1932, this art deco building just outside of the walls was originally a public pool before being converted into a concert hall. After undergoing major reconstruction in 2007, Palais Montcalm has emerged as one of the main centers for artistic life in the city. Seating close to 1,000, this is the home stage of chamber orchestra **Les Violons du Roy** (the King's Violins) as well as the site of many jazz, classical, and world music concerts. Along with the large auditorium, it also has a multipurpose café/theater and café/bar.

MAP 1: 995 Place d'Youville, 877/641-6040, www.palaismontcalm.ca; $25-90

Vieux-Québec's Lower Town Map 2

GALLERIES

GALERIE MADELEINE LACERTE

Housed in an old car garage on a corner lot in the Vieux-Port, Galerie Madeleine Lacerte is one of the most prominent contemporary art galleries in Québec City. It was founded by Madeleine Lacerte in 1986, and her son Louis Lacerte is now the gallery director. It's dedicated to supporting Québec and Canadian artists on both national and international levels. The artists they represent are all based in Canada. Exhibits range from painting and photography to installation and conceptual pieces and feature both established and emerging artists. They continue to be on the forefront of contemporary art.

MAP 2: 1 Côte Dinan, 418/692-1566, www.galerielacerte.com; noon-5:30pm Wed.-Fri., noon-5pm Sat.-Sun.; free

★ GALERIE MICHEL GUIMONT

This bright and airy gallery in Lower Town has been going strong, exhibiting contemporary Québécois artists, for decades. You'll find established and emerging artists working in a variety of media—painting, sculpture, photography. Check the website in advance to see if you can catch a vernissage (exhibition opening) or special event while you're in town.

MAP 2: 273 rue St-Paul, 418/692-1188, www.galeriemichelguimont.com; 11am-5pm Tues.-Sat., noon-5pm Sun.; free

GALERIE PERREAULT

At the base of Côte de la Montagne, this large contemporary gallery favors bright and colorful paintings from the 20th and 21st centuries, mostly large-scale, and often commercially appealing. Check the event calendar—they often hold vernissages when introducing new works to the gallery.

MAP 2: 122 Côte de la Montagne, 418/692-4773, www.galerie-perreault.com; 10am-5pm Mon.-Fri.; free

GALERIES D'ART BEAUCHAMP AND BEAUCHAMP

Six commercial galleries make up this large collection of exhibition spaces located in the Vieux-Port. Each gallery has its own mandate, allowing for a huge variation in the types and the prices of work, as well as its own layout; some galleries have so many pieces on the walls you can barely see the wall. The galleries represent over 140 artists, particularly local ones. Both classical and contemporary works are on view, as well as photography. Though typical closing time is 5:30pm, they often stay open later on busy summer days.

MAP 2: 10 rue du Sault-au-Matelot, 877/694-2244, www.galeriebeauchamp.com; 9:30am-5:30pm daily; free

MUSEUMS

MUSÉE NAVAL DE QUÉBEC

This small museum in the Vieux-Port is dedicated to the city's naval history. The permanent exhibits look at the major historic events that have taken place on the St. Lawrence River, from the first First Nations settlements to the numerous invasion attempts by the British to the German U-boat attacks that happened in the river. Personal stories add a human face to the history, and objects include bows and arrows, 18th-century muskets, and a model of the hull of a World War II warship. The museum also hosts traveling exhibitions. The museum is dedicated to Lieutenant-Commander Joseph Alexis Stanislas Déry (its alternative name is the Musée Naval Stanislas-Déry), who made major contributions to the museum's initial collection.

MAP 2: 170 rue Dalhousie, 418/694-5387, www.mnq-nmq.org; 10am-5pm daily; free (donations accepted)

THEATER

LA CASERNE DALHOUSIE

This center for the multidisciplinary arts was established by Robert Lepage and his creative collaborators—actors, writers, set designers, technicians, opera singers, and puppeteers—in 1997. The ultramodern venue looks almost mechanical, with visible pipes, scaffolding, and stairs. It's used primarily as a workspace for the company, called Ex Machina, to try out and create new performances. They occasionally hold public events to show off new works.

MAP 2: 103 rue Dalhousie, 418/692-5323, www.acaserne.net; cost varies

CONCERT VENUES

★ THÉÂTRE PETIT CHAMPLAIN

Situated in the pretty Quartier du Petit-Champlain, this small venue was built in the mid-19th century and was originally used as a theater, but since 1994 it's become a mecca for emerging and established musicians and stand-up comics. It consists of two smaller stages: La Salle Ulric Breton, which seats 140, and the Mezzanine, which seats 90. The shows are always intimate. The exposed brick walls and balcony seating give both rooms a cozy, cavern-like atmosphere. Many popular, and cool, French-language performers play here as well as the occasional English-language band. Check out their "Souper-Spectacle" package deals (dinner and a show) with nearby restaurants Le Cochon Dingue and Sapristi.

MAP 2: 68 rue du Petit-Champlain, 418/692-2631, www.theatrepetitchamplain.com; $20-30

Parliament Hill and the Plains

Map 3

GALLERIES

GALERIE LINDA VERGE

A cozy gallery in a redbrick building, Galerie Linda Verge exhibits contemporary Québécois painters, sculptors, and print-makers—everything from figurative to abstract work. Art here tends to be of a higher quality than some of the work you'll find at larger commercial galleries in Vieux-Québec, and it's worth checking out.

MAP 3: 1049 ave. des Érables, 418/525-8393, www.galerielindaverge.ca; 11:30am-5:30pm Wed.-Fri., 1pm-5pm Sat.-Sun.; free

MUSEUMS

MAISON HENRY-STUART

Take afternoon tea and cake in this charmingly authentic 19th-century cottage. Built in 1849 for Mrs. William Henry, the wife of a rich wood merchant, the house today is found on one of the biggest boulevards in the city, but inside it has retained its elegant and rich decor. Tours of the garden and house give visitors an idea of what life was like for well-to-do

Clockwise from top left: Galeries d'art Beauchamp and Beauchamp; Musée Naval de Québec; Maison Henry-Stuart.

English families in Québec at the turn of the 20th century, and tea-time is part of the hour-long tour.

MAP 3: 82 La Grande-Allée W., 418/647-4347, www.maisonhenrystuart.qc.ca; tours on the hour 11am-4pm Tues.-Sat. mid-June-early Sept.; $8 adult, $6 senior, $3 child 6-12

THEATER

★ GRAND THÉÂTRE DE QUÉBEC

The largest arts complex in Québec City, the Grand Théâtre was built to commemorate the country's centennial in 1967. Designed by Montréal-based architect Victor Prus, the large concrete structure opened in 1971. Home to the Québec Symphony Orchestra, l'Opéra de Québec, and the Théâtre du Trident, it's here that most large-scale performances happen, whether it's a dance piece by the Ballet du Québec or a concert by Canadian jazz pianist Diana Krall or Québec indie favorite Karkwa.

MAP 3: 269 blvd. René-Lévesque E., 877/643-8131, www.grandtheatre.qc.ca; $23-264

CINEMA

CINÉMA CARTIER

This repertory cinema, located above a pharmacy, might bring you back to your adolescence if you grew up watching unlikely films in unlikely places. It's devoted to screening original films that have never before been screened in Québec City, and the emphasis is on classics, modern-day masterpieces, and of course, independent features. With 117 seats, it's intimate without being uncomfortable. English films are screened with French subtitles, but no matter the language, this place is for film buffs.

MAP 3: 1019 ave. Cartier, 418/522-1011, www.cinemacartier.com; $11.25 adult, $8.75 senior and student, $7.75 child under 13

Saint-Jean-Baptiste and Saint-Roch

Map 4

GALLERIES

CENTRE MATERIA

This artist-run center is dedicated to the field of fine crafts. With an aim to broaden the public's familiarity with and recognition of this art form, they host openings and exhibits by diverse artists, everything from glasswork to textiles. Both emerging and established artists exhibit here, but unlike conventional galleries, Materia doesn't represent the individual artists. In a bright, open space on the busy boulevard Charest, the gallery has an industrial feel with white walls and exposed pipes and ceiling beams. An on-site shop adjacent to the gallery offers fine crafts for purchase.

MAP 4: 395 blvd. Charest E., 418/524-0354, www.centremateria.com; 11:30am-5:30pm Wed.-Sun.; free

LE LIEU

Situated in Saint-Roch, this artist-run center was established in 1982 and focuses on multidisciplinary arts. The floor-to-ceiling windows of the sparse space look out onto the street—perfect for catching the attention of passersby. Le Lieu works with artists both at home and abroad, and the contemporary work shown focuses on practices like installation, performance, and audio and visual art. It's often quite conceptual, so don't expect to show up and see a row of neatly hung paintings. They also host Rencontre Internationale d'Art Performance (RAIP), a yearly international festival dedicated to performance art.

MAP 4: 345 rue du Pont, 418/529-9680, www.inter-lelieu.org; 9am-4pm Mon.-Thurs., 9am-3pm Fri., 1pm-5pm Sat.-Sun.; free

★ MÉDUSE

Established in 1995, Méduse is a co-op arts complex filled with galleries, studios, and offices dedicated to arts and culture. Made up of linked buildings, some of them modern, others refurbished historical structures, it's the home of 10 different businesses, from artists' collectives to art galleries. L'œil de Poisson, which exhibits contemporary works, and VU, an artist-run center dedicated to contemporary photography, are always worth checking out. This hub has become integral to all forms of the city's contemporary arts scene, and some spaces offer open-to-the-public workshops. If you want to check out a specific space, check the times before you leave since they often vary.

MAP 4: 541 rue St Vallier E., 418/640-9218, www.meduse.org; 9am-5pm daily; free

THEATER

THÉATRE LA BORDÉE

Established in 1976 by a group of young actors directly out of theater school, this independent theater company in Saint-Roch mounts a handful of larger productions, and a few smaller productions with shorter runs, every year. Walking the line between classical and experimental, their aim is to produce excellent theater that is also accessible to a large public. They focus on plays from Québec, but there is also variety in their programs, and past seasons have included productions of Shakespeare's *Richard III*, Dumas's *Le Reine Margot*, and *The Pillowman* by Irish playwright Martin McDonagh. Consisting of two presentation halls, an Italian-style theater that seats 350 and one that seats 60, the settings are decidedly intimate. All productions are in French.

MAP 4: 315 rue St-Joseph E., 418/694-9721, www.bordee.qc.ca; $34-41 adult, $29-36 senior, $24-31 under 30

CONCERT VENUES

LE CERCLE

Not only does it serve up a mean meal and cool bar atmosphere, but it's also the place where you'll find the coolest music shows. This Saint-Roch staple is all concrete floors, high ceilings, great acoustics, and even better acts. If you want to dance the night away to the sounds of Berlin's latest electro sensation, this is your destination. Since it's one of the few places to catch new music in the city, it's become quite popular. Get your tickets ahead of time, and if you want a decent view, arrive early. In addition to live music, they also host film and art events.

MAP 4: 226 and 228 rue St-Joseph E., 418/948-8648, www.le-cercle.ca; $10-30

IMPÉRIAL BELL THEATRE

This theater and concert hall in Saint-Roch has a long history. Originally the site of the neighborhood's cemetery, this was a factory before becoming a theater with a second-floor art gallery in 1912. Rebuilt in 1917, in the style that was popular at the time—a flat, square marquee, and the Impérial's sign illuminated and protruding from the center of the building—this facade still exists and is one of the few theaters in Québec that recall the golden age of silent films. Inside, the old-time charm remains, with balustrades adorned with winged cherubs and moldings framing the stage. It's a midsize venue; bands like Gwar, Timber Timbre, and Bruce Cockburn have hit the stage, along with cabaret acts and the occasional movie screening.

MAP 4: 252 rue St-Joseph E., 418/523-3131, www.imperialdequebec.com; $15-50

Greater Québec City — Map 5

MUSEUMS

MUSÉE HURON-WENDAT

Take a half-hour drive northwest of the city to the Musée Huron-Wendat, which was created in Wendake in 2008 to celebrate and protect the history and heritage of the Wendat people. The permanent exhibition, located in the museum's circular main building, delves into Wendat ancestral traditions and pre-contact history. Visitors learn the Wendat creation myth and are introduced to the Wendat way of life through archival materials such as tools, clothing, and even a canoe. Temporary installations include contemporary art and culture exhibits. The on-site gardens, featuring traditional regional plants, are also worth a visit.

MAP 5: 15 Place de la Rencontre, Wendake, 418/847-2260, www.museehuronwendat.ca; 9:30am-noon and 1pm-5pm daily mid-May-late Oct., 10am-noon and 1pm-4pm Wed.-Sun. late Oct.-mid-May, 10am-noon and 1pm-4pm daily winter holidays and March break; $11.50 adult, $10 senior and student, $5.75 child 6-17

CINEMA

LE CLAP

If you can get past the slightly unfortunate name, Le Clap is a great repertory cinema that plays films that don't always get wide distribution in the province. It plays English movies with French subtitles. Fans of international and art-house cinema will enjoy their selection of festival hits from festivals like Cannes, TIFF, and Festival Nouveau Cinéma. With none of the bells and whistles you find at bigger name cinemas, the smaller auditoriums and intimate setting aren't for everyone.

MAP 5: 2360 chemin Ste-Foy, 418/653-2470, www.clap.qc.ca; $11.50 adult, $9 senior, $8 student and child

Festivals and Events

There's no helping Québec—it's simply a province that wants people to get together and have a good time. If you had to spend six months locked up indoors, you'd want to get out and celebrate too, which is why one of the biggest festivals of the year, Québec City's Carnaval de Québec, is held during the coldest months. Of course, when the warm weather finally arrives, Québec City throws it a big party too, in the form of the Festival d'Été de Québec.

WINTER

NEW YEAR'S EVE

Winter is bitterly cold and snowy in Québec, but that just means that residents embrace every chance for an outdoor party (in a heavy-duty parka, wearing warm tuques—winter hats—and boots). The New Year's Eve celebration, taking place over four days, culminates in a concert and New Year's countdown on the 31st. But it also includes heated terraces, outdoor bars, dance performances, an urban zipline, a Ferris wheel, and a giant slide. Time to bundle up and embrace the winter!

Parliament Hill and the Plains: La Grande-Allée, 418/626-3716, www.jourdelan.info; Dec. 27-31; free

CARNAVAL DE QUÉBEC

The most iconic of all the festivals in the province, Carnaval de Québec has its roots in the early days of New France, when everyone got together in the weeks leading up to Lent to drink and let loose. Following tradition, the festival runs for just over two weeks between the end of January and early February. The first big Carnaval took place in 1894 as a way of combating the winter blahs, and in this spirit the festival has taken place every winter since 1955. Led by Bonhomme, a life-size snowman with a floppy red hat and a *ceinture fléchée* (a traditional Québécois belt), the festival is all about fun in the outdoors. From parades to dog-sled races, tobogganing to ice-canoeing, ice-skating to outdoor dance parties and snow sculpture competitions, there's always something going on. It's also the only festival to give adults full rights to wander the town in snowsuits without shame while sipping on something to keep them warm. Early-bird "effigies" (small Bonhomme figurines allowing access to Carnaval sites) purchased in December cost $10, and the regular price is $15—very reasonable for two weeks of daily activities!

Various locations: 418/626-3716, www.carnaval.qc.ca; end of Jan.-early Feb.; $15, free children 8 and under

MOIS MULTI

The international festival Mois Multi, founded in 2000, focuses on multidisciplinary and electronic arts. Artists from such diverse countries as Russia, Australia, and Mexico have exhibited here, bringing with them their various light and sound installations and multimedia performances that explore topics like synesthesia, sound-architecture, and light chaos. Throughout the month-long festival in February, visitors are invited to witness these man-made realms, making it more than just an event—it becomes an experience.

Various locations: 418/524-7553, www.moismulti.org; Feb.; festival passes $90 31 and over, $75 under 31

SPRING

QUÉBEC EXQUIS!

For gourmands interested in seeing and tasting the latest in cuisine and wine, Québec Exquis! brings out the best in new merchandise. Over 12 days in mid-April, diners are encouraged to make reservations for reasonably priced tasting menus at the city's top restaurants. The 2017 festival theme invited participating restaurants to pair the wines of Languedoc with suitable tasting menus, which cost $20 at lunch and $40-50 at dinner. Eat your way across the city for a song.

Various locations: 418/683-4150, www.quebecexquis.com; mid-Apr.; $20 lunch, $40-50 dinner

MANIF D'ART

Manif d'Art is Québec City's biennial, held for a month from early May to early June. Every even-numbered year, the city and the world's established and up-and-coming artists present their works at what is the biggest contemporary art festival in Québec City. Events outside of the exhibitions are held as well, including colloquiums and forums, and satellite activities with other disciplines such as live performances and shows. A nominal fee allows visitors to see all the exhibitions and gives them access to guided tours, theme-related events, and creative workshops. You can also enter events separately (cost varies; some events are free).

Various locations: 418/524-1917, www.manifdart.org; May-June; passes $15 adults, $10 students, children under 12 free

CARREFOUR INTERNATIONAL DE THÉÂTRE DE QUÉBEC

The city's preeminent theater festival, Carrefour International de Théâtre de Québec presents innovative theater work from Canada and beyond. Though established playwrights often present here, there's an eye on emerging playwrights and artists as well. Held for just over two weeks from the end of May to early June, all the productions presented are premieres in the province—they do not accept pieces that have already been mounted in Québec. Since it is an international festival, there are often a few English or bilingual selections.

Various locations: 418/692-3131, www.carrefourtheatre.qc.ca; end of May-early June; single-play tickets $49.50, multi-play ticket packages (on sale mid-Apr.-mid-May) $120-330

SUMMER

FESTIVAL COMEDIHA! QUÉBEC

The Québec City equivalent of Just for Laughs, Festival ComediHa! caters to a Francophone audience. Occasionally, however, they have some big-name English acts like Jerry Seinfeld on the bill. It runs for two weeks in early to mid-June, and with over 100 shows on the schedule, there are often a few offered in English. Shows take place at indoor and outdoor venues all over the city. A $50 pass will get you into 100 shows, everything but the big-name events at the Grand Théâtre.

Various locations: 418/647-2525, www.festivalcomediha.com; June-early July; $10 and up, children under 12 free

INTERNATIONAL POW WOW OF WENDAKE

A super-fun, three-day family-friendly event, the International Pow Wow of Wendake draws indigenous folks from all over to participate and compete in traditional dances. Pow wows have taken place for centuries, and this one, which aims to bring together people of different nations to share their cultures and traditions, is no different. The site venue is drug- and alcohol-free, and when you're there it's best to remember your best guest manners—read up about traditions before visiting, and always ask before you take any photos (including some parts of the pow wow itself, which hold spiritual significance and are not to be photographed).

Greater Québec: Wendake, 418/847-1835, www.tourismewendake.ca; last weekend in June; $15 adults, $7.50 children, under 6 free

FÊTE NATIONALE SAINT-JEAN-BAPTISTE

Fête Nationale Saint-Jean-Baptiste is Québec's national holiday, which takes place on June 24. "Nationale" refers to the nation of Québec; this holiday isn't celebrated elsewhere in Canada. Though Saint-Jean-Baptiste Day has been celebrated in Québec since the first European settlers, it took a patriotic turn in 1834 after Ludger Duvernay, who would later found the Saint-Jean-Baptiste Society, was inspired by Saint-Patrick's Day celebrations in Montréal. In celebration of the province's national holiday, the people of Québec usually spend the afternoon with an aperitif before heading out to the free concert on the Plains of Abraham in the evening, featuring famous Québécois performers and stars.

Parliament Hill and the Plains: Plains of Abraham, 418/640-0799, www.fetenationale.quebec/fr/programmation/zone-capitale; June 24; free

Clockwise from top left: ice slides at Carnaval de Québec; an ice glass full of Caribou—a whiskey-based Québécois alcohol; La Cour Arrière du Festibière is an outdoor pub that runs all summer, even after Festibière has wrapped.

FESTIVAL D'ÉTÉ DE QUÉBEC

One of the biggest events in the entire calendar year, Festival d'Été de Québec (Québec Summer Festival) is essentially one 12-day-long concert. With literally hundreds of shows—some of them for free—happening during the beginning of July, this event gives the city the attitude of a nonstop party. Started in 1968, the focus was mainly on Francophone and world artists, but since 2000 the festival has presented some of the world's most interesting international acts, including P!nk, Amadou et Mariam, Caribou, Black Eyed Peas, and emerging talents. The biggest outdoor shows take place on the Plains of Abraham and in the past have featured musicians such as Metallica, Arcade Fire, and Paul McCartney.

Various locations: 888/992-5200, www.infofestival.com; early to mid-July; $95 early-bird adult pass; $105 regular adult pass

FESTIVAL DES JOURNÉES D'AFRIQUE, DANSES ET RYTHMES DU MONDE

Celebrating African dance and music, the three-day Festival des Journées d'Afrique, Danses et Rythmes du Monde, which occurs late July to early August, sees artists from all over the world performing a diverse range of African-roots music. Everything is represented, from soukous from the Congo to Trinidadian calypso, South African Afro-beat, and roots reggae from Québec.

Vieux-Québec's Upper Town: Place d'Youville, 418/640-0572, www.festivaljourneedafrique.com; late July; free

LES FÊTES DE LA NOUVELLE-FRANCE

For four days in August, the public is invited to step back in time during Les Fêtes de la Nouvelle France to experience Québec as it was during the French regime. Bringing to life over a dozen sites in the Vieux-Québec's Lower Town, each year is centered around a theme in order to give viewers a fuller picture of what life was like in New France. Past events have dramatized early parts of colonial religious history, including the baptism of a First Nations person and a public blessing of women's pregnant bellies. Visitors are encouraged to dress up in period costumes, which are available to buy or rent.

Various locations: 418/694-3311, www.nouvellefrance.qc.ca; early Aug.; $10 early-bird adult, $12 on-site adult, children under 12 free

PLEIN ART QUÉBEC

For the first two weeks of August, over 100 professional artisans meet to hawk their wares at Plein Art Québec in the Old Port, in Vieux-Québec's Lower Town. The Conseil Métiers d'Art du Québec, which represents 1,000 artists across the province, puts on this impressive event. Many of the artists who attend inherited their craft from a parent, who inherited it from their parent—these are talented folks who take their work seriously.

Vieux-Québec's Lower Town: Espace 400e, Old Port of Québec, 418/861-2727, www.metiersdart.ca; early to mid-Aug.; free

LES GRANDS FEUX LOTO-QUÉBEC

During the first three weeks of August, Loto-Québec sponsors a huge firework show, Les Grands Feux Loto-Québec, every Wednesday and Saturday night after sunset, starting around 9pm. The fireworks are set off from a platform in the middle of the St. Lawrence River and are visible from the Old Port, in Lower Town, and the Terrasse Dufferin, in front of Château Frontenac. Bring your popcorn, but leave your dog at the hotel.

Vieux-Québec's Lower Town: Old Port of Québec, 418/692-3736, www.lesgrandsfeux.com; Aug.; free

FESTIVAL CELTIQUE DU QUÉBEC

Celebrating Québec's Celtic heritage, the four-day Festival Celtique du Québec features fun and zany events, including a waiter's obstacle course, where servers compete head to head to defend their restaurant's reputation. Taste-test whiskeys, visit a mythical garden, watch the bagpipers do their thing. Oh, and don't forget to check out the Highland Games, where amateurs and pros alike compete in the caber toss and the heavy hammer throw, among others.

Various locations: www.festivalceltique.com; mid-Aug; free

FESTIBIÈRE

Festibière takes place along the waterfront for three days in mid-August and couldn't be better located. In order to expand the taste buds of beer lovers everywhere, tents feature various beers, both local and international brews. There's also a conference dedicated to the art of brewing where you can test your knowledge of hops against that of the experts. Legal drinking age in Québec is 18, so don't be surprised to find yourself surrounded by a few amateur yet eager beavers. The site is free to enter, but to taste beer you'll need to buy the festival's official glass ($15) and tasting tickets—$10 for 10 tickets. If you miss the festival, you can still take advantage of its outdoor pub, complete with wading pool, **La Cour Arrière du Festibière** (check website for details—it's usually open daily July-Sept.).

Vieux-Québec's Lower Town: 100 Quai St-André, 418/948-1166, www.festibieredequebec.com; mid-Aug.; $15 for the official festival glass, $10 for 10 tickets.

BORDEAUX FÊTE LE VIN

Taking place over the Labor Day weekend, the four-day Bordeaux Fête le Vin offers Bordeaux wine tasting, local gastronomic delights, and workshops. You'll also be treated to suitably French—often accordion-heavy—musical accompaniment. Located in the Old Port, the tented outdoor venue draws a nice breeze from the water.

Vieux-Québec's Lower Town: Espace 400e, Old Port of Québec, www.bfvq.ca; early Sept; $35 early-bird pass, $40 regular pass

FÊTE ARC-EN-CIEL DE QUÉBEC

Taking place in early September, usually over Labor Day weekend, Fête Arc-en-Ciel de Québec (Rainbow Celebration) is Québec's three-day gay pride celebration. Each year, the three-day event is based on a different theme, usually one that can be loosely interpreted and allow for some great street decorations. Though the center of the celebrations is the gay pride parade, the festival also includes free performances, concerts, and conferences that look at important topics like homophobia and transphobia in high schools.

Various locations: 418/809-3383, www.arcencielquebec.ca; early Sept.; free

FALL

ENVOL ET MACADAM

The alternative music festival Envol et Macadam was founded in 1996, with the aim of both nurturing up-and-coming talent and bringing established artists to the city who wouldn't necessarily play here otherwise. Taking place for three days in early September, the festival hosts a few outdoor stages (often downtown) and takes over a number of indoor venues during the fest. Though "alternative" isn't as defining a moniker as it was in the 1990s, bands are still outside of the mainstream and have included acts like Bloc Party and Metric as well as punk, hardcore, and metal bands like Propagandhi, Pennywise, and Bad Religion.

Various locations: 418/522-1611, www.envoletmacadam.com; early Sept; $35 festival pass, $121 VIP pass (individual shows $13 and up)

JOURNÉES DE LA CULTURE

The province-wide Journées de la Culture opens various cultural and artistic hubs to the public by inviting visitors into architecture offices, design studios, and local theaters for a behind-the-scenes look. Also called "Days of Culture," this free, three-day event begins on the last Friday of September and runs for the next two consecutive days. Cities offer complimentary shuttle services to various sites and events, so there's no excuse to miss out. Various workshops and kid-specific events make it an adventure for the whole family.

Various locations: 866/734-4441, www.journeesdelaculture.qc.ca; end of Sept.; free

FESTIVAL DE JAZZ DE QUÉBEC

The Festival de Jazz de Québec is for real jazz buffs only; you won't find any Top 40 artists here. The target audience for this fest, running for 10 days in mid- to late October, is jazz aficionados. You'll find entire sets dedicated to greats like Charles Mingus and John Coltrane. Local jazz musicians also take to the stage, including younger avant-garde artists.

Various locations: www.festivaldejazzdequebec.com; mid-late Oct.; $26-43 per show

FESTIVAL DES MUSIQUES SACRÉES DE QUÉBEC

The Festival des Musiques Sacrées de Québec (Québec Festival of Sacred Music) is just that: a three-day-long October festival filled with compositions inspired by spirituality. Taking place at the Église Saint-Roch, where they are the proud owners of a (partly) Casavantes organ, programs include standards like Brahms's and Verdi's requiems, as well as occasional dance performances, gospel concerts, and compositions from lesser-known sources like sacred songs from Anatolia.

Saint-Jean-Baptiste and Saint-Roch: Église St-Roch, 590 rue St-Jean, 866/524-3577, www.musiquessacreesquebec.com; early Nov.; festival passport $80

PARADE DES JOUETS

Held annually on the second Saturday of November, the Parade des Jouets (Parade of Toys) has a long history. It was started at the end of World War II by fireman Marcel Bourassa. Firefighters of the city worked together to repair old toys and make new ones for the less-fortunate children in the city. The tradition continues today, and since 2004, 900 underprivileged children are the recipients of new and refurbished toys each year. The parade is run in celebration of that event and includes floats and marching bands.

Various locations: 418/780-3004, www.paradedesjouets.ca; 2nd Sat. in Nov.; free

MARCHÉ DE NOËL ALLEMAND

Snowy and picturesque in the wintertime, Québec City is the ideal place for a Christmas market. The Marché de Noël Allemand (German Christmas Market) takes place for a month from late November to late December. You can find gifts for friends and family, decorations for your home, and—perhaps best of all—a range of German meals and snacks, like bratwurst, mulled wine, and gingerbread, to sate any shopping-induced hunger.

Vieux-Québec's Upper Town: Place de l'Hôtel-de-Ville and Jardin de l'Hôtel-de-Ville, www.noelallemandquebec.com; late Nov. to early Dec.; free

Sports and Activities

Québec City is blessed with huge green spaces, a waterfront, and a cliff face perfect for scaling. Even in its most populated areas, citizens and visitors will feel close to nature and all the outdoor activities it offers—even a trip to the local store can sometimes feel like a hike. The city offers intense inclines with unbeatable views, the promise of mountains looming to the north, and the beauty of one of the world's largest rivers. Quebeckers embrace this proximity to nature, taking up summer and winter sports like canoeing and skiing in their urban environment. The whole family gets involved and the emphasis is on enjoying the sun and snow—there's no need to be a pro, and it's a great place to try out a new sport you've always been curious about.

In the winter, when the ground is buried under four feet of snow, cross-country skiing and snowshoeing become part of getting around in the city. What better way to see the historical sights than skiing from one place to the next? There's no shortage of outdoor skating rinks, many of which are frozen rivers and ponds. Ice-skating is an idyllic and truly Canadian pastime. Not far from the city center are mountains perfect for exploring with snowboards and downhill skis. For the less sporty, ice slides and tubing are a great way to enjoy the snow.

The city is on one of the largest waterways in North America, so boating is a popular sport, and in summer the St. Lawrence is dotted with white sails and even the occasional sea kayak.

Though it's quite hilly, Québec City is also home to two of the longest bike paths in the country, both fairly flat and fairly picturesque, as they run alongside the river; a trip down the Promenade Samuel-De Champlain,

Previous: a Croisières AML boat tour on the St. Lawrence River; the Glissades de la Terrasse Dufferin.

Look for ★ to find recommended activities

Highlights

★ **Best Winter Sledding:** At 250 meters high, the biggest (and only) winter slide in Québec City is the **Glissades de la Terrasse Dufferin;** speeding from the top down to the *terrasse* at speeds of up to 70 kilometers per hour has been a tradition since 1884 (page 139).

★ **Best Bike Path:** Running alongside the St. Lawrence River and through Cap-Blanc and various parks, **Corridor du Littoral** is a great path for exercise and to see some of the lesser-known parts of the city (page 139).

★ **Best Place for Snow Sports:** With everything from cross-country skiing to ice-skating and snowshoeing available, **Parc des Plaines d'Abraham** is your outdoor sports paradise (page 141).

★ **Best Place to Have a Picnic:** Once the grounds of the governor-general's residence, **Parc du Bois-de-Coulonge** boasts groomed gardens and amazing views of the St. Lawrence that are still worthy of royalty (page 145).

★ **Best Summer Activity:** Nothing says summer like a game of baseball. **Les Capitales de Québec** are among the best in the Can-Am league (page 147).

Parc des Plaines d'Abraham

which runs 4.3 kilometers eastward from the Aquarium du Québec, is like a mini-break from the city. And, of course, come winter the bike path becomes one of the best ski trails.

Vieux-Québec's Upper Town Map 1

ICE-SKATING

PATINOIRE DE LA PLACE D'YOUVILLE

Directly in front of the Palais de Montcalm, this outdoor skating rink is a veritable winter wonderland once the snow has settled. A great place to bring the kids, it is frequented by tourists and locals alike who want to go for a skate in the shadow of the old city walls. Skate rental and sharpening are available during opening hours, as is a warm changing room fitted out with lockers, but visitors have to bring their own padlock.

MAP 1: 995 Place d'Youville, 418/641-6256; noon-10pm Mon.-Thurs., 10am-10pm Fri.-Sat. Nov.-early Mar.; free

SLEDDING

★ GLISSADES DE LA TERRASSE DUFFERIN

This entertainment of sliding down a steep 250-meter run at speeds of up to 70 kilometers per hour has been around since 1884. The Glissades de la Terrasse Dufferin *(les glissades)* are a Québec tradition. In front of the Château Frontenac, with great views of the St. Lawrence, families line up in full winter regalia to ride a toboggan down to the base of the wooden structure. Up to four people can ride down on a single toboggan, though you're also allowed to try it solo and in pairs. A mini sugar shack full of refreshments is available on the spot—pick up a slide and hot chocolate combo for $6. Lines can be long, especially on weekends, so be prepared to wait.

MAP 1: Terrasse Dufferin, at rue des Carrières and Place d'Armes, 418/528-1884, www.au1884.ca; 11am-11pm daily mid-Dec.-mid-Mar.; $3 pp per ride

Vieux-Québec's Lower Town Map 2

BIKING

Bike Paths

★ CORRIDOR DU LITTORAL

This 48-kilometer bike path stretches all the way from Saint-Augustin-de-Desmaures west of Québec City way to Chute Montmorency to the east. Running alongside the St. Lawrence, the path includes the **Promenade Samuel-De Champlain;** redone for the city's 400th anniversary in 2008, this section of the path is below the Plains of Abraham and includes various parks and rest stops. It takes you along Cap-Blanc, a charming working-class area built directly against the cliff.

Though it's mainly a bike path, runners, walkers, in-line skaters, and those in wheelchairs are free to use the path for both recreation and mobility. Open throughout the year, it becomes an ideal place to snowshoe and cross-country ski in winter.

MAP 2: St-Augustin-de-Desmaures to Chute Montmorency, 418/641-6290, www.routeverte.com; free

Bike Rentals and Tours

CYCLO SERVICES

Offering both rentals and tours, Cyclo Services has different types of bikes on offer, including hybrids, road bikes, tandem, and children's bikes. All rentals come with a helmet, lock, and map. Located across the street from the Corridor du Littoral, it couldn't be easier to jump on your bike and go. Six bike tours are available throughout the summer season; some, like the one through Lower Town and the Vieux-Port, stay closer to home, while others, like Huron-Wendake, take you farther afield. Prices vary and times change often, so call or email ahead. For those with their own wheels, an on-site mechanic is available seven days a week.

MAP 2: 289 rue St-Paul, 418/692-4052, www.cycloservices.net; 8am-6pm daily; tours May-Oct.; rentals $38 per day and up

ECHO SPORTS

Near the Vieux-Port, Echo Sports is perfectly situated right next to the Corridor du Littoral, the longest bike path in the city. They rent hybrid bikes and road bikes, ideal for getting around the hilly city, and they also offer electric bikes to help give your pedaling a bit of a push, as well as tandems and kids' bikes. You can rent by the hour, half day, or full day—renting a hybrid costs $15 for two hours, $35 for the first full day, and $20 for each subsequent day. They also offer six guided tours, such as a full-day bike and cruise tour that includes a hearty Italian lunch.

MAP 2: 39 rue Dalhousie, 418/692-3643, www.locationechosports.ca; 9am-5pm daily May-Oct.; rentals $15-25 for 2 hours, $35-65 per day; tours $60-125

BOAT TOURS

CROISIÈRES AML

Cruises are available on the *Louis Jolliet,* a restaurant boat; zodiac tours and combination bus-boat whale-watching packages are also available. The largest boat tour operation in town, Croisières AML offers a wide range of experiences based on the season. Options include the brunch cruise with activities for kids, a tour of Île d'Orléans, a fireworks cruise, and a five-course dinner cruise. The captain's lounge, three dining rooms, and terraces are on board, as well as a gift shop and a bistro. Entertainment is part of every cruise, and guide Louis Jolliet—an early Canadian explorer—will reveal all the area's secrets. An orchestra plays in the evenings; passengers can dance the night away.

MAP 2: Quai Chouinard, 10 rue Dalhousie, 866/856-6668, www.croisieresaml.com; cruises $35-200 adults, $20-100 children under 13 (some cruises are suitable only for ages 13 and up)

Parliament Hill and the Plains

Map 3

CROSS-COUNTRY SKIING AND SNOWSHOEING

★ PARC DES PLAINES D'ABRAHAM

Come winter, this historic site becomes an outdoor sport paradise. For beginners and pros, the 13.9 kilometers of cross-county trails and the 3.8-kilometer (round-trip) trail for snowshoers are the best place to experience winter in the city's own backyard. Five classic ski trails, made up of one easy trail, three intermediate trails, and one expert trail, are open, as well as one snowshoe trail. Those without their own equipment—boots, poles, skis, and snowshoes—can rent them from the Information and Reception Centre. A waxing room and two heated rest areas are available around the plains, and they also offer tours and events involving snowshoes.

MAP 3: Information and Reception Centre, 835 rue Wilfrid-Laurier (equipment rental), 418/649-6157, www.ccbn-nbc.gc.ca; 8:30am-4pm daily late Dec.-mid-Mar.; free

ICE-SKATING

PARC DU MUSÉE

This outdoor skating rink, directly in front of the Musée National des Beaux-Arts and right on the Plains of Abraham, is a great place to bring the kids. Easily accessible and popular with locals, it was completely renovated in 2011 and can accommodate up to 350 skaters at a time. Rental equipment and hot chocolate are available at the on-site skaters' chalet. Access to the ice is free; skates cost $8 for the first hour and $4 for each additional hour.

MAP 3: Parc des Champs-de-Bataille, 418/641-6100; 10am-10pm daily mid-Dec.-mid-Mar.; free

SWIMMING

PISCINE PARC DU MUSÉE

Located on the Plains of Abraham, this public pool and wading pool were renovated in 2011, giving them a brand-new look. Conveniently located right on La Grande-Allée, it's easily accessible from all points in the city. A haven for locals, this is a great place to bring the kids, especially to let them go a little wild after an afternoon at the museum.

MAP 3: Parc des Champs-de-Bataille; noon-7pm daily mid-June-mid-Aug., 2pm-5pm daily mid-Aug.-early Sept.; free

Top: Cyclo Services offers bike rentals and bike tours. **Bottom:** Visitors disembark the *Louis Jolliet* after a sightseeing tour with Croisières AML.

PISCINE PARC NOTRE-DAME-DE-LA-GARDE

This L-shaped pool a little off the beaten path is 25 meters long—larger than the Piscine Parc du Musée, and suitable for older children and adults as well as younger children. A trip to this pool is worth it if the whole family is looking to cool off on a hot summer's day.

MAP 3: Parc Bassin-Brown; noon-7pm daily mid-June-mid-Aug., 2pm-5pm daily mid-Aug.-early Sept.; free

Greater Québec City

Map 5

PARKS

DOMAINE MAIZERETS

Across the St. Charles River, Domaine Maizerets is both a public park and a historical site. Bought by the church in 1705, the land served as a farm, and some of the church's old buildings are still standing. Tours of the beautifully landscaped gardens and arboretum are available, and concerts are often held on the park grounds. Four bike paths cut through the park, and in the winter it's a popular place for skating, cross-country skiing, snowshoeing, and tobogganing.

MAP 5: 2000 blvd. Montmorency, 418/666-3331, www.domainemaizerets.com; dawn-dusk daily; free

PARC CARTIER-BRÉBEUF AND CARTIER-BRÉBEUF NATIONAL HISTORIC SITE

South of Saint-Roch, this national historic site commemorates both the winter of 1535, when Jacques Cartier and his shipmates spent the season near the Iroquoian village of Stadacona, and the site of the Jesuit missionaries' first home in Québec. Commemorative monuments are set up around the park, which is divided into east and west by a small river. With 6.8 hectares, it's a popular place for outdoor sport, and a bike path cuts through most of it. An interpretation center is open on-site from late June to early September, offering guided tours and various family activities.

MAP 5: 175 rue l'Espinay, 888/773-8888, www.pc.gc.ca; park dawn-dusk daily, interpretation center 1pm-5pm daily late June-early Sept.; free

PARC DE LA PLAGE JACQUES-CARTIER

Located outside of the city, just on the other side of the Québec Bridge, this waterfront park gives visitors direct access to the St. Lawrence River. The winding paths and roads that take you to the shore, coupled with the boulders and pebbles that line the beach, make you feel as though you're somewhere else entirely. Since swimming is prohibited, boating is the summer's most popular sport, along with the 2.5 kilometers of hiking trails.

MAP 5: 3636 chemin du Pavillon, Ste-Foy, 418/654-4443; dawn-dusk daily; free

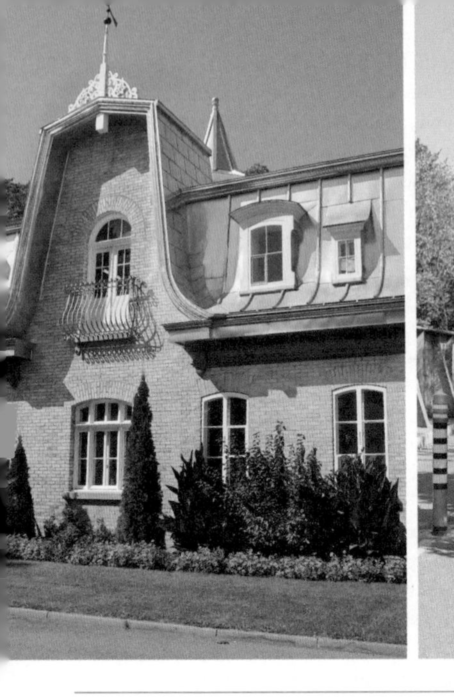

Clockwise from top left: the former stables at the Parc du Bois-de-Coulonge; biking on the Corridor des Cheminots; Piscine Parc du Musée.

★ PARC DU BOIS-DE-COULONGE

The former home of the governor-general of United Canada, Spencer Wood was bought by the Québec government in 1870 and was home to the province's lieutenant-governors until 1966. Though a fire destroyed the main residence, the splendid gardens remain, including a park that runs along the St. Lawrence, offering great views of the city. The park is a favorite for picnicking, self-guided tours, and hiking. There's also a children's playground and sledding in winter. From late June to early September, Café 47 is open to serve coffee, tea, and snacks (11am-6pm daily).

MAP 5: 1215 La Grande-Allée W., 800/442-0773; 7am-11pm daily; free

PARC LINÉAIRE DE LA RIVIÈRE SAINT-CHARLES

Starting at the Vieux-Port and running on for a total of 32 kilometers, this park follows the banks of the St. Charles River, covering both urban and natural environments. Open year-round, it has seven kilometers of bike and rollerblade paths, ice-skating, snowshoeing, and over 10 kilometers of cross-country skiing in winter. An interpretation center is in the middle of the park.

MAP 5: 332 rue Domagaya, 418/691-4710, www.societerivierestcharles.qc.ca; dawn-dusk daily; free

PARC VICTORIA

Situated along the northwestern edge of Saint-Roch on the banks of the St. Charles River, Parc Victoria has been one of the few green spaces in the area since 1897. Almost completely surrounded by water, the small park was named after Britain's Queen Victoria. It provides excellent views of the river and it's here that you'll catch a baseball game by Les Capitales de Québec.

MAP 5: Rue Robert-Rumilly, 418/641-6654; dawn-dusk daily; free

AMUSEMENT PARKS

MEGA PARC DES GALERIES DE LA CAPITALE

A child's paradise, this amusement park in the middle of a mall is designed for toddlers through tweens. Nineteen different rides are waiting for kids to take them for a whirl, from physical fun like the Magic Castle's ball pit, slides, and rope games and the Baby Jungle's plush obstacle course to more traditional fairway staples like mini-bumper cars, a miniature train, a merry-go-round, Ferris wheel, and a rollercoaster. For kids wanting a bit more sport, there's also a climbing wall, an ice rink, and mini-putt. Each ride requires a varying number of tokens, anywhere from two to five, with each token costing 85 cents.

MAP 5: 5401 blvd. des Galeries, 418/627-5800, www.mega-parc.com; noon-5pm Mon.-Wed., noon-9pm Thurs.-Fri., 9:30am-5pm Sat., 11am-5pm Sun. Sept.-mid-June; 10am-5pm Sun.-Mon., 10am-9pm Wed.-Fri., 9am-5pm Sat. mid-June-Aug.

BIKING

Bike Paths

CORRIDOR DES CHEMINOTS

Intersecting with the Corridor du Littoral just outside Saint-Roch, the Corridor des Cheminots is 22 kilometers long and takes riders from the city to Haute Saint-Charles in the north. Since it passes through various areas, including the St. Charles River and Wendake Village, riders can view a diverse landscape. Open to cyclists, walkers, runners, and inline skaters, it becomes a popular place for cross-country skiing and snowshoeing in the winter.

MAP 5: North of Estuaire de la Rivière St-Charles to Haute St-Charles, 418/641-6412, www.routeverte.com; free

CLIMBING

LE PYLÔNE

This natural climbing wall can be accessed from rue Champlain. Just outside of the city, near the Pont de Québec, this outdoor climbing area is a popular place with local climbers and caters to both learners and intermediate climbers. Le Pylône, known as the "School of Rock," features 30 routes ranging in difficulty from 5.3 to 5.11. Daily site access through the FQME (Fédération Québécoise de la Montagne et de l'Escalade) is $10; an annual FQME membership is $22 for adults, $11 for ages 19 and under. Visit the FQME website for more details about area regulations and climbing preparation.

MAP 5: Near Pont de Québec, www.fqme.qc.ca; dawn-dusk daily; $10 daily site access

ROC GYMS

Opened in 1993, Roc Gyms is a climbing school that offers indoor climbing lessons. Dozens of routes are available in their large main room, while three bouldering rooms are also available on-site, as are indoor aerial courses. Experienced climbers can sign up for courses in outdoor and ice-climbing. Located in Limoilou, it's easily accessible from downtown and Vieux-Port.

MAP 5: 2350 ave. du Colisée, 418/647-4422, www.rocgyms.com; 9am-10pm daily; $18.50 day rental with equipment

GOLF

LA TEMPÊTE

Situated across the water in the city of Lévis, La Tempête is one of the top courses in the metropolitan area (of course, the greens fees reflect this). It hosted the World Skins tournament in 2009 and has been called the first 18-hole golf course of international caliber in the area. Designed by golf architect Darrell J. Huxham, the 7,203-yard course is topped with a luxurious clubhouse and high-class restaurant.

MAP 5: 51 rue des Trois Manoirs, Lévis, 418/832-8111, www.golflatempete.com; dawn-10pm daily May-Nov.; $105-165 for 18 holes

ICE-SKATING

POINTE-AUX-LIÈVRES

When the St. Charles River, which separates Saint-Roch from Limoilou, freezes over, it becomes a natural skating rink, measuring 1.5 kilometers long. You'll find people playing pickup hockey and families teaching the youngest members how to skate. If you want a real Canadian experience, there's nothing like plopping your bum on a cold park bench to lace up your skates. Of course, a warm changing room and heated pavilion with hot chocolate and skate rental ($7 per hour) are also available. Bonus: You can also rent inner tubes ($4 per hour) to slide down the toboggan hill, as well as cross-country skis ($10 for 2 hours).

MAP 5: 25 rue de la Pointe-aux-Lièvres, 418/641-6345; noon-10pm Mon.-Thurs., 10am-10pm Fri.-Sun. mid-Dec.-mid-Mar.; free

SPECTATOR SPORTS

Baseball

★ LES CAPITALES DE QUÉBEC

Members of the Can-Am Baseball League, Les Capitales are one of the most successful teams in the league. Making the playoffs almost every year since they entered the league in 1999, they garnered league titles in 2006, 2009, and 2010-2013. They play at the Stade Canac, which seats approximately 5,000 and is in Parc Victoria. The stadium opened in 1938 and has a long history within local baseball legend. This rich history and the affordable tickets give you the feeling that you're still in touch with what sports used to be and should be.

MAP 5: Stade Canac, 100 rue de Cardinal-Maurice-Roy, Parc Victoria, 418/521-2255, www.capitalesdequebec.com; tickets $12 general admission, $19 box seats

Football

ROUGE ET OR

This university football team has amassed a strong following in a city craving more spectator sports. Rouge et Or (Red and Gold, which are Université Laval's school colors) won the Vanier Cup, the highest distinction for a Canadian university football team, an amazing eight times between 2003 and 2016. They also hold the record for the longest winning streak in Canadian Interuniversity Sport football with 25 consecutive wins. If you happen to be visiting in the fall, a trip to Sainte-Foy to see a game is worth it; the bleachers are always packed and the energy is palpable.

Université Laval's outdoor stadium can hold up to 10,000 spectators but fit double that in 2005 with standing room only. The team's loyal fan base has also mastered the art of tailgating, getting to the stadium parking lot early on game day mornings.

MAP 5: PEPS de l'Université Laval, 2300 rue de la Terrasse, 418/656-7377, www.rougeetor.ulaval.ca; tickets $12-52 adults, $6-52 students, children under 12 free for general admission

Hockey

REMPARTS DE QUÉBEC

Ever since they won the Memorial Cup (the Canadian Junior Championships) in 2006, the Remparts, Québec's Major Junior Hockey team, have become the hottest show in town. And things will probably stay that way so long as this crazy-about-hockey city doesn't have an NHL team. Their home rink is the Centre Vidéotron. Famous Remparts alumni include legendary player Guy Lafleur, ex-NHL Québec Nordiques Michel Goulet, left-winger Simon Gagné, center Mike Ribeiro, and right-winger Alexander Radulov.

MAP 5: Centre Vidéotron, 250 blvd. Wilfrid-Hamel, 418/525-1212, www.remparts.qc.ca; tickets $17-19 adults, $14-16 seniors, $11-13 students, $8-10 children 6-12, under 6 free

WATER SPORTS

BAIE DE BEAUPORT

A world of boating fun is only a five-minute drive from downtown Québec City. This beach is the only one in the city where swimming is permitted in the river. In addition, paddle board, canoe, kayak, sailboard, dinghy, and catamaran rentals are offered at various rates and lengths, and those looking to learn how to sail can sign up for classes. Beach soccer and volleyball courts are free for all to use, and the large children's park keeps the kids busy.

MAP 5: Eastern end of blvd. Henri-Bourassa, 418/266-0722, www.baiedebeauport.com; 10am-9pm daily mid-June-mid-Aug.; $2 adults, free age 17 and under, parking $10/day

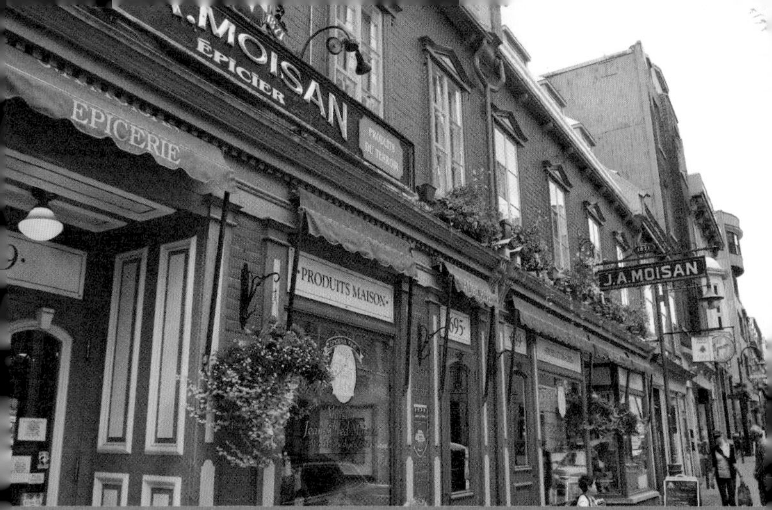
J.A.MOISAN
ÉPICIER
EPICERIE
PRODUITS MAISON
J.A.MOISAN

Shops

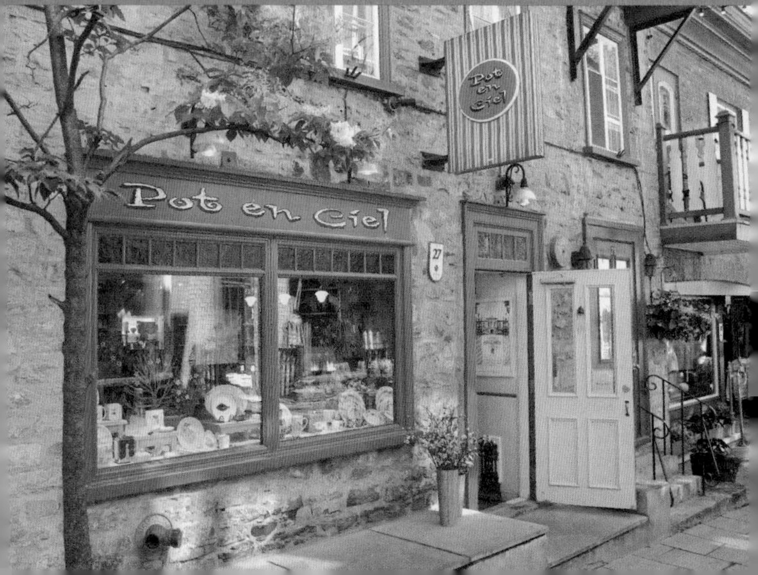
Pot en Ciel
Pot en Ciel

Look for ★ to find recommended shops

Highlights

★ **Best Hat Store: Bibi et Compagnie** has approximately 3,000 men's and women's hats for all kinds of weather and in all kinds of styles (page 154).

★ **Unique Gifts:** Connoisseur of kitsch, Mr. Blouin carries everything from old milk jugs to vintage magazines at the cabin-esque **Magasin Général P.L. Blouin** (page 157).

★ **Best Artisanal Crafts:** Carrying the work of over 125 local artisans, **Boutique des Métiers d'Art** is a perfect one-stop shop for everything from jewelry to salad bowls (page 159).

★ **Best Woolen Goods:** Tucked into a small basement storefront, **Charlevoix Pure Laine** features goods handmade from local sheep (page 162).

★ **Best Place to Rock:** If you're a fan of rock, specifically garage, punk, hardcore, and indie, and specifically on vinyl, then **Le Knock-Out** has got you covered (page 169).

★ **Best Toy Store:** Parents can let kids run wild and kids can let parents do the same at toy emporium **Benjo** (page 169).

★ **Best Selection of Local Designers:** Dedicated to local designers, **Jupon Pressé** exclusively carries lines from some of the province's most exciting emerging designers and does it with some fun in a bright, eclectic boutique (page 171).

★ **Best Chocolate:** Featuring a cocoa museum, **Érico Chocolatier** blends tradition with invention, offering everything from homemade ice cream to lavender-infused truffles (page 173).

★ **Best Outdoor Gear:** If you're headed for an outdoor adventure, **Latulippe** has everything from bike gear to arctic sleeping bags to get you ready (page 175).

Magasin Général P.L. Blouin

Québec has a long history with commerce. As the site of the first settlement in New France, its entire founding was based on trade with First Nations such as the Huron and Algonquin peoples. As the colony grew, trade became vital to its survival.

Its genetic makeup as a commercial city is still apparent, and over the centuries it has created some of Canada's most recognized stores and brands.

Many of those same stores exist today. La Maison Simons and J.A. Moisan (the oldest grocery store in North America) are businesses that first bloomed in Québec and whose rich past can still be seen when you enter their establishments.

With all that history, however, it's important to have something new, and the revival of **rue St-Joseph** in Saint-Roch has been one of the most important developments of the past decade or so. The area was abandoned by businesses that opted for the malls of the late 1950s, but new customers and retailers are now emerging in the area. Filled with young, modern stores and independent boutiques, it has given the city a much-needed boost of unpretentious fresh blood. **Rue St-Jean,** outside of the walls, is experiencing a similar rejuvenation, with youthful stores popping up, many with an eye on local products and design. If you want to pick up some vintage Félix Leclerc after an inspiring night at a *boîte à chansons,* you'll find both new and used vinyl and CDs along rue St-Jean.

Unlike most major Canadian cities, Québec sticks to its roots when it comes to the **downtown** core. Here, stores like H&M, Gap, and Zara are relegated to the malls, about a 15-minute drive away. Though some chains can be found (mostly in Upper Town), they are few and far between.

Previous: J.A. Moisan is the oldest grocery store in North America; Pot en Ciel sells charming ceramics and kitchenware.

Instead, the historical houses and beautiful Beaux-Arts buildings are small independent boutiques or established businesses.

There are independent jewelry stores throughout Québec City. **Rue du Petit-Champlain** has a good mix of high-end and more artsy offerings. In fact, these are the two main kinds of jewelry stores found all over the city: super kitsch costume jewelry and high-end designer pieces. One thing that remains the same in upscale or costume jewelry is that it's all handcrafted.

If you're on the hunt for antiques, look no further than the narrow cobblestone **rue St-Paul,** where just about every other store is dedicated to antiques. The stores are stocked full of everything from antique bedposts to silverware.

Many of the stores that line the streets of **Vieux-Québec's Upper and Lower Town** cater to tourists and blend into one another. The stores included here, however, all offer something a bit different and less well known.

Though Québec doesn't have crafts in the traditional sense, there is a certain aesthetic found in the various artisanal works. A mix of materials is one element, as is an unexpected juxtaposition of colors and shapes. Inuit art, though not exclusive to the province, can also be found in arts and craft shops, since the northernmost part of Québec is home to and part of the traditional territory of the Inuit (while shopping for these goods, make sure to keep an eye out for the real deal—buying Inuit-made arts and crafts instead of knock-offs helps to support indigenous artisans and will ensure you take home an authentic piece instead of a factory-made imitation).

English books are hard to come by in Québec City. Magazines, however, are much easier to find, and both European and North American versions are readily available.

It's not surprising that in a city so defined by its food, its best markets revolve around farmers and fresh produce. And though winters can be harsh, the farmers markets keep going all year long.

In high tourist season, boutiques in Upper and Lower Town stay open late, some even as late as midnight, if the crowds are still out. In winter, stores often close early, or for months at a time, depending on the nature of their business. If there's a store you particularly want to visit, it's always best to call ahead in the off-season.

ACCESSORIES AND JEWELRY

ZIMMERMANN

Having studied jewelry design and gemology in Paris, Michel Zimmermann returned to Québec in the late 1970s to open his very own jewelry shop. Zimmermann has since become one of the most respected jewelers in the business, known for unique handcrafted gems. The pieces are all meticulously handcrafted without the use of any cast, working exclusively with 925/1000 silver and 18-carat gold or platinum. Styles vary from simple, leaf-shaped earrings to detailed wedding bands and teardrop birthstone pendants.

MAP 1: 46 Côte de la Fabrique, 418/692-2672, www.zimmermann-quebec.com; 9:30am-5:30pm Mon.-Wed. and Sat., 9:30am-9pm Thurs.-Fri.

ARTS AND CRAFTS

GALERIE D'ART LES TROIS COLOMBES

Situated in a beautiful old house complete with a red-peaked roof and white-washed facade, Galerie d'Art les Trois Colombes is one of the most picturesque of arts and craft stores. Filled with selections from both Québécois and Canadian arts and crafts, it also carries Inuit and First Nations works, including thick-wool parkas trimmed with fur and moccasins and mukluks in both child and adult sizes. Authentic snowshoes, soapstone sculptures, and weavings occupy the downstairs, while, upstairs, visitors will find handmade hats, rag dolls, and sweaters.

MAP 1: 46 rue St-Louis, 418/694-1114; 9:30am-7pm Mon.-Wed., 9:30am-9pm Thurs.-Sun.

LAMBERT & CO.

This teeny-tiny store in the interior courtyard of Château Frontenac, approximately two meters wide, is a splendid gem. The emphasis is on quality not quantity, and their finely made striped wool socks, black-and-red checkered blankets, and fur-trimmed hats have become a recognized brand in this region. Alongside the cozy woolen goods (and pillows that make great souvenirs), they sell a few natural beauty products, like moisturizer, body wash, and shampoo, for both people and their pets.

MAP 1: 1 rue des Carrières, 418/694-2151, www.lambertco.ca; 9am-7pm Mon.-Wed., 9am-10pm Thurs.-Sat., 9am-9pm Sun.

BATH, BEAUTY, AND SPAS

LE SPA DU MANOIR

Located inside the Hôtel Manoir Victoria, this full-service spa offers manicures ($50), pedicures ($70), and signature treatments like deep-cleansing facials ($95), bamboo and eucalyptus massage ($115), and maple body scrubs ($65). A 30-minute Swedish massage will set you back $65. It's frequented by hotel guests, but nonguests may also make a reservation here.

Many of the treatments use products made with local, organic ingredients, and spa packages also give visitors access to the hotel's gym, sauna, and indoor pool, all of which have an early-20th-century, Turkish-bath feel with mosaic tiles and arched columns around the pool.

MAP 1: 44 Côte du Palais, 800/463-6283, www.manoir-victoria.com; 9am-9pm daily

BOOKS AND MUSIC

LIBRAIRIE PANTOUTE

Founded in 1972 by a bunch of counterculture kids, Librairie Pantoute (its name means "not at all" in Québécois lingo) is one of the most important independent bookstores in the province. Situated in the heart of Upper Town, this location has high ceilings and walls full of bookshelves. They carry popular English titles, mostly best-sellers like John Grisham and Ken Follett, although they usually have a title or two by still popular but slightly lesser-known authors. No matter what you're looking for, the well-informed, usually bilingual staff will be able to help.

MAP 1: 1100 rue St-Jean, 418/694-9748, www.librairiepantoute.com; 9:30am-10pm daily

PREMIÈRE ISSUE

Die-hard comic fans will want to make Première Issue a definite stop. Sitting at a 45-degree angle in Vieux-Québec's Upper Town directly across from Les Fortifications, this comic book paradise is filled with back issues of DC and Marvel comics, as well as cult classics like *The Watchman*. Local fans can be found browsing and reading or having an intense discussion about *Tintin* with staff. The atmosphere is laid-back with a bit of whimsy. Though they also carry comics from Québec and France, known as *bande dessinée*, the focus is on classic English-language comics.

MAP 1: 27A rue d'Auteuil, 418/692-3985, www.librairiepremiereissue.com; 9am-9pm Mon.-Fri., 10am-7pm Sat., noon-7pm Sun.

CLOTHING AND SHOES

★ BIBI ET COMPAGNIE

If you ask the owner of this headwear wonderland tucked down a quiet side street how she would describe her store, she will tell you, "I sell hats. That's it. Point final." And she's right. Men's hats, women's hats, they are all available, from panamas to fedoras, caps to cloches, and in an array of colors and sizes, stacked up along the shelves or modeled by body-less mannequins. The service is hands-off, unless customers show real interest, and the atmosphere quite sober, depending on the mood of the staff, who are mostly mature Québécois wearing fine hats.

MAP 1: 42 rue Garneau, 418/649-0045, www.bibietcie.com; 9am-7pm Mon.-Sat., 10am-6pm Sun. Feb.-Oct.; noon-7pm Thurs.-Sun. Nov.-Jan.

LA MAISON DARLINGTON

One of the oldest boutiques in Québec, La Maison Darlington is named after an English tailor who took over a business that sold military garments

Clockwise from top left: Librairie Pantoute is one of Québec's most significant independent bookstores; it's always Christmas at La Boutique de Noël; Confiserie C'est Si Bon is the ideal place to sate your sweet tooth.

and turned it into a wool and cashmere boutique. The antique till and specialized wooden sweater shelves are reminders of times past, and though the styles may have changed since he opened in 1872, the ethos remains the same. You'll find accessories, tuques, berets, mittens, and scarves of only the highest quality from brands such as Ballantyne, Johnston of Elgin, and Tilley Endurables. Dapper gentlemen who still wear caps are fans, as are well-heeled older women who come for their cozy knits.

MAP 1: 7 rue de Buade, 418/692-2268; 9:30am-6pm Mon.-Sat., 10am-6pm Sun.

DEPARTMENT STORES

LA MAISON SIMONS

One of the city's most important businesses, La Maison Simons was started in 1840 by 17-year-old John Simons, who opened a dry goods store near Porte Saint-Jean. In 1870, the store moved to a new location close to the basilica, where it remains. Though opened in the late 19th century, it has a definite art deco feel, with a beautiful, concave ceiling made of pearl glass. A large section has recently been remodeled and features high ceilings, sleek white modern stairs, and a live DJ on weekends. They carry labels both midrange (Canada Goose) and luxury (Kenzo, Chloe), as well as their private label collection. Locations include Place Ste-Foy (2450 blvd. Laurier, 418/634-1840) and Galeries de la Capitale (5401 blvd. des Galeries, 418/626-1840).

MAP 1: 20 Côte de la Fabrique, 418/694-3630, www.simons.ca; 9:30am-5:30pm Mon.-Wed., 9:30am-9pm Thurs.-Fri., 9:30am-5pm Sat., noon-5pm Sun. winter; 9:30am-9pm Mon.-Sat., noon-5pm Sun. summer

GIFTS AND HOME

BOUTIQUE ARTISANS CANADA

Open since World War II, this large, spacious boutique in Vieux-Québec's Upper Town has subsequently been run by three generations of the Théberge family. It stocks jewelry, leather goods, fur hats, plush toys, sweaters, T-shirts, and outerwear. The majority of the lines are made and designed in Québec. It's recommended by the *New York Times* as a store to visit, and staff will remind you of this designation. The back of the store is dedicated to toy soldiers, and they have a huge collection of figurines, including the French battling the English at Waterloo and on the Plains of Abraham.

MAP 1: 30 Côte de la Fabrique, 418/692-2109, www.artisanscanada.com; 9am-10pm daily summer, 10am-6pm daily winter

LA BOUTIQUE DE NOËL

No matter the time of year, it's always Christmas at La Boutique de Noël. In a three-story building whose facade is permanently decorated with fairy lights, the interior is painted a deep hunter green with red trim and high-flying angels. Fully decorated Christmas trees line the aisles, while the

The Oldest Grocery Store in North America

If you're tired of museums but still want a trip back in time, head to **J.A. Moisan** (695 rue St-Jean, 418/522-0685, www.jamoisan.com, 8:30am-7pm Mon.-Wed. and Sat., 8:30am-9pm Thurs.-Fri., 10am-7pm Sun.), the oldest grocery store in North America, established in 1871. The Victorian-era look of the store has been meticulously recreated. Every little detail has been accounted for, from the crisp white shirts of the serving staff to the large wood-framed display cases to the tin roof, wooden shelves lined with goods, and the French music from the 1930s and '40s piping in over the speakers.

When it first opened, Moisan's aim was to offer the area's well-to-do clients gourmet foods, and that tradition continues today with items like charcuterie, imported foie gras, biscuits, chocolates, and even soaps filling the walls of the two-room grocery store. One change, however, is the addition of a small café near the entrance, where locals come to grab a quick lunch or indulge in a fresh pastry and coffee. Built in the early 1800s, it is one of the oldest buildings in Saint-Jean and was one of the few structures that weren't destroyed by the great fire of 1881, which decimated the area. Though it retains a Victorian aesthetic, it is still a functioning grocery store, with locals popping in to get their morning bread and fresh produce. It may look and feel like the oldest grocery store in North America, but it is also very modern. The owners run a small auberge if you're looking for quaint accommodations.

walls are hung with countless ornaments, from Disney characters to sophisticated icicles and everything in between. They also carry nativity scenes, stockings, tinsel, and anything else you want to hang on your tree. If you're unsure of the number of days left until the big event, this place has a running countdown.

MAP 1: 47 rue de Buade, 418/692-2457, www.boutiquedenoel.ca; 10am-5pm daily Jan.-Apr., 9am-10pm daily May-June and Oct., 8am-midnight daily July-Aug., 9am-11pm daily Sept., 9am-9pm daily Nov.-Dec.

★ MAGASIN GÉNÉRAL P.L. BLOUIN

Without a doubt one of the best stores in the city, Magasin Général P.L. Blouin is filled with novelty items and pieces of historical kitsch. Old Québec license plates line the walls, along with models of old cars. They stock everything here, from brand-new checkered hunters' caps to vintage magazines, old Coca-Cola paraphernalia, magnetic Elvises, and Carnaval de Québec souvenirs. Owner Mr. Blouin is a connoisseur of kitsch, and people wanting to get rid of 40 years' worth of junk in the attic come to him first.

MAP 1: 1196 rue St-Jean, 418/694-9345, www.magasingeneralplblouin.com; 9am-6pm Sun.-Wed., 9am-9:30pm Thurs.-Sat. Nov.-Apr.; 9am-10pm daily May-Oct.

GOURMET TREATS

CONFISERIE C'EST SI BON

This picturesque shop has the feel of an old-time *confiserie,* or candy shop. The shelves are lined with containers full of candy, old-fashioned treats, novelty cups and saucers, magnets, and bowls, making it a great place to pick up a gift. Homemade chocolate, fudge, and hot chocolate are made on the premises, and there's an emphasis on local products like spices, teas, candies, and maple goodies. It's been open since 1990, and just about everything is for sale, from the antique display case to the squares of maple sugar candy sitting temptingly at the cash register.

MAP 1: 1111 rue St-Jean, 418/692-5022, www.sibon-lesplats.com; 9am-9pm daily summer; 9am-5pm Mon.-Wed., 9am-9pm Thurs.-Fri., 9am-5:30pm Sat.-Sun. winter

DÉLICES ÉRABLE & CIE

Everything here is drizzled with maple, from the blueberry gelato to the fleur du sel. Part store, part café, one side of this large, open store is dedicated to pastries, coffees, desserts, and gelatos, while the other is filled with rows of gourmet maple syrup, maple cookies, maple pork rub, coffees, teas—you get the idea. A small seating area at the back is a pleasant place to try a taste of their hot maple-flavor milk, but the real draws are the gourmet products.

MAP 1: 1044 rue St-Jean, 418/692-3245, www.deliceserableetcie.com; 7am-9pm Mon.-Thurs., 7am-10pm Fri., 9am-10pm Sat., 10am-10pm Sun. fall and spring; 7am-8pm Mon.-Thurs., 7am-9pm Fri., 9am-9pm Sat., 10am-9pm Sun. winter; 7am-midnight Mon.-Fri., 9am-midnight Sat., 10am-midnight Sun. summer

MARKETS

ARTISANS DE LA CATHÉDRALE

This outdoor market, established in 1973, runs throughout the summer on the grounds of the Holy Trinity Anglican Cathedral, in the shadow of Château Frontenac. The cozy, makeshift stalls put you in direct contact with the artist or crafter who made the goods, making the shopping and browsing experience all the more memorable. The products are completely unique and different than what you'll find in other artisan and gift shops. Vendors sell everything from jewelry to sweaters to glass and woodwork.

MAP 1: Corner of rue Ste-Anne and rue du Trésor, www.artisansdelacathedrale.com; 10:30am-10pm daily mid-June-early Sept.

SHOPPING DISTRICTS AND CENTERS

QUARTIER DU PETIT-CHAMPLAIN

Full of artisanal shops, many of which double as artists' workshops, Quartier du Petit-Champlain is the perfect place to support the local arts and pick up some unique gifts. It's run as a co-op, and there is a real neighborhood spirit and camaraderie, partly because many of these stores have been here since its inception in the late 1980s. Expect to find silk scarves, leather goods, gourmet fudge, maple syrup, expensive handmade jewelry, and more.

MAP 2: Between Place Royale and rue du Petit-Champlain

RUE ST-PAUL

This narrow cobblestone street in the Vieux-Port is Québec City's antiques row. With the exception of some cafés, bars, restaurants, and artisanal craft spots, almost all of the stores are filled with antiques. There is a real emphasis on classic antiques—that is to say, don't expect to walk in and find a midcentury modern gem (though it could happen). The pieces aren't often dated later than the 1940s, and even objects from that period can be hard to find. Instead, the focus in many stores is on traditional Québécois antiques.

MAP 2: Between rue St-Pierre and rue Rioux

ANTIQUES

ANTIQUITÉS BOLDUC

Owned and staffed by a helpful and friendly young couple, Stéphanie and Frédéric Bolduc, this small antiques store situated in an old stone house is bright, uncluttered, and artfully laid out with furniture, chandeliers, and just about anything else. Clocks and sconces line the walls, while tables, cabinets, and dressers are topped with children's toys, rotary telephones, firefighters' helmets, china tableware, steak knives, and vanity sets.

MAP 2: 89 rue St-Paul, 418/694-9558, www.lesantiquitesbolduc.com; 9:30am-5pm Mon.-Fri., 10:30am-5pm Sat.

ARTS AND CRAFTS

★ BOUTIQUE DES MÉTIERS D'ART

Devoted to the work of Québécois artisans, the Boutique des Métiers d'Art showcases the work of over 125 craftspeople, all members of the Québec Craft Council. Situated on the famous Place Royale, it couldn't be better located, with huge, floor-to-ceiling windows and shelves and display cases lining the stone walls. Everything is well plotted out. Goods are divided by materials and include wood, ceramic, metals, and glass, though other materials can be found in the work throughout the shop. Whether it is simple

Clockwise from top left: Rue St-Paul is Québec City's antiques row; Antiquités Bolduc sells antique furniture, clocks, and accessories; Charlevoix Pure Laine sells locally made wool and woolen goods.

wood kitchen utensils you're looking for, a tin candelabra, or a unique silver pendant, you'll find it here.

MAP 2: 29 rue Notre-Dame, Place Royale, 418/694-0267, www.metiers-d-art.qc.ca; 10am-5pm daily

PAULINE PELLETIER

Pauline Pelletier's ceramic and porcelain artwork is unconventional yet modern. Using unusual shapes as a base—a square teapot, for example—the ceramic is then smoke-fired to create the final effect, giving it a marbled finish. The unusual pieces of art, popular with tourists and locals alike, include vases, tea sets, and serving platters. The colors are unconventional—navy blue, red, and jade, many with a touch of rich gold adorning the edges. The boutique, open since 1983, also carries the work of other Québec artisans and jewelers, giving it a more dynamic atmosphere and added quirkiness.

MAP 2: 38 rue du Petit-Champlain, 418/692-4871, www.paulinepelletier.com; 9:30am-5:30pm Mon.-Wed., 9:30am-9pm Thurs.-Fri., 9am-5pm Sat.-Sun. Oct.-May; 9am-9pm daily June-Sept.

SOIERIE HUO

This unique shop is run by artist Dominique Huot, who has been creating her one-of-a-kind silk products since the late 1970s. A descendant of Québécois artist Charles Huot, Dominique uses natural silk and wool fibers to create her scarves and men's ties. The designs on many of the scarves are spontaneous, though she continually recreates certain themes, including abstracts, florals, and maple leaves. The shop itself is quite small, with the scarves predominantly displayed throughout.

MAP 2: 91 rue du Petit-Champlain, 418/692-5920, www.soieriehuo.com; 9:30am-9pm daily summer, 9:30am-5pm daily winter

CLOTHING AND SHOES

ATELIER LA POMME

This store in the quaint Petit-Champlain district carries lines by Québécois designers, from young, lesser-known labels like Huguette Facteau (who creates made-to-measure leather coats) to the mixed-textile playfulness of Myco Anna. Situated in a historical building, the interior is plain, featuring white walls with red trim. Carrying both men's and women's wear, it's a popular tourist shop for watches, jewelry, leather bags, and seasonal products like fur coats and hats, all made in Québec.

MAP 2: 47 rue Sous-le-Fort, 418/692-2875; 10am-5pm Sat.-Wed., 10am-9pm Thurs.-Fri.

LE CAPITAINE D'ABORD

If you need a pea coat, a striped Breton sweater, or some boat shoes, this is a good place to start. The goods all have a nautical flair and evoke Cape Cod even when it's mid-January outside. The bright blue walls, low ceilings, and high-gloss wood floors give the vague impression you're on a ship, but the thick, knitted sweaters and heavy down jackets will remind you of the weather outside. They are exclusive carriers of yachting brands like Paul & Shark, Armor-Lux, and Meyer, and if you're sailing the St. Lawrence, this is the only store you need.

MAP 2: 59 and 63 rue du Petit-Champlain, 418/694-0694, www.capitainedabord.com; 9am-9pm daily

BOUTIQUE BILODEAU

Look out for the black bear and the mounted moose and deer heads: This shop has opted to play up its out-on-the-land Canadiana. Despite the touristy storefront, Boutique Bilodeau is the real deal when it comes to Québec-made winter garments, everything from gloves and mitts to boots and coats. Stylish, comfortable and warm, these products are designed to get you through the toughest of winters. They also sell pelts and rugs—if you're traveling with kids, that may be a push or a pull factor.

MAP 2: 20 rue Cul-de-Sac, 581/742-6595, wwwl.bilodeaucanada.com; 10am-6pm daily

★ CHARLEVOIX PURE LAINE

This small shop tucked into a basement suite under Le Capitaine d'Abord is a true gem. The wool comes directly from Charlevoix, Québec, and is made into signature socks, hats, scarves, mitts, and felt. Depending on how busy it is when you visit, you may even get to see the salespeople in action, knitting or making felt art. Staff is very friendly and knowledgeable, happy to talk shop about knitting and crocheting, and to talk through the craftsmanship necessary to produce the store's beloved goods.

MAP 2: 61½ rue du Petit-Champlain, 418/692-7272; 9:30am-5:30pm Sat.-Wed., 9:30am-9pm Thurs.-Fri., 9:30am-5pm Sat.-Sun.

OCLAN

This two-floor store on the tiny rue du Petit-Champlain carries contemporary designer brands, including house brand FLM (Fuck La Mode). Entering the menswear section, you'll find a fairly small floor space tastefully packed with the latest from Matinique, Nikben, and RVLT, among others. Down a camouflaged staircase you'll reach the women's floor (which you can also enter or exit from the larger rue Champlain), similar in size but much more stocked, with pieces from La Fée Maraboutée, Melissa Nepton, and Part Two, among others.

MAP 2: 67½ rue du Petit-Champlain, 418/692-1214, www.oclan.net; 10am-5:30pm Sat.-Wed., 10am-9pm Thurs.-Fri.

RICHARD ROBITAILLE SIGNATURE

Established in 1894, Richard Robitaille is a family business passed down through four generations. The boutique, located in an old gray stone building with stone arches and rich dark-wood-trimmed windows on Place Royale, showcases a large selection of original, handmade garments made down the street in the business's workshop. Selling everything from simple key rings and fur-lined mittens to ready-to-wear and custom coats, this shop is not for the PETA-inclined—but its wares will keep you warm if you live in a cold northern climate.

MAP 2: 19 rue St-Pierre, 418/692-9699; 10am-5pm Mon.-Sat.

GIFTS AND HOME

MACHIN CHOUETTE

This place takes things you love but seemingly have no real use for, like that first pressing of the Grateful Dead's "Anthem to the Sun," and turns them into something useful like a CD rack. The brainchild of Lyse Maheu, this large, open boutique in the Vieux-Port has some great pieces, from the aforementioned vinyls-turned-CD racks. They also turn old butter boxes into ottomans and teapots into lights and carry various kinds of furniture, from old country pine tables to contemporary pieces that would look just as good in a loft as in a 19th-century townhouse.

MAP 2: 225 rue St-Paul, 418/525-9898, www.machinchouette.com; 10am-5pm Mon.-Wed. and Sat., 10am-6pm Thurs.-Fri. and Sun.

POT EN CIEL

This split-level store in Petit-Champlain carries ceramics and kitchenware. On the lower floor they carry an array of charming things for the home, including mugs with mustaches, checkered canisters, and artisanal pieces like carved owls and polar bears, as well as a few gourmet products like dried pasta imported from Italy and loose-leaf teas from France. On the upper level, it's all serious kitchen stuff like baking sheets, cookie cutters, and French brands like Emile Henry, as well as Bodum presses.

MAP 2: 27 rue du Petit-Champlain, 418/692-1743; 10am-5pm Mon.-Wed. and Sat.-Sun., 10am-9pm Thurs.-Fri.

GOURMET TREATS

LA FUDGERIE

As the name suggests, this place is a fudge fanatic's fantasy. Well established outside of the city, this cozy, old-timey store is the company's first in downtown Québec. The low ceilings, old wood floors, and exposed ceiling beams make you feel as though you're stepping into the past, a feeling added to by the workers in pristine white coats who circle the store with a platter offering tastes of their divine homemade fudge. Nougat, gourmet hot chocolate, and candied pecans are also made here.

MAP 2: 16 rue du Cul-de-Sac, 418/692-3834, www.lafudgerie.com; 9:30am-5:30pm Mon.-Wed., 9:30am-9pm Thurs.-Fri., 9:30am-5pm Sat.-Sun.

MADAME GIGI CONFISERIE

This sweets shop in Petit-Champlain boasts one of the most dangerous sounding treats—chocolate pizza. With floor-to-ceiling windows and display cases prettily decorated with the day's chocolate special, this place will easily break your resolve and lure you in to try their various goodies,

Top: Try La Fudgerie's homemade fudge, nougat, and hot chocolate. **Bottom:** Le Petite Cabane à Sucre de Québec offers a year-round sugar shack experience.

including fudge, chocolate-dipped fruit kebabs, and Belgian chocolate. In summer, they also have homemade ice cream, and their homemade jam is available year-round.

MAP 2: 84 rue du Petit-Champlain, 418/694-2269; 9am-5:30pm Mon.-Wed., 9am-9pm Thurs.-Fri., 9am-6pm Sat.-Sun. winter; 10am-9pm daily summer

LA PETITE CABANE À SUCRE DE QUÉBEC

This little shop at the end of rue du Petit-Champlain is all kitted out in wood paneling, both inside and out. Exclusively selling maple goods, it is the downtown extension of a sugar shack outside of the city. "The little sugar shack" sells maple syrup, maple candy, ice cream, maple lollipops, nougat, butter and spreads, and a ton of other maple products.

MAP 2: 94 rue du Petit-Champlain, 418/692-5875, www.petitecabaneasucre.com; 10am-5pm Sat.-Wed., 10am-9pm Thurs.-Fri. winter, 9:30am-9pm daily summer

MARKETS

MARCHÉ DU VIEUX-PORT

Right on the marina, this is the city's largest farmers market. A tradition since 1841, the Marché du Vieux-Port continues the practice of country farmers bringing their goods to city dwellers. Everything is locally grown and produced, and many products are organic. You'll find everything from fruits and vegetables to cheese, meats, and seafood to wine and beer. If seeing all that food makes you hungry, there are places to grab a sandwich or a light lunch. A section is dedicated to gifts and artisanal goods, including handmade jewelry, knitted scarves and socks, artwork, and leather goods.

MAP 2: 160 Quai St-André, 418/692-2517, www.marchevieuxport.com; 9:30am-5pm Thurs.-Sun. Jan.-mid-Mar.; 9am-6pm Mon.-Fri., 9am-5pm Sat.-Sun. mid-Mar.-Sept.; 9am-5pm daily Oct.-late Nov.; 9am-5pm Sat.-Wed., 9am-9pm Thurs.-Fri. late Nov.-Dec.

Parliament Hill and the Plains

Map 3

ARTS AND CRAFTS

KETTO

Located in a skinny corner house decorated with deep blue trim, lots of flower pots, and their unmistakable yellow sign, Ketto has an aesthetic all its own. In the late 1990s, Onge was working at a ceramic store when the pieces with her cutesy, big-headed, stick-limbed characters painted on them started flying off the shelves. Today, Ketto carries hand-painted ceramics, jewelry, clothing, glassware, and stationery all with Onge's signature style. The interior can be a bit chaotic, but everything is perfectly laid out, with a simple wood cabinet full of cups and saucers taking up almost an entire wall.

MAP 3: 951 ave. Cartier, 418/522-3337, www.kettodesign.com; 10am-5pm Mon.-Wed. and Sat.-Sun., 10am-9pm Thurs.-Fri.

CLOTHING AND SHOES

URBAIN PRÊT-À-PORTER

This corner boutique in a well-heeled part of town carries fashion-forward brands aimed at women of various ages. The decor changes throughout, from the deep gray walls and designs that cater to more mature women to an adjoining white space that features younger brands like Diesel and Nolita. The store also has its own shoe section, with seasonal footwear from the likes of Matinique and Ilse Jacobsen, among others, as well as a wall dedicated to denim.

MAP 3: 996 ave. Cartier, 418/521-1571; 10am-5:30pm Mon.-Wed., 10am-9pm Thurs.-Fri., 10am-5pm Sat.-Sun.

GIFTS AND HOME

ZONE

This modern living and design store carries an array of products, all chic, sleek, and sophisticated for your home. The all-white store is artfully decorated with stock arranged as you might arrange it in your own home. The store takes up not only the corner lot but the one next to it, with mirrors, chandeliers, table lamps, drinking glasses, tableware, shower curtains, jewelry boxes, cool wall clocks, and furniture from kitchen tables to small couches and chairs.

MAP 3: 999 ave. Cartier, 418/522-7373, www.zonemaison.com; 9:30am-6pm Mon.-Wed., 9:30am-9pm Thurs.-Fri., 9:30am-5:30pm Sat., 10am-5pm Sun.

MARKETS

LES HALLES CARTIER

Less like a market than a mini gourmet shopping center, Les Halles Cartier is a brick and mortar building filled with great shops. It's popular with locals. An organic fruit and produce stand, a fishmonger, butcher, cheese shop, fresh pasta shop, and a bakery all offer top-quality products. It also boasts not one but two coffee shops, where you can take a break with a cappuccino; get one to go as you carry on with your browsing.

MAP 3: 1191 ave. Cartier, 418/688-1635, www.hallesdupetitquartier.com; 7am-7pm Mon.-Wed. and Sat., 7am-9pm Thurs.-Fri., 7:30am-7pm Sun.

Saint-Jean-Baptiste and Saint-Roch

Map 4

SHOPPING DISTRICTS AND CENTERS

RUE ST-JEAN

Whether inside or outside the walls, rue St-Jean is Québec City's main shopping street. In Vieux-Québec's Upper Town you'll find a string of well-known stores, including Québec chains like Bizou and La Maison Simons, as well as internationally recognized brands like Crocs, Aldo, and Foot Locker. Bookstores sell English-language material. If you want to shop like the locals, check out the independent clothing boutiques and record stores in Faubourg Saint-Jean-Baptiste, a continuation of the same street; you'll find interesting shops just beyond the fortifications.

MAP 4: Between rue Couillard and ave. Salaberry

RUE ST-JOSEPH

The main shopping strip in the Saint-Roch neighborhood, this street has an illustrious past that has recently been revived. Once the Fifth Avenue of Québec City, it is now the city's coolest shopping district. You won't find many well-known chains here except for Urban Outfitters, the only store of its kind in the city. Independent lingerie boutiques can be found, as well as some great shoe stores, home stores, and other fashion-forward boutiques. The best children's store in the province, Benjo, is here, with a VIP entrance especially for the little ones.

MAP 4: Between rue St-Dominique and rue Caron

ACCESSORIES AND JEWELRY

MADEMOISELLE B

This narrow storefront would be easy to miss if it weren't for the floor-to-ceiling windows and the old-fashioned sign that pops out over the door. Situated in a newer building in the Saint-Roch neighborhood, Mademoiselle B has an old-world charm with dark chocolate parquet floors, soft pink walls, and plush velvet display shelves. In keeping with the romantic interior, the costume jewelry is very girly, with collections coming from France, the south of Italy, and, of course, Québec.

MAP 4: 541 rue St-Joseph E., 418/522-0455; 10am-5:30pm Mon.-Wed., 10am-9pm Thurs.-Fri., 10am-5pm Sat., 11am-5pm Sun.

ROSE BOUTON

A lot of time could be spent in this kitschy store filled with overwhelming amounts of jewelry and accessories, vibrantly decorated with bubble-gum pink walls, bright florals, pink fur, and circle motif wallpaper. Expect to find fabric-covered earrings, hand-drawn pins, long-fringe pendants and earrings, and bracelets and necklaces made with buttons, the store's namesake *bouton*. A fun and vibrant store, it also carries seasonal accessories like bags, scarves, and hats.

MAP 4: 387 rue St-Jean, 418/614-9507; 11am-5pm Tues.-Wed., 11am-7pm Thurs.-Fri., 11am-5pm Sat., noon-5pm Sun.

ANTIQUES

DÉJÀ VU

Specializing in furniture and objects from the 1930s to the 1970s, Déjà Vu's selection is much more midcentury modern than what you'll find in most antiques stores in the city. Full of Formica tables, colored-glass cocktail sets, and electric blue sectionals from the late 1950s, it's a fun place to stop in. Unlike flea market finds, the treasures here have been lovingly and expertly restored by owners Marie-Claude and François Gagnon. Prices can be higher than anticipated, but knickknacks and anything to do with cocktail hour—ice buckets, martini shakers—are well priced and the perfect unique souvenir.

MAP 4: 832 rue St-Joseph E., 418/914-2483, www.dejavumeubles.com; 10am-5pm Wed., 10am-6pm Thurs.-Fri., 10am-5pm Sat., noon-5pm Sun.

ARTS AND CRAFTS

POINT D'EXCLAMATION

Founded by Diane Bergeron of Euphory Design in 2004, Point d'Exclamation was at the forefront of the movement to champion Québec-based designers. Nowadays, the neighborhood is full of shops dedicated to locally produced and designed goods (Jupon Pressé, Rose Bouton), but it was Bergeron and her eye for local artisanal work that got the ball rolling. The boutique carries the work of 30-40 local designers at any one time, and the goods range from jewelry to accessories and clothes. The all-white interior is a bit too bright at times but puts the focus on the work, while their constantly changing storefront window is always a feast for the eyes.

MAP 4: 762 rue St-Jean, 418/525-8053, www.pointdexclamation.ca; 10am-6pm Mon.-Wed., 10am-9pm Thurs.-Fri., 10am-5pm Sat., noon-5pm Sun.

BATH, BEAUTY, AND SPAS

COSMÉTIQUES BLOOMI

This sleek and modern cosmetics store is reminiscent of the international chain Sephora. Products are beautifully arranged on white high-gloss lacquered shelves, and the whole interior is given an added bit of warmth thanks to the exposed brick walls. It carries high-end makeup lines, a large range of perfumes, and just about any color of polish you could want. Pop in to get a manicure or pedicure, your makeup done for a special occasion, or just to get some tips from the beauticians, who are always ready to give you some pointers and a bit of a touchup.

MAP 4: 507 rue St-Joseph E., 418/529-7470, www.bloomi.ca; 10am-5:30pm Mon.-Wed., 10am-8pm Thurs.-Fri., 10am-5pm Sat., noon-5pm Sun.

MASSOTHÉRAPIE LA QUINTESSENS

This urban spa in Saint-Roch is great for a massage or a quick bit of pampering. The decor is relatively simple, with the rooms filled with massage tables and not much else. Though they offer treatments, the focus is on massage, and five kinds are available: Swedish, Californian, Amma (also known as Japanese massage), Thai-yoga massage, and massage with hot stones. Hour-long massages cost $65, and body wraps, including chocolate, algae, and sea salt, are $75. They also offer half-hour lunchtime massages (11:30am-1:30pm, $25) and 15-minute chair massages ($15).

MAP 4: 656 rue St-Joseph E., 418/525-7270; 10am-7pm Tues.-Fri., 10am-5pm Sat.

BOOKS AND MUSIC

CD MÉLOMANE

Established in 1996, this is the best record store in the city. Totally unpretentious, the staff simply know their stuff, with certain clerks knowing the store's entire stock almost by heart. New and used CDs are available, as are racks upon racks of vinyl, which take up the majority of the space. Brick arches divide the store. They'll happily transfer your cherished 33s, 45s, and 78s onto CD.

MAP 4: 248 rue St-Jean, 418/525-1020, www.cdmelomane.com; 10am-5:30pm Mon.-Wed., 10am-9pm Thurs.-Fri., 10am-5pm Sat., noon-5pm Sun.

★ LE KNOCK-OUT

Vinyl is king at this Saint-Roch record store. Tired of having to buy vinyl on the internet, owners Jean-Philippe Tremblay and Roxann Arcand decided to open a store dedicated to genres and media they most wanted to hear played. Specializing in rock (indie, math, pop), garage, punk, and local, the shop has an impressive collection of both new and used records. The space is open concept and airy: There's even a foosball table near the large floor-to-ceiling window and a makeshift stage where shows are played at the back. The walls are lined not only with music but also books, zines, DVDs, and magazines about the bands and genres they love. The walls are fairly sparse, but the work of Mathieu Plasse, illustrating the history of rock through outfits, is pretty much all you need.

MAP 4: 832 rue St-Joseph E., 581/742-7625; 11am-6pm Tues.-Wed., 11am-9pm Thurs.-Fri., 11am-5pm Sat., noon-5pm Sun.

CHILDREN'S STORES

★ BENJO

You could spend all day at this 25,000-square-foot store, and that's exactly the point. It's filled with educational toys, accessories for infants, model trains, planes, automobiles, party favors, candy, books, and a whole lot of costumes; if it's meant for children you'll likely find it here. Take the kids to lunch at the Benjo restaurant, or sign them up for a ceramic-painting, jewelry-crafting, or paper-making workshop. The staff is always helpful

Clockwise from top left: Benjo is a beloved, massive children's store; Le Knock-Out sells an impressive collection of new, used, and vintage vinyl records; Jupon Pressé sells clothing from emerging designers from Québec City, Montréal, and beyond.

and delightfully off-kilter, as is mascot Benjo, a frog, with whom the kids can take a train ride on the weekends (10:15am-4:15pm Sat.-Sun.).

MAP 4: 550 blvd. Charest E., 418/640-0001, www.benjo.ca; 10am-5:30pm Mon.-Wed., 10am-9pm Thurs.-Fri., 9:30am-5pm Sat.-Sun.

CLOTHING AND SHOES

BOUTIQUE LUCIA F.

Boutique Lucia F. is a vintage store carrying everything from old 45s to women's pumps. Owned by a young graduate of design, there is an easy feel to how the whole place has been put together; carefully organized dresses line the wall, bric-a-brac and paintings decorate the tops of shelves and racks, and an inviting mustard-yellow couch is flanked by a rubber plant near the front window. Styles for men and women are carried, and most prices are $10-20. And if you like that magazine rack currently holding scarves, well, you can likely buy that too.

MAP 4: 34 rue St-Joseph E., 418/262-2629; 11am-5pm Wed. and Sat.-Sun., 11am-6pm Thurs.-Fri.

FANAMANGA

Fans of manga and cosplay congregate at this store turned hangout that brings a touch of Tokyo to Québec. It's filled with Gothic Lolita outfits, cosplay accessories, manga, and magazines; Japanese treats like bubble tea, Okonomiyaki chips, and curry-flavored sweets; and trinkets, dolls, and ephemera associated with the culture. The tables at the center of the store are sometimes filled with fans in cosplay. They also have a karaoke box you can rent by the hour that has songs in Japanese, English, Korean, Chinese, and Vietnamese, or you can visit their Facebook page to learn about when they're holding their next in-store karaoke session.

MAP 4: 650 rue St-Joseph E., 418/614-5052, www.fanamanga.com; noon-5pm Sun.-Mon., 10:30am-6pm Tues.-Wed., 10:30am-9pm Thurs.-Fri., 11am-8pm Sat.

★ JUPON PRESSÉ

This inviting women's boutique on St-Jean is dedicated to emerging designers from Québec City, Montréal, and beyond. Brightly decorated with purple walls, flashes of yellow, bright floral wallpaper, and an inflatable moose head, the shop has an especially clean layout with pieces from designers like Eve Gravel, Supayana, and Valérie Dumaine. Nicely hung and spaced, nothing looks too crowded. T-shirts are perfectly piled on Formica tables, while accessories are laid out deliciously on cake plates; jewelry is displayed like art, framed and hung on the wall, though always easily accessible. Along with things for you to wear, they also carry cute, kitschy finds for the home.

MAP 4: 790 rue St-Jean, 418/704-7114; 10am-6pm Mon.-Wed. and Sat., 10am-9pm Thurs.-Fri., 10:30am-5:30pm Sun.

SCHÜ'Z

Casual shoes for men and women can be found at this relaxed boutique on St-Jean. Steve Madden, Camper, and Maians are available for women, while men's brands include Sperry, Vans, and Dr. Martens. Though there is definitely more of a choice for women, men looking for something unfussy, masculine, and modern, or just a new pair of everyday sneakers, are sure to find it here. The decor is minimal with the shoes displayed on the wall and the center of the room taken up with seating and seasonal displays. Winter boots are one of their specialties, so they always have a range of styles for both sexes come autumn.

MAP 4: 748 rue St-Jean, 418/523-4560, www.schuz.ca; 10am-9pm Mon.-Sat., 10am-6pm Sun. mid-June-mid-Oct.; 10am-6pm Mon.-Wed. and Sat., 10am-9pm Thurs.-Fri., 11am-5:30pm Sun. mid-Oct.-mid-June

SIGNATURES QUÉBÉCOISES

This Saint-Roch shop is dedicated to local designers. If you're interested in a snapshot of Québécois fashion as it's made here, then this shop is a must. Taking over the semi-basement of a church, the space has been completely refurbished and modernized. Open and sprawling, it features the work of different designers and different styles and price ranges. Expect everything from province favorite Myco Anna to specialty brands like Yoga Jeans and Kollantaï. The clothes and accessories suit just about any age and style, though there's much less choice for men.

MAP 4: 560 rue St-Joseph E., 418/648-9976, www.signaturesquebecoises.com; 10am-6pm Mon.-Wed., 10am-9pm Thurs.-Fri., 10am-5pm Sat.-Sun.

SWELL & GINGER

Proof that Saint-Roch is indeed the fastest-growing (and coolest) neighborhood in the city, style savvy womenswear boutique Swell & Ginger put down roots here in mid-2013. Modern, open, and sparsely decorated with heavy wood tables and steel fixtures, the boutique would fit right in in New York's East Village or London's Portobello Road. Labels include Honey Punch and Melissa Nepton. Though the clothes lean toward upscale and beachy, prices are surprisingly reasonable.

MAP 4: 765A rue St-Joseph E., 581/742-7080, www.swellandginger.com; 10am-6pm Mon.-Wed., 10am-9pm Thurs.-Fri., 10am-5pm Sat.

DEPARTMENT STORES

LALIBERTÉ

In May 1867, 24-year-old Jean-Baptiste Laliberté founded a modest fur shop that by the early 20th century was one of the best fur stores in North America. From its humble beginnings, the store eventually grew to become an arresting five-floor department store with huge arched windows and a corner clock tower looking over St-Joseph. When many stores upped and moved to the new malls outside of town, Laliberté was one of the few that stayed. Though the store has since been scaled back (the unused floors are now lofts), Laliberté continues to be a leader in furs. Bring your old furs to be remodeled or browse their seasonal collections.

MAP 4: 595 rue St-Joseph E., 418/525-4851, www.lalibertemode.com; 9:30am-5:30pm Mon.-Wed., 9:30am-9pm Thurs.-Fri., 9:30am-5pm Sat., noon-5pm Sun.

GOURMET TREATS

CHAMPAGNE LE MAÎTRE CONFISEUR

This chocolate and sweets shop has a few unique specialties. With only a few marble-topped tables to sit at, this fairly small store serves up some of the best marzipan treats in the city and also offers a range of fine sugar-free chocolate made in the European tradition in flavors that range from saffron to goat cheese with honey. Port glasses made of chocolate are the ultimate companion to the aged wine, as are their buttery French biscuits. The most unusual treat, though, is the cherry blossom—cherries soaked with champagne and cherry kirsch, covered in dark chocolate, and topped with a chocolate-dipped marshmallow. Totally decadent.

MAP 4: 783 rue St-Joseph E., 418/652-0708, www.champagnechocolatier.com; 8am-7pm Mon.-Wed., 8am-9pm Thurs.-Fri., 10am-5pm Sat.-Sun.

EPICERIE EUROPÉENNE

This shop was founded in 1959 by two Italians nostalgic for their homeland. The massive wooden shelves are stocked with imported products. Italian coffees, olive oils, pestos, and balsamic vinegars take center stage, while at the back you'll find a cheese and meat counter where you can order a great panini—but hurry up, they go fast. Along with the groceries, they also sell imported kitchen accessories, coffeemakers, crockery, and the famous French Laguiole knives. Stop in and try one of their specialties, an authentic *espresso ristretto*—the shortest coffee around.

MAP 4: 560 rue St-Jean, 418/529-4847, www.epicerie-europeenne.com; 9am-6pm Mon.-Wed., 9am-7pm Thurs.-Fri., 9am-5pm Sat., 11am-5pm Sun.

★ ÉRICO CHOCOLATIER

Established in 1987, this artisanal chocolatier is one of the most decadent stops in the city. Chocolate lines the walls in this quaint kitchen and boutique, with an array of seasonal treats (like nachos dipped in chocolate) on one side and displays of freshly made chocolates (with flavors like chestnut cream, rum, and allspice) on the other. Line up to get your gourmet hot chocolate, ice cream, or dessert—the brownies and chocolate cake are said to be among the best in the province. There's no seating in the shop. The Chocolate Museum in an adjoining room provides a history of the treat, lets you taste some wares, and allows you to watch the magic being made in the kitchen.

MAP 4: 634 rue St-Jean, 418/524-2122, www.ericochocolatier.com; 10:30am-6pm Mon.-Wed. and Sat., 10:30am-9pm Thurs.-Fri., 11am-6pm Sun.

SHOPPING DISTRICTS AND CENTERS

GALERIES DE LA CAPITALE

About a 20-minute drive from downtown Québec City, Galeries de La Capitale is one of the most fascinating malls in the province (especially for kids). Opened in 1981, it was the brainchild of businessman Marcel Adams and was filled with Canadian department store heavyweights Eaton's, The Bay, Simons, and Woolco. Today, it has 280 stores, 35 restaurants, the biggest IMAX theater in Canada, and an indoor amusement park. Called Le Mega-Parc, it has 19 attractions, including a Ferris wheel, a rollercoaster, a skating rink, and smaller rides and games that will make kids go wild.

MAP 5: 5401 blvd. des Galeries, 418/627-5800, www.galeriesdelacapitale.com; 10am-9pm Mon.-Fri., 9am-5pm Sat., 10am-5pm Sun.

LAURIER QUÉBEC

Laurier Québec, formerly called Place Laurier, is three levels high and boasts 350 stores. Opened in 1961, it is the largest mall in eastern Canada and one of the city's top tourist attractions. Well-known stores like Old Navy, H&M, Sears, Bench, and Aldo are all here, as are specialized boutiques including Calin Caline, which carries clothes for babies and kids, and Vision Rock, where you can get a piercing while you pick up a Kiss wall-clock and a T-shirt from your favorite hard-rock band. Laurier Québec offers free shuttle service between Vieux-Québec and the mall as well as to the nearby Aquarium du Québec.

MAP 5: 2700 blvd. Laurier, 418/651-5000, www.laurierquebec.com; 10am-6pm Mon.-Wed., 10am-9pm Thurs.-Fri., 9am-5pm Sat., 10am-5pm Sun.

PLACE DE LA CITÉ

Part of the large shopping complex on boulevard Laurier in Sainte-Foy, Place de la Cité stands out thanks to the 17-story office building that's attached to the mall's concourse. It's home to 150 stores and restaurants, and you'll find independent boutiques including Simone Paris, which caters to sizes 6-18, and Québécois label Myco Anna. La Maison Anglaise, the only bookstore dedicated to English books in the region, is here, as are sports stores including Bikini Village, Sport Select, and Québec brand Chlorophylle.

MAP 5: 2600 blvd. Laurier, Ste-Foy, 418/657-6920, www.placedelacite.com; 10am-6pm Mon.-Wed., 10am-9pm Thurs.-Fri., 9:30am-5pm Sat., 10am-5pm Sun.

PLACE STE-FOY

One of the three shopping malls that make up the impressively large complex in the region close to Université Laval just outside of the city, Place Ste-Foy is also one of the oldest. Built in 1958, it is considered the best shopping center in Québec City for upscale boutiques and labels. Among the mall's over 135 stores you'll find standards like Banana Republic and the Gap alongside more niche shops like Le Creuset, Lululemon, and Saks Fifth Avenue.

MAP 5: 2452 blvd. Laurier, 418/653-4184, www.placestefoy.ca; 10am-6pm Mon.-Wed., 10am-9pm Thurs.-Fri., 9:30am-5pm Sat., 10am-5pm Sun.

BOOKS AND MUSIC

LA MAISON ANGLAISE

The only bookstore dedicated to English books in Québec City is in Place de la Cité, one of the mega malls on the outskirts of town. The staff knows their English-language stuff and is always ready to help. The selection is, unsurprisingly, unbeatable, from *New York Times* bestsellers to literary fiction, humor, philosophy, travel, and children's books. It might not be as big as your local Barnes & Noble, but it does have the most comprehensive collection of English books in the city and the atmosphere is quiet and calm—like it should be.

MAP 5: Place de la Cité, 164-2600 blvd. Laurier, 418/654-9523, www.lamaisonanglaise.com; 9:30am-5:30pm Mon.-Wed., 9:30am-9pm Thurs.-Fri., 9am-5pm Sat., 10am-5pm Sun.

CHILDREN'S STORES

UNIVERS TOUTOU

A special treat for kids of all ages, this store is in one of the malls outside of the city. Over 20 different kinds of plush toys are available, from teddy bears to rabbits, moose, and pigs. Once the selection has been made, the plush is then stuffed and given a passport with its date and place of birth printed inside. The staff is kid-friendly and excited about helping kids pick a companion. Choices hang at kid level all around the brightly decorated store. Clothing like bathrobes and boxers and accessories like sunglasses and jewelry can be added to give the new plush toy a bit of its own personal style.

MAP 5: Galeries de la Capitale, 5401 blvd. des Galeries, 418/623-5557, www.universtoutou.com; 10am-9pm Mon.-Fri., 9am-5pm Sat., 10am-5pm Sun.

OUTDOOR GEAR

★ LATULIPPE

Founded in 1940, Latulippe is one of the highly regarded stores in the region when it comes to gear for hunting and fishing. What used to be just a tiny, family-run store was recently renovated and is now a large, modern, two-floor store with everything you need for an outdoor adventure—boots, bags, tents, waterproof outerwear, and accessories. They even have gear for snowmobiling and ammunition, guns, and knives for hunting. And the staff is always full of advice and helpful tips, so just ask.

MAP 5: 637 rue St-Vallier W., 418/529-0024, www.latulippe.com; 8:30am-5:30pm Mon.-Tues., 8:30am-9pm Wed.-Fri., 9am-5pm Sat., 10am-5pm Sun.

MOUNTAIN EQUIPMENT CO-OP

Better known as MEC, this co-op was started by a couple of Canadian climbers in the 1970s and now has almost three million people as registered members. You must sign up to become a member in order to make a purchase, but the $5 good-for-life membership pays for itself by the time you get to the checkout. The open-concept store design offers lots of room for the goods, which include everything from cycling gear to hiking boots, tents to sleeping bags. Rental equipment is available. Eco-friendly and pro-sustainability, the store hires clerks that are friendly, patient, and know their stuff.

MAP 5: 1475 blvd. Lebourgneuf, 418/522-8884, www.mec.ca; 10am-9pm Mon.-Fri., 9am-5pm Sat., 10am-5pm Sun.

Hotels

Look for ★ to find recommended hotels

Highlights

★ **Best Hostel:** One of the few hostels in the city center, **Auberge Internationale de Québec** is friendly, affordable, and couldn't be closer to the action (page 181).

★ **Most Romantic Hotel:** Situated in two of the most beautiful buildings in Vieux-Québec's Upper Town, **Auberge Place d'Armes** has a 17th-century-meets-21st-century decor that makes it perfect for a getaway for two (page 181).

★ **Most Luxurious Hotel:** The **Fairmont Le Château Frontenac** is one of the most recognized hotels in the world. A stay is nothing short of a fantasy (page 182).

★ **Best Location:** Tucked away on an unassuming side street near the old walls, **Hôtel Manoir Victoria** makes for an easy walk to just about anywhere in the city (page 185).

★ **Best Budget Hotel:** A charming bed-and-breakfast in Vieux-Québec's Upper Town, **La Marquise de Bassano** is affordable, well located, and, above all, welcoming (page 186).

★ **Most Relaxing Hotel:** Located in a converted 17th-century monastery, the nonprofit **Monastère des Augustines** preserves Québec heritage and promotes health and wellness (page 186).

★ **Most Distinctive Building:** A former marine warehouse, **Auberge Saint-Antoine** has high ceilings, exposed beams, and stone floors that match perfectly with the minimal but opulent decor (page 187).

★ **Best Place to Bring the Gang:** Situated in the Old Port and with modern suites at reasonable prices, **Hôtel Port-Royal** is ideal if you're traveling with the kids (page 188).

★ **Best Boutique Hotel:** With an accommodating staff and awesome views of the St. Lawrence River and Lower Town, chic **Hôtel 71** is a great home-away-from-home (page 188).

★ **Best Guesthouse:** Situated above the oldest grocery store in North America, **Auberge J.A. Moisan** is authentically Victorian without being stuffy (page 189).

Monastère des Augustines

PRICE KEY

$ Less than CAN$150 per night
$$ CAN$150–250 per night
$$$ More than CAN$250 per night

Staying in Québec City can be expensive. There is a lack of choice when it comes to affordable accommodations; it can sometimes feel as though hotels are taking advantage of a lucrative situation. The majority of the time, however, this isn't the case, and service, at both moderately priced and more expensive hotels, couldn't be better.

Like restaurants, hotels don't lack in numbers, and the highest concentration of hotels can be found in **Vieux-Québec's Upper Town,** where you'll find a couple of smaller inns on just about every little street. The Fairmont Le Château Frontenac is also in Upper Town, standing sentinel on the cliff and casting a shadow on some lesser-known but equally good hotels. Because of its proximity to sights such as the Château Frontenac and the Citadelle, as well as a number of restaurants, Upper Town is the most sought-after area, but by extension it's also the most touristy.

If you're a fan of sleek, minimal boutique hotels, opt for something in **Vieux-Québec's Lower Town** or **Vieux-Port,** once the center of the city's financial district. Old banks, office buildings, and warehouses have been converted into some of the most exciting new hotels. Though it's just as much a tourist attraction as Upper Town, the area has a more relaxed vibe. And although you step out of your hotel into one of the oldest places in North America, it maintains a neighborhood feel that gives it a unique touch of authenticity.

If you want to be close to the action but also want to experience a bit of the city's hipper, younger side, check out hotels in the **Saint-Roch** and **Saint-Jean Baptiste** areas. Since they are not traditional tourist areas,

Previous: Fairmont Le Château Frontenac; Hôtel Port-Royal.

the rates can be more competitive, and though you might not find yourself looking out onto the oldest square in North America, the history is just as rich.

One thing that stands out in Québec City's hotel landscape is the lack of major chains. The Delta and Hilton can be found in Upper Town on René-Lévesque just outside of the city walls, but they are just about the only ones. Most chain hotels are outside of the city center, close to a collection of shopping malls in **Sainte-Foy** on the aptly named Avenue des Hôtels. Most of these hotels offer competitive rates and daily shuttles to downtown in the summer. In winter, this service doesn't necessarily apply—though city buses are available and fairly easy to navigate. If you're traveling without a car, it might be more practical to spring for something closer to downtown.

CHOOSING A HOTEL

When choosing a hotel in Québec City, one of the first things to consider is mobility and how you travel. Charles Dickens famously called it the "Gibraltar of America," and that's still a fitting description. Though it's possible to spend your entire trip in either Upper Town (on the hill) or Lower Town (below the hill), it is unlikely, and even then you'll encounter inclines and hills no matter where you go. Québec isn't a large city by any stretch, but, if you're limited in mobility or by the length of your stay, getting a hotel near the sights you most want to see makes sense. Upper and Lower Town are easily accessible by the funicular and city transit (Réseau de Transport de la Capital, or RTC), but if you like boutique hotels, for example, and only have a night, plan it all in the Vieux-Port and spend the next morning doing the rounds in Upper Town. Driving to the sights, especially in summer and unless they are far way, will be much more hassle than it's worth.

The competitive prices of Sainte-Foy hotels might be tempting, but if you're arriving by train or bus at the main station, you'll end up crossing the entire city just to get there. Instead, pick something more modest in the Vieux-Port or Saint-Roch that can be easily accessible when you arrive. Or make sure you get a ticket to the Sainte-Foy station instead.

The majority of hotels have standard North American-style rooms and amenities like air-conditioning and coffee in the room. But since many of the hotels are also in historical buildings, the rooms in Québec City are usually more European in size. If you book a room in a quaint-looking Victorian house, avoid disappointment and expect it to be smaller than usual. Since they are old homes, it means some of them might not have elevators; it's worth inquiring before you book, though most will have a bellhop.

Breakfasts also come in European sizes or not at all. Many hotels don't include breakfast as part of the room, or if they do, they are continental with fresh pastries, breads, cheeses, and fruit. In some cases it's wisest to skip the hotel breakfast altogether and head to one of the city's many bistros for a filling first meal instead.

Packages offer different options for guests when they book and can include breakfast as part of the deal as well as things like tours, museum entrances, and bottles of champagne. Parking, even at bigger hotels, can be hard to come by, but most paid parking lots are safe and relatively affordable. If you're staying near the Plains you might be lucky enough to find free street parking amid the upscale homes. Even if they don't provide parking themselves, the hotels are usually more than willing to help you find a spot or at the very least give you various options.

Vieux-Québec's Upper Town Map 1

★ AUBERGE INTERNATIONALE DE QUÉBEC $

This hostel is a member of Hostelling International, and you won't find a more affordable place to stay in Vieux-Québec. Situated in what used to be a convent, this comfortable youth hostel has been providing sparse but spacious and spotless rooms for over 40 years. Along with dormitories—male, female, or mixed—they also offer private rooms available for 1-5 people, perfect if you're traveling with a group. Communal areas include a self-serve kitchen and a café bistro, a great place to relax and chat with fellow travelers. In summertime, you can enjoy breakfast in the charming little interior courtyard. The bilingual staff is warm and welcoming and offers activities from tours outside the city to organized pub crawls.

MAP 1: 19 rue Ste-Ursule, 418/694-0755, www.aubergeinternationaledequebec.com

★ AUBERGE PLACE D'ARMES $$

Spread throughout two buildings, one an old hotel and the other an old wax museum, Auberge Place d'Armes is one of the most beautiful hotels in the city, situated in the shadow of the Fairmont Le Château Frontenac. Although walls date back to the 17th century, there is nothing old about this hotel; it's just charming. The rooms are all decorated in a mix of modern meets antiques, the most lavish of which is, appropriately, the Marie Antoinette Suite. With its eggshell-blue walls, ornate gold moldings, and rich fabrics, the room is kept light by the addition of pieces like a Plexiglas take on a baroque lamp and Philippe Stark-inspired Louis XIV chairs. Complimentary breakfast is served at Chez Jules, their on-site restaurant. Those traveling with pets can bring them (for a small extra fee) but must request a specific room at time of booking.

MAP 1: 24 rue Ste-Anne, 418/694-9485, www.aubergeplacedarmes.com

HÔTEL DU CAPITOLE $$

Blink and you might miss the sliver of a sign marking this discreet hotel. Tucked into an old building near the Saint-Jean Gate that includes Il Teatro restaurant and Le Capitole theater—special packages for all three are available—this small four-floor hotel with 40 rooms is in a great location. The interior is distinctly contemporary, with bright colors and modern takes on classic furniture shapes. Rooms, however, can be quite small, and though they all boast en suite bathrooms, some tubs—Jacuzzi or antique claw-foot—are located next to the bed. It may be romantic, but it's not necessarily practical.

MAP 1: 972 rue St-Jean, 800/363-4040, www.lecapitole.com

CHEZ HUBERT $

Tucked away on a quiet side street, this small, three-room bed-and-breakfast is a good option for those looking for the Upper Town experience without the cost. This grand old Victorian townhouse has chandeliers in every room, stained-glass windows, and a beautiful curved staircase at the entrance. Owner Hubert is warm and amiable and offers guests a hearty buffet breakfast. Each of the rooms is decorated in soft hues, and one room looks out on the Château Frontenac while another has a balcony. Each room has a private bathroom, but the common room, featuring a fridge and microwave, is shared.

MAP 1: 66 rue Ste-Ursule, 418/692-0958, www.chezhubert.com

★ FAIRMONT LE CHÂTEAU FRONTENAC $$$

This is luxury at its finest. And having undergone major renovations and refurbishing, this historic hotel and landmark is one of the chicest and most sought-after temporary addresses in the city. Just entering the sumptuously decorated lobby you feel as though you've stepped into a Victorian salon, with its rich wood-paneled walls and ceilings, wall sconces in the shape of candelabras, and antique chandelier hung above the grand staircase. The decor of the 618 rooms and suites follows suit with high ceilings, classic fabrics, and Victorian-style wood furnishings. Like most fine hotels, it has all the amenities you'd expect: restaurants, bar, pool, spa, gym, and ballroom.

MAP 1: 1 rue des Carrières, 418/692-3861, www.fairmont.com/frontenac-quebec

HÔTEL CAP DIAMANT $$

Located in a historical building on a small and quiet street not far from the walls of the Citadelle, Hôtel Cap Diamant is a charming bed-and-breakfast. Each of the 12 rooms is furnished with rich antiques, giving it a European charm. It's run by Mme. Guillot and her daughter, and the staff is warm, welcoming, and helpful. Guests are treated to a complimentary continental breakfast, which they're welcome to eat in the hidden backyard, full of flowers in the summer. Though there's an elevator for luggage, guests will have to climb the stairs to their rooms, some of which are on the fourth floor.

MAP 1: 39 ave. Ste-Geneviève, 418/694-0313, www.hotelcapdiamant.com

HÔTEL CHÂTEAU BELLEVUE $$

Located in front of the Parc des Gouveneurs just behind the Château Frontenac, this 48-room hotel offers great views of the St. Lawrence River and access to all the major sites on foot. Taking over four stately homes that were built at the turn of the 20th century, the rooms are smaller than

Clockwise from top left: Auberge Place d'Armes; La Marquise de Bassano; a room at the Fairmont Le Château Frontenac.

Chill Out at the Ice Hotel

Come winter, the **Hôtel de Glace** (www.hoteldeglace-canada.com) is one of the most magical places to lay your head. Started in 2001, it was the first ice hotel in North America and has since become one of the most extraordinary hotel experiences in the city. Open from January to March, and situated just outside of the city, the hotel takes roughly a month and a half and 60 workers to construct, with the ice built around a metal base that forms its foundations. Entirely redesigned and rebuilt every year, each incarnation is built around a different theme.

Though the design, theme, and architecture change, the materials don't. The interior is always decked out with ice furniture, sculptures, and touches of fur and animal hide to soften and warm up the space. Everything here, except for the heated bathrooms in a separate building, is made of ice, from the glasses at the bar to the bar itself, the lobby chairs, the serving plates, and, of course, the beds. Made of blocks of ice, the base of the bed is then layered with solid wood as well as a mattress, which is topped with an insulating bed sheet and pillow that are brought to your room just as you're getting ready for bed, along with an arctic sleeping bag. Though temperatures outside might dip to -25°C (-13°F), the four-foot thick walls keep the room between -3°C and -5°C (27°F and 23°F) no matter the temperature outside.

A typical night at the Ice Hotel starts at three in the afternoon with a check-in at the Four Points by Sheraton, the base for the ice hotel; this is also where guests eat a hot breakfast the following morning. A free shuttle takes guests out to the hotel, where they can spend the afternoon and evening drinking in the ice bar, trying out the gigantic ice slide, or warming up in the outdoor hot tubs before heading to their rooms later in the night. Some rooms and suites even come with an optional fireplace or both a fireplace and private spa, perfect for a romantic getaway. The hotel even has its very own ice chapel for midwinter marriages. A stay at the hotel will typically cost around $500 per person, which includes a concurrent night as well as an additional night at another nearby hotel, along with breakfast, among other perks. A simple stay at the Ice Hotel will run about $200 per person per night, though you won't be able to access a second room with your luggage and will need to use the on-site showers.

If you're not convinced sleeping in -3° weather is for you but feel oddly compelled to visit the **Winter Playground** (and who could blame you), it's open 10am-9pm daily December-March (12 years and up $29.95, ages 5-11 $22.95, ages 3-4 $10.95).

what you might be hoping for but are comfortably appointed with homey touches like throw pillows and antiques. The hotel offers a complimentary breakfast as well as free Internet and access to a fitness facility. Guests may also access on-site spa and massage services.

MAP 1: 16 rue de la Porte, 418/692-2573, www.hotelchateaubellevue.com

HÔTEL CLARENDON $$

Built in 1858 and designed by Charles Baillairgé, this historic hotel is the oldest in Vieux-Québec. First a home, then offices, it became a hotel in 1870. Originally a four-story building, it underwent two additions in the

20th century, one to include two floors and the mansard roof and the other a six-floor art deco extension, making it particularly striking. It's across the street from city hall and next door to Édifice Price. Upon entering the Clarendon you're immediately hit with the art deco feel—wood beams feature on the ceiling and large mirrors are placed throughout. The rooms themselves are rather modest with simple decor, though some feature gorgeous circular windows.

MAP 1: 57 rue Ste-Anne, 418/692-2480, www.hotelclarendon.com

HÔTEL LE CHAMPLAIN $$

Completely renovated in 2016, Hôtel Le Champlain is a welcoming boutique hotel. Surrounded by historical buildings, the hotel is distinctly modern, though the hardwood floors and exposed brick walls add a bit of European charm to the 49 rooms. Ideally located on a quiet street, it is close to everything but avoids the noise and bustle of streets like St-Jean and St-Louis. Guests are treated to a complimentary breakfast, and cappuccinos and espressos are available throughout the day in the lobby.

MAP 1: 115 rue Ste-Anne, 418/694-0106, http://hotelsduvieuxquebec.com/en/hotel-champlain

HÔTEL LE CLOS SAINT-LOUIS $$

If you're an old-fashioned romantic, you will swoon at Hôtel Le Clos Saint-Louis. Calling itself the "most romantic Victorian hotel in the city," it's fastidiously decorated with period antiques, including wardrobes, four-poster beds, and fainting couches. Its location close to the Saint-Louis Gate makes sights both inside and outside the walls walkable. Catering to couples, this isn't a place for kids. Packages include Honeymoon, Anniversary, and Romance and Culture, which includes tickets for the Musée National des Beaux-Arts or the Musée de la Civilisation.

MAP 1: 69 rue St-Louis, 418/694-1311, www.clossaintlouis.com

★ HÔTEL MANOIR VICTORIA $$

Though the building that now houses the Hôtel Manoir Victoria was built in 1904, the hotel's history dates back to the 1830s, when Thomas Payne opened the city's most exclusive hotel across the street from its current location. Situated just off of St-Jean in Upper Town on a street that connects to Lower Town and the Saint-Roch area, Hôtel Manoir Victoria is sumptuously decorated with rich, embellished fabrics and classically comfortable furnishings. The rooms are modern but still traditional, and there's a hominess to both the superior rooms and more luxurious suites. Though still beautiful, the hotel enjoyed its heyday in the 1920s, and no place is this more evident than with the pool. With its Grecian columns and small black-and-white tiles, it's like something out of *The Great Gatsby.* It's also connected to the Chez Boulay Bistro Boréal, so you don't have to leave the premises to eat well.

MAP 1: 44 Côte du Palais, 418/692-1030, www.manoir-victoria.com

HÔTEL SAINTE-ANNE $$

Chic and sophisticated is the best way to describe the feel of this 20-room hotel just across the square from Château Frontenac. Located on a busy cobblestone street, this historical building has been perfectly transformed into a sleek, boutique-style hotel. The stone walls, exposed ceiling beams, and Norman-style windows are the perfect complement to the simple, clean lines of the furnishings and the ultramodern bathrooms—black slate tiles, glass shower doors. The rooms can be small, however, so keep size in mind if you're choosing between a superior room and a junior suite.

MAP 1: 32 rue Ste-Anne, 418/694-1455, www.hotelste-anne.com

★ LA MARQUISE DE BASSANO $

Located on a quiet street lined with historical homes in Vieux-Québec's Upper Town, this charming bed-and-breakfast is steps away from Château Frontenac and Les Fortifications. It's run by a young, outgoing couple, and the five rooms of this gray-stone townhouse are uniquely decorated (and priced), with touches like a full bookshelf, writing desk, and vintage typewriter in the Library Room, a claw-footed bathtub, or antique pieces. Only two rooms have their own bathrooms, however; the other three must share. Breakfast is served in the European style with meats, hardboiled eggs, and various breads and pastries.

MAP 1: 15 rue des Grisons, 418/692-0316, www.marquisedebassano.com

★ LE MONASTÈRE DES AUGUSTINES $$

In a converted 17th-century monastery that blends the restored gray stone and wood building with a bright, contemporary glass and steel addition, this hotel used to house hundreds of Augustinian sisters, a hospital-devoted order of nuns who came to Québec to work as healers and help France achieve its colonial and religious goals. Though about a dozen nuns remain in the building today—you can join them for religious services in the hotel's chapel—the goal of the hotel is to provide a secular, wellness-based stay to guests. Both spartan traditional rooms (restored nuns' cells, with shared hallway bathrooms) and contemporary rooms (redesigned to offer more familiar hotel accommodations, including en suite bathrooms) are available, and though you won't find amenities like in-room television, you will find quietude and calm. Breakfast is complimentary and eaten in silence; the restaurant provides healthy, hearty fare in a buffet style with a strong emphasis on vegan and vegetarian options. If you need a break from the hustle and bustle of your city exploration, join daily yoga or meditation classes or check out the hotel's museum, dedicated to exploring the history of the Augustinian order.

MAP 1: 77 rue des Remparts, 418/694-1639, www.monastere.ca

★ AUBERGE SAINT-ANTOINE $$$

Once a port-side warehouse, Auberge Saint-Antoine retained its high ceilings, exposed beams, and stone floors, all the things that make it one of the most inviting hotels in the city today. It was built on the archaeological site of Ilôt Hunt, an area full of wharfs and warehouses at the peak of Québec's port history, and artifacts that were found on this site have been incorporated into the hotel design. The rooms are sleek and modern with a touch of luxury: plush headboards with unique motifs and heated bathroom floors. Many also have balconies, terraces, or fireplaces, so request one when you book. Unique services include an archaeological tour and an on-site cinema. One of the city's top restaurants, Chez Muffy (formerly Panache), is also here, in what was once the warehouse lobby.

MAP 2: 8 rue St-Antoine, 418/692-2211, www.saint-antoine.com

AUBERGE SAINT-PIERRE $$

The first boutique hotel to open in Québec City, Auberge Saint-Pierre has a charm all its own. Though it has been remodeled with slightly sleeker furniture and more minimalist decor, the Saint-Pierre still makes you feel as though you're staying with a close friend or family (but without the bickering). Brick walls and classic black-and-white photos are the backdrop for cozy white wooden furniture and pops of bright color. Each room comes with its own coffeemaker, iron, mini fridge, and umbrella. The feeling of home continues in the main area, with a complimentary gourmet breakfast in the relaxed dining room and a library with a roaring fireplace, perfect for relaxing with a nightcap.

MAP 2: 79 rue St-Pierre, 418/694-7981, www.auberge.qc.ca

HÔTEL BELLEY $

Looking out over the marina and farmers market, Hôtel Belley is a close walk to sights in both Upper and Lower Town, a stone's throw from the cool Saint-Roch area, and reasonably close to the bus and train stations. This tiny eight-room, six-loft hotel has a definite laid-back atmosphere, perhaps helped in part by the historic tavern on the ground floor, which provides an excellent place to socialize and relax all year long. The rooms are small and simply furnished, but the views, especially at night, are lovely. Come summer, *terrasses* are open in both the front and back of the building, attracting locals and tourists alike.

MAP 2: 249 rue St-Paul, 418/692-1694, www.hotelbelley.com

L'HÔTEL LE GERMAIN $$$

With its grandiose neoclassical facade and modern, understated interior, you'd never guess that this chic boutique hotel started off as a fish warehouse. In the former financial district, this nine-floor hotel, the first of Le

Germain's to open in North America, offers great views over both the St. Lawrence and Lower Town. The large, open lobby with big windows, comfy couches, and a laid-back atmosphere is immediately inviting. You'll want to spend all morning in the adjoining dining room, sinking back into your plush seat with a paper while you finish off breakfast. The rooms themselves are equally inviting, with big windows, simple, uncomplicated design, and a Nespresso machine making it the ultimate getaway.

MAP 2: 126 rue St-Pierre, 418/692-2222, www.legermainhotels.com/en/quebec

HÔTEL LE PRIORI $$

At the base of Cap Diamant in the Vieux-Port on one of the oldest streets in North America, Hôtel Le Priori occupies the former home of architect Jean Baillairgé. In summer, its white-washed facade is punctuated with color from hanging flowers and vines that crown the entrance. Inside, a modern interior contrasts with stone walls that date as far back as 1734. The emphasis is on minimalist chic but with a touch of art deco. The boutique hotel features 16 regular rooms and four suites. Furniture in asymmetrical shapes and unusual colors like deep purple or bright red can be found in most rooms. Each suite, however, is uniquely decorated. Make sure to take advantage of the secluded outdoor *terrasse* or make reservations at the in-house restaurant Toast!

MAP 2: 15 rue du Sault-au-Matelot, 418/692-3992, www.hotellepriori.com

★ HÔTEL PORT-ROYAL $$

This old storehouse with gray-stone exterior in the center of the Vieux-Port has since been converted exclusively into suites. Offering three types of suites (classic, deluxe, and superior), Hôtel Port-Royal provides a home away from home, with each suite equipped with living room and kitchenette, a great option if you want to save costs by eating in. The decor throughout is simple and modern with wood floors, sandy-colored walls, and each suite decorated just so, whether with dramatic striped wallpaper or a colorful, floral couch. It's perfect if you're traveling with family.

MAP 2: 144 rue St-Pierre, 418/692-2777, www.leportroyal.com

★ HÔTEL 71 $$$

Located on a cobblestone street in what was once the city's financial district, Hôtel 71 is in a building that was once the National Bank's head office. The neoclassical facade of this boutique hotel is juxtaposed against the sleek, modern interior. Rooms are uncluttered, with earth-toned furniture giving them an especially Zen feeling. The bathrooms, too, are relaxing, with gray slate tiles and geometric lines. Large windows in almost every room allow not only for natural light but also for great views of the city and surrounding area. It's the choice of design lovers with a larger budget (there's even a penthouse). Breakfast is served in the adjoining restaurant and offers a delicious cappuccino to wash down your hearty continental breakfast.

MAP 2: 71 rue St-Pierre, 418/692-1171, www.hotel71.ca

Parliament Hill and the Plains

Map 3

HÔTEL CHÂTEAU LAURIER $$

Set back from the Plains of Abraham and a two-minute walk to Vieux-Québec's Upper Town, Hôtel Château Laurier is ideally located. The newly renovated lobby is open and inviting with a blazing fire in the winter. Rooms run the gamut from smaller European-style to big, bright, newly renovated rooms with updated modern furniture and more of a Zen quality. Eight of the hotel's rooms are wheelchair accessible. No matter your room type, all guests are welcome to try the indoor saltwater pool. Continental and American-style breakfasts are both available.

MAP 3: 1220 Place Georges-V W., 418/-522-8108, www.hotelchateaulaurier.com

Saint-Jean-Baptiste and Saint-Roch

Map 4

★ AUBERGE J.A. MOISAN $$

This four-bedroom guesthouse invites you to be a part of history by sleeping above the oldest grocery store in North America. Charmingly decorated with impeccable moldings, antique furniture, homemade quilts, and Laura Ashley prints, it gives just a taste of what it was like to be a successful businessman in the 19th century. The beautifully restored Victorian house also boasts a living room, library, solarium, and *terrasse,* all of which guests have access to. Just to take things a little bit further tea is served 3pm-8pm.

MAP 4: 699 rue St-Jean, 418/529-9764, www.jamoisan.com

AUBERGE L'AUTRE JARDIN $$

This 28-room hotel is dedicated to sustainable and responsible tourism, with organic breakfasts made with fair-trade products and furnishings that come from sustainable sources. Owned by Carrefour Tiers-Monde, a Québec-based charity that raises awareness on issues in developing countries, the hotel is one of the money-making sides of the business. The rooms are tastefully decorated and feel more like a friend's place, with classic bedding and neutral and earth-toned walls and furniture. Rooms are decorated with ethically sourced art from Africa, Asia, and India. The hotel also has a fair-trade store selling coffee, jewelry, and different international art crafts and accessories.

MAP 4: 365 blvd. Charest E., 418/523-1790, www.autrejardin.com

Clockwise from top left: Auberge J.A. Moisan; Hôtel Château Laurier; a room at Auberge Saint-Antoine.

AUBERGE LE VINCENT $$

The keyword here is "concierge." Every effort is put into making your stay nothing less than fantastic and tailor-made. From the made-to-order breakfasts to in-house movie rentals (there are over 100 to choose from at the front desk), the staff evinces old-school charm, taking care of dinner reservations, walking tours, and more—you name it and they're on it. Of course, they can handle it all because this is a small, 10-room hotel in the trendy Saint-Roch area. It is impeccably designed. Each room is uniquely decorated, but all feature exposed brick walls, 400-thread-count sheets, and the most modern bathrooms, often separated by a crystal-clear glass window—with optional blind.

MAP 4: 295 rue St-Vallier E., 418/523-5000, www.aubergelevincent.com

CHÂTEAU DES TOURELLES $$

This light and airy bed-and-breakfast, marked by a turret, stands out on this strip of Saint-Jean, which is lined with neighborhood bistros and small boutiques. Climb a flight of stairs into this warm and welcoming place. Wood floors and exposed brick give the rooms a cozy and a little bit country feel, without being kitschy. A filling breakfast is served in the sunny dining room, and a roaring fire in the sitting room is great for guests in the winter, while the rooftop terrace offers views of (nearly) all of the sights in the city.

MAP 4: 212 rue St-Jean, 418/647-9136, www.chateaudestourelles.qc.ca

LE CHÂTEAU DU FAUBOURG $

Set back from the road on busy rue St-Jean is a huge Second Empire-style château. Built by the rich Imperial Tobacco family in the 1800s, it retains its original grandeur and is one of the city's most impressive bed-and-breakfasts. A gilded staircase and chandelier greet you as you enter and set the tone for the rooms, which give off the air of an old manor house with rich antique furnishings, sumptuous fabrics, and, in the case of one room, an entire library as headboard. Each room has its own bathroom. Breakfast is served in a grand library, and the owners are lovely and charming.

MAP 4: 429 rue St-Jean, 418/524-2902, www.lechateaudufaubourg.com

HÔTEL PUR $$

This chic, boutique-style hotel in the heart of up-and-coming Saint-Roch couldn't be cooler. Standing 18 floors tall, it's the highest building in the area, so just about every room has a view from the floor-to-ceiling windows, looking out on to the city, the Laurentian Mountains, or the newly refurbished Saint-Roch church. The sleek design and minimal color palette—gray, black, and white with bursts of orange—give it an uncluttered but still relaxed vibe. The slate-gray bathrooms give it an added calming touch, as do the accessible Japanese-style baths and glass-door showers. Visitors can dine in the equally chic adjoining restaurant Table, with long communal tables, comfy couches, and breakfast, lunch, and dinner services.

MAP 4: 395 rue de la Couronne, 418/647-2611, www.hotelpur.com

Greater Québec City

Map 5

LE BONNE ENTENTE $$

This large, sprawling hotel outside of the city offers an alternative to those who want the feel of a country getaway with proximity to the downtown. Just about every room in this cottage-style hotel with mansard roofs and soft-yellow clapboard is distinctly decorated, from the hardwood floors and country fabrics of the Cocooning room to the carpeted, sleek but comfortable decor of the Business room. With an on-site spa, large outdoor pool and hot tub, and golf course, relaxation is never far away.

MAP 5: 3400 chemin Ste-Foy, 418/653-5221, www.lebonneentente.com

HÔTEL SÉPIA $$

Located outside of the city center and close to other hotels, the city's largest shopping malls, and the aquarium, Hôtel Sépia is a bit of urbanity in suburbia. With its sleek modern design—rain showerheads, Barcelona chairs, and refinished wood floors—this boutique-style hotel will make you feel like you're in the middle of downtown. It's approximately a 15-minute drive to downtown, and the hotel offers free shuttle services during the summer months; those traveling without a car, however, might find it impractical come winter. This hotel might not give you a great view of the Vieux-Port, but it will give you a great view of the famous Pont de Québec.

MAP 5: 3135 chemin St-Louis, 418/653-4941, www.hotelsepia.ca

Excursions

Look for ★ to find recommended sights and activities

Highlights

★ **Best Historic Road:** One of the oldest roads in North America, **Route de la Nouvelle France** is lined with ancestral homes dating back hundreds of years (page 198).

★ **Best Waterfall:** Taller than Niagara Falls, **Chute Montmorency** is an impressive sight, especially when you're on the suspension bridge over the falls with 360-degree breathtaking views (page 198).

★ **Oldest Pilgrimage Site:** Built in honor of Sainte-Anne, the patron saint of shipwrecked sailors, the **Basilique Sainte-Anne-de-Beaupré** is one of the oldest pilgrimage sites in the world (page 199).

★ **Best Place to Pick Your Own Fruits and Vegetables: Île d'Orléans** is an island in the middle of the St. Lawrence River. It has some of the oldest homes in the region and some of the best agriculture. Head to the island to pick your own fresh fruit and vegetables (page 199).

★ **Most Artistic Town:** The birthplace of Cirque du Soleil, **Baie-Saint-Paul** is full of galleries and folk art boutiques (page 206).

★ **Best Skiing:** Overlooking the St. Lawrence River and cutting through the boreal forest, the hills at **Le Massif** offer views just as stunning as the slopes themselves (page 209).

★ **Best Bike Excursion:** Only 11 kilometers long and 3 kilometers wide, the **Isle-aux-Coudres,** near Tadoussac, is filled with old churches, windmills, and other rarities best explored by bike (page 212).

★ **Best Hiking:** The gorges and fjords of **Parc National des Hautes-Gorges-de-la-Rivière-Malbaie,** along with its unique mix of tundra and taiga, make it one of the most breathtaking sites to hike in the region (page 215).

★ **Best Whale-Watching:** At the confluence of the Saguenay and St. Lawrence Rivers, the shores surrounding the historic town of **Tadoussac** have one of the most diverse ecosystems in the world. This is the annual meeting place for 10 species of whales, from humpbacks to belugas (page 216).

While visiting Québec City might give you a picture of Québec's urban population, if you really want to get to see the culture and nature that have shaped the province, you have to go north.

Referred to as the *régions* (regions), the forests and the jagged cliffs of the St. Lawrence provide a real sense of Québec and its rugged beauty. Barely a half-hour drive from Québec City, you'll find yourself in the picturesque Côte-de-Beaupré, lined with quaint ancestral homes—most continue to be residential homes. Not every historical event took place in and around the city; in fact, this area is where General Wolfe and his men camped before they laid siege to the city.

Once mostly farmland, the area is now a large tourist destination thanks to pilgrimages to the Basilique Sainte-Anne-de-Beaupré and the popularity of the impressive Chute Montmorency. Across the water on the Île d'Orléans, however, things have stayed much the same as they have for hundreds of years. Agri-tourism comprises a large part of the livelihood of the island, which is full of vineyards and farms; visitors should take full advantage by picking their own fruits and vegetables and sampling the cheeses, wines, ciders, and chocolate on offer at local artisanal producers.

Navigating the Côte-Nord (North Coast) couldn't be easier; two highways take you to the same destination, and it all depends on whether you want the scenic route, Route 362, or the faster route, Route 138. Truth be told, even the faster route could be described as scenic—it features high cliffs, rolling hills, and even patches of tundra landscape as you head farther north. Baie-Saint-Paul seems to emerge like a mirage, its church steeple sparkling on the shores of a low valley flanked by stone cliffs and the

---

Previous: snowboarding at Le Massif, Charlevoix's largest ski mountain; the beach at Baie Saint-Paul.

Excursions

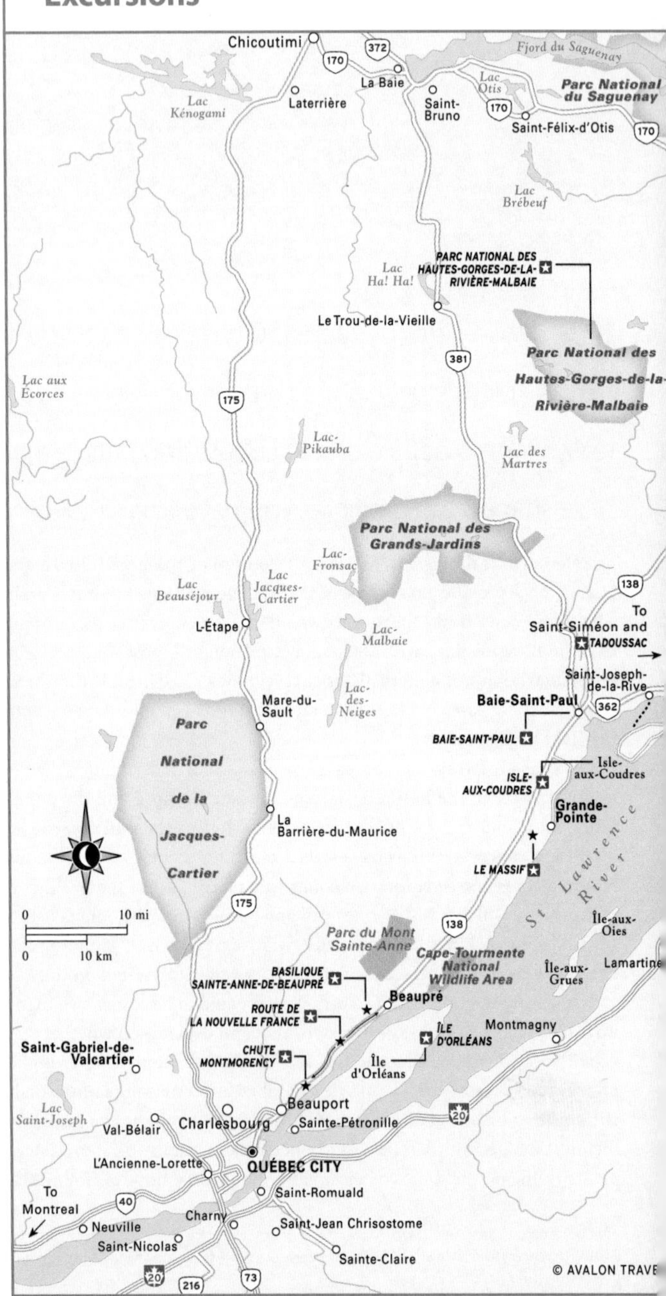

Chicoutimi
La Baie
Laterrière
Lac Kénogami
Saint-Bruno
Lac Otis
Fjord du Saguenay
Parc National du Saguenay
Saint-Félix-d'Otis
Lac Brébeuf
PARC NATIONAL DES HAUTES-GORGES-DE-LA-RIVIÈRE-MALBAIE
Lac Ha! Ha!
Le Trou-de-la-Vieille
Parc National des Hautes-Gorges-de-la-Rivière-Malbaie
Lac aux Écorces
Lac-Pikauba
Lac des Martres
Parc National des Grands-Jardins
Lac-Fronsac
Lac Jacques-Cartier
Lac Beauséjour
L'Étape
Lac-Malbaie
To Saint-Siméon and TADOUSSAC
Saint-Joseph-de-la-Rive
Lac-des-Neiges
Mare-du-Sault
Baie-Saint-Paul
BAIE-SAINT-PAUL
Parc National de la Jacques-Cartier
Isle-aux-Coudres
ISLE-AUX-COUDRES
Grande-Pointe
La Barrière-du-Maurice
LE MASSIF
St Lawrence River
0 10 mi
0 10 km
Île-aux-Oies
Parc du Mont Sainte-Anne
Cape-Tourmente National Wildlife Area
Lamartine
Île-aux-Grues
BASILIQUE SAINTE-ANNE-DE-BEAUPRÉ
Beaupré
ROUTE DE LA NOUVELLE FRANCE
ÎLE D'ORLÉANS
Montmagny
CHUTE MONTMORENCY
Saint-Gabriel-de-Valcartier
Île d'Orléans
Lac Saint-Joseph
Beauport
Val-Bélair
Charlesbourg
Sainte-Pétronille
L'Ancienne-Lorette
QUÉBEC CITY
To Montreal
Saint-Romuald
Neuville
Charny
Saint-Jean Chrisostome
Saint-Nicolas
Sainte-Claire
170
372
175
381
138
362
40
20
73
216
© AVALON TRAVE

St. Lawrence. More picturesque than most of the other towns, it's worth a wander.

North again, La Malbaie sneaks up on you from the corners of the twisting, turning road, and though the sights aren't much, the landscape is lovely. Once you're this far north you might as well continue to the jewel of Charlevoix and cross the majestic Saguenay by ferry to Tadoussac. The massive cliffs that plunge into the river make for breathtaking scenery, and if you're lucky enough to catch a view of the diverse whale life that thrives in these waters, you'll understand the atypical beauty that defines the region and the province.

PLANNING YOUR TIME

Some of these excursions can be done by day or even an afternoon by car. However, some places, including Tadoussac and the Saguenay Fjord, are three hours away (or sometimes more, depending on traffic and road conditions), so plan to spend at least a night in these locations. Of course, no matter how far afield you're willing to travel, if you have the time, it's always fun to stay a bit longer in order to really get to know a place.

Most of the sights are accessible by national highways, though in some places these highways slim down to two lanes. If you're driving in winter, the journey could take longer, especially if the weather is bad. Snow tires are required by law December-March; if you don't have them on your car, avoid trips into the rocky and hilly Charlevoix, or rent a car with the right tires. North of Côte-de-Beaupré, the distance between towns lengthens, so it's a good idea to keep an eye on your gas gauge and fill up when you have the chance.

High season is May-October; those traveling north to Charlevoix later in the year should make sure to plan well ahead or opt for a package deal at places like La Massif. Getting a hotel, dinner, and recreation in one deal will allow you to see the beauty of the area without worrying about whether you'll be able to find an open restaurant.

Côte-de-Beaupré and Île d'Orléans

Minutes outside of Québec on Route 138, you'll reach the Côte-de-Beaupré. Located on the banks of the St. Lawrence River, this historical area boasts ancient ancestral homes and open farmland running along the Route de la Nouvelle France, one of the oldest roads in North America. As you travel along the 50 kilometers of roadway, you'll pass through small towns between the high cliffs of the Laurentians and the shores of the river.

From the Côte-de-Beaupré you can see the Île d'Orléans, an island in the stream of the St. Lawrence. Linking the two historical areas is the Île d'Orléans Bridge, which can be used by car, bike, or foot. The island itself has one main road, Chemin Royal, which circles the entire island. It's dotted with towns, but much of the island is devoted to local agriculture and can be visited year-round.

SIGHTS

★ ROUTE DE LA NOUVELLE FRANCE

Leave Québec City heading northeast and you'll soon be on the **Route de la Nouvelle France** (www.cotedebeaupre.com/en/route-de-la-nouvelle-france.php), one of the oldest roads in North America. In 1626 Samuel de Champlain established a livestock farm on Cap-Tourmente farther along the river, but it was Saint François de Montmorency-Laval (also known as Monseigneur de Laval) who originally traced the road, which brought provisions from the Côte-de-Beaupré to the city.

All along the 50-kilometer road are heritage homes, some dating as far back as the 1600s. Each is designed in its own particular style, indicative of early New France architecture. Though many of the homes are private residences, the public can visit **Aux Trois Couvents** (7976 chemin Royale, 418/824-3677, www.auxtroiscouvents.org; 10am-5pm daily early June-early Sept.; 9am-4pm Wed.-Fri., 1pm-5pm Sat.-Sun. early Sept.-early June; $6 adults, $5 seniors, $4 students, free children 12 and under). A museum and exhibition space, Aux Trois Couvents shares cultural and historical knowledge about the settlement of the Côte-de-Beaupré. **Centre de Généalogie** (277 rue du Couvent, 418/824-3079, www3.telebecinternet.com/archives.chateau-richer, 9:30am-4:30pm Mon.-Thurs. July-Aug., 1pm-4pm Mon.-Thurs. Sept.-Oct., 1pm-4pm Wed.-Thurs. Nov.-June, free) can help you with genealogical research, a popular Québécois pastime.

From mid-June to mid-November, stop in at **Ferme le Comte de Roussy** (6167 ave. Royale, 418/822-1649, www.lecomtederoussy.com; 9am-6pm Mon.-Fri., 9am-5pm Sat., 9:30am-5pm Sun. mid-June-mid-Nov., free) to pick apples, visit with goats and bunnies, and purchase fresh pies and produce.

As you travel along the road, you'll notice cavern-like structures built directly into the hillsides; these are root cellars, some of which date back more than 300 years. Also along the route is **Chez Marie** (8706 ave. Royale, 418/824-4347, www.boulangeriechezmarie.com; 9am-5pm daily summer; noon-4pm Mon.-Fri., 9am-5pm Sat.-Sun. winter, $5), a fourth-generation family bakery located in a homestead that dates back to 1652.

★ CHUTE MONTMORENCY

Near the bridge to the Île d'Orléans, you'll find **Chute Montmorency** (4300 blvd. Ste-Anne, 800/665-6527, www.sepaq.com/ct/pcm; hours vary by season), an 83-meter-high waterfall (even taller than Niagara Falls, as everyone will point out) that dominates the landscape between the cliffs of the Laurentians and the St. Lawrence. It's a stunning natural wonder in the middle of lush greenery, and visitors can discover the falls by foot, via steps alongside and a suspension bridge that allows you to cross along the top. For more expansive views, take the cable car ($14.06 adult, $7.03 child round-trip); for the most adventurous, try the zipline, which stretches in front of the falls ($25 adult, $18.75 child). Any way you slice it, you'll get great views of Île d'Orléans, the falls, the river, and even Québec City.

There's access at either side of the falls year-round. Basic access is free, but a fee is charged for parking ($7.05 per car late Oct.-late Apr., $10.57 per car late Apr.-late Oct.). There are lots at the top and bottom of the falls.

★ BASILIQUE SAINTE-ANNE-DE-BEAUPRÉ

This is the oldest pilgrimage site in North America, and people have been coming to **Basilique Sainte-Anne-de-Beaupré** (10018 ave. Royale, 418/827-3781, www.sanctuairesainteanne.org; 7am-5pm daily early May-early June, 7am-9pm daily early June-early Sept., 7am-5:30pm daily early Sept.-early Oct., 8am-5pm daily early Oct.-early May) since the 1660s. The first chapel was constructed on the site in 1658 as a place of worship for the area's new settlers and to house a statue of Sainte-Anne, Québec's patron saint. She's also the patron saint of shipwrecked sailors, and it was a group of Breton sailors caught in a storm who vowed to erect a chapel in Sainte-Anne's honor if they got safely back to land. While the chapel was being constructed, a man with rheumatism was said to have been cured after laying just three bricks, and a pilgrimage site was born.

The first basilica was built in 1876 to accommodate the legions of pilgrims who visited the shrine. The structure that exists today, built in the shape of a Latin cross and featuring 214 stained-glass windows, was constructed in 1926 after the first church was destroyed by fire in 1922. A small museum in the church's parking lot exhibits some of the church's treasures as well as donations made by pilgrims.

★ ÎLE D'ORLÉANS

Located five kilometers from downtown Québec City, Île d'Orléans is an island in the middle of the St. Lawrence and one of the oldest parts of New France to have been colonized. It measures 34 kilometers long and 8 kilometers wide. Explorer Jacques Cartier first called it Île de Bacchus, because of the amount of wild grapes found growing on the island. Today, it's home to small villages, but agriculture is still a large part of life on the island.

The first parish was founded in 1661, and a visit to **Maison Drouin** (4700 chemin Royal, 418/829-0330, www.fondationfrancoislamy.org; 10am-6pm daily mid-June-early Sept., noon-4pm Sat.-Sun. mid-Sept.-Oct.; $6 adult, children under 12 free) will give you an idea of what the early houses looked like. Built in 1730, it has been preserved in its original state.

Agri-tourism is a big draw to the island; you can pick your own strawberries, apples, pumpkins, and other produce at many farms across the island, including **Cidrerie Verger Bilodeau** (1868 chemin Royal, 418/828-9316, http://en.cidreriebilodeau.com; U-pick 9am-5pm daily late-Aug-early Oct., check website for store hours at other times of the year; free). Though many farms on the island don't have a web presence, they're chockablock along

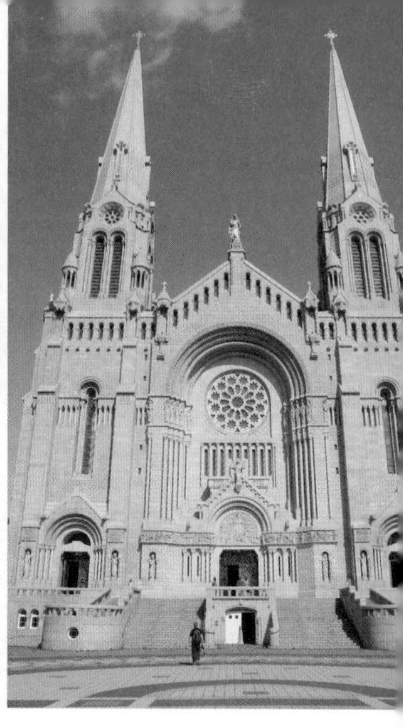

Clockwise from top left: Les Fromages de l'isle d'Orléans; Basilique Sainte-Anne-de-Beaupré; Chute Montmorency.

the main road; if you visit in late summer or fall, you won't go astray taking the main road along the island and stopping wherever your fancy takes you.

Visit **Cassis Monna & Filles** (721 chemin Royal, 418/828-2525, www.cassismonna.com, 10am-6pm daily May-Nov., free) and learn about how they make their black currant liqueur, or go for a tasting at **Vignoble de Sainte-Pétronille** (1A chemin du Bout-de-l'Île, 418/828-4554, http://vs-p.ca; 10am-5pm Wed.-Sun. Apr., 10am-5pm daily May, 10am-6pm daily June, 10am-8pm daily July-Aug., 10am-5pm daily Sept.-Oct., 10am-5pm Wed.-Sun. Nov.-Dec.; $2-5 tasting) and try their reds and whites as you look at the Chute Montmorency (bonus: Québec City staple Chez Muffy holds a mobile restaurant, **Panache Mobile**, here in the summer—check www.saint-antoine.com for details). Try delicious heritage and artisanal cheeses (including frozen cheese and fried cheese) at **Les Fromages de l'isle d'Orléans** (2950 chemin Royal, 418/829-0177, www.fromagesdeliledorleans.com; 10am-6pm daily late June-early Sept., 11am-5pm daily early Sept.-Canadian Thanksgiving; free).

RESTAURANTS

If you left Québec City early in the morning, stop in at **Pâtisserie Praline et Chocolat** (7874 ave. Royale, 418/824-3677, http://pralinechocolat.ca; 8am-6pm Mon.-Sat., 8am-5pm Sun. Mar.-Nov.; $5-10) for some mouthwatering pastries. They offer several different kinds of *viennoiseries* (baked goods) made fresh daily, as well as artisanal bread, jams, and other treats. If you're visiting Chute Montmorency, you can't go wrong with **La Terrasse du Manoir** (2490 chemin Royale, 844/522-4883, www.sepaq.com/ct/pcm; 11:30am-3pm daily May-Oct.; $12-29), on-site.

If you're looking for a fancy meal, **Bistro Nordik** (355 rue Dupont, 418/827-5748, www.chateaumontsainteanne.com; dinner 5pm-10pm daily, check ahead for other meals; $12-40, reservations recommended) at the Château Mont-Sainte-Anne has you covered with fresh, seasonal cuisine cooked with care—chef Frédéric Delsault lets his ingredients shine without excess salt or sugar. If you're in the mood for something less refined, **Chez Bolduc** (10969 blvd. Ste-Anne, 418/827-4660, www.restaurantchezbolduc.com; 11am-11pm daily summer, 11am-10pm daily winter; $10) serves up poutine, burgers, club sandwiches, and dairy bar selections.

On Île d'Orléans, tuck into some traditional cuisine or take part in the *cabane à sucre* (sugar shack) experience at **Le Relais des Pins** (3029 chemin Royal, 418/829-3455, www.lerelaisdespins.com; 11:30am-2:30pm daily June-Sept., winter by reservation only, Mar.-Apr. check website for sugar shack season offerings; $17-30). This delightful log cabin has lots of natural light and a modern take on decor.

If you've got a sweet tooth, **Chocolaterie de l'Île d'Orléans** (150 chemin du Bout de Île, 418/828-2250, www.chocolaterieorleans.com; $10) will satisfy with rich chocolate desserts, homemade ice cream, and delicious coffees. Their adjoining café also offers soups, salads, and sandwiches.

Treat yourself to fine dining overlooking the St. Lawrence at **La Goéliche**

(22 chemin de Quai, 418/828-2248, www.goeliche.ca; 8am-8:30pm daily; $16-36), where breakfast includes dishes like waffles and bacon, and dinner has choices like ribs with truffle oil and farm-fresh duck breast.

RECREATION

Bird-Watching and Hiking

CAP-TOURMENTE

The site of a livestock farm established by Samuel de Champlain in the early 1600s, **Cap-Tourmente** (570 chemin du Cap-Tourmente, 418/827-4591, www.ec.gc.ca/ap-pa; 8:30am-5pm daily early Apr.-early Nov., 8:30am-4pm daily early Nov.-mid-Dec. and Jan.-Mar.; $6) became a farm headed by Monsignor de Laval in 1664. It was an active farm well into the 20th century, and some of the early buildings remain. Today the area is mostly a nature reserve; it's a great place to bird-watch and learn about the greater snow goose and American bulrush marshes. Interpretive guides and 20 kilometers of hiking trails are available.

Golf

LE GRAND VALLON

One of the best courses in eastern Canada, **Le Grand Vallon** (100 rue Beau-Mont, Beaupré, 418/827-4561, www.legrandvallon.com; dawn-10pm daily May-Sept.; $29-79 for 18 holes), designed by Howard Watson, was once nicknamed the "minister's club" because of the number of high-level politicians that frequented the links. Along the 6,583-yard course there are four lakes and 42 white-sand bunkers, and the changing scenery moves from rolling tree-lined fairways to a large open plan at mid-course. Equipment rentals, golf carts, driving range, and lessons are also available, and use of the practice range is included in the greens fee.

Skiing, Snowboarding, and Snowshoeing

MONT-SAINTE-ANNE

About an hour's drive north of the city, the most popular ski station in the Québec City region, **Mont-Sainte-Anne** (2000 blvd. Beau Pré, Beaupré, 888/827-4579, www.mont-sainte-anne.com; 9am-4pm Mon.-Fri., 8:30am-4pm Sat.-Sun. early Dec.-early Apr.; $79 adult, $69 senior, $56 youth, $39 child 7-12), offers downhill skiing and snowboarding as well as snowshoeing and cross-country skiing. Sixty-six trails cover the north and south faces of the mountain. Officially opened in 1966, the history here goes back to 1947, when the Canadian Championships were held on these slopes.

HOTELS

Cozy but modern, the 31 rooms at **Hotel la Camarine** (10947 blvd. Ste-Anne, 800/567-3939, www.camarine.com; $104-204) in the Côte-de-Beaupré are often fitted with a warming gas fire, perfect after a long day outdoors.

Top: Chocolaterie de l'Île d'Orléans. **Bottom:** skiing at Mont-Sainte-Anne.

First Nations Culture and Heritage: Wendake Reserve

Drive northwest out of Québec City and you'll soon come across Wendake, a First Nations reserve that is home to over 3,000 residents. The home of the Huron-Wendat tribe since 1697, this unique reserve offers both a historical and modern perspective on the nation and its people. While many of the 19th-century buildings resemble those found back in the city—whitewashed houses and clapboard churches—look a little closer and you'll see something entirely different.

Shaped like an old Algonquin smokehouse, the **Musée Huron-Wendat** (15 Place de la Rencontre, 418/847-2260, www.museehuronwendat.ca; 9:30am-noon and 1pm-5pm daily mid-May-late Oct., 10am-noon and 1pm-4pm Wed.-Sun. late Oct.-mid-May, 10am-noon and 1pm-4pm daily winter holidays and March break; $11.50 adult, $10 senior and student, $5.75 child 6-17) conserves and promotes the history and heritage of the Wendat people. The permanent exhibition delves into Wendat ancestral traditions and pre-contact history. Visitors learn the Wendat creation myth and are introduced to the Wendat way of life through archival materials. Temporary installations include contemporary art and culture exhibits. The on-site gardens are also worth a visit.

Those who want to experience the past firsthand can head over to **Onhoüa Chetek8e** (575 Chef Stanislas-Koska St., 418/842-4308, www.huron-wendat.qc.ca), a traditional Huron site, where a tour guide will take you through typical buildings and rituals of the Huron First Nations people. Several different packages and activities are available, including snowshoeing, Huron storytelling, and craftsmanship workshops, so check the website for more details.

One of the latest additions to Wendake is the **Hôtel-Musée Premières Nations** (5 Place de la Rencontre, 866/551-9222, www.hotelpremieresnations.ca; $180-400), a beautiful hotel connected to the museum. Its 55 rooms seamlessly blend minimal contemporary design with natural accents, including tree trunks and stone. While you're here, have dinner at **La Traite Restaurant,** which takes inspiration from traditional Huron cooking to create dishes like grilled bison and pan-seared seal.

To orient yourself, head to the **Wendake Tourism Center** (10 Place de la Rencontre, Wendake, 418/847-0624, www.tourismewendake.ca; 8:30am-5pm daily mid-June-mid-Oct., 8:30am-4:30pm Mon.-Fri., 10am-4pm Sat.-Sun. mid-Oct.-mid-June) for useful maps and other information.

On Île d'Orléans, grab a room with a view at **Auberge La Goéliche** (22 chemin de Quai, 418/828-2248, www.goeliche.ca; $119-179). Named after a small schooner, the white clapboard house has charm in spades; the views of the river and the well-appointed rooms with country touches like handmade quilts make it an ideal choice.

Total country charm is the best way to describe **Auberge Le Canard Huppé** (2198 chemin Royal, 800/838-2292, www.moteliledorleans.com/chambres/#auberge; $110-150), now managed by the Auberge & Motel Île d'Orléans. The oversized wood furniture, pine paneling, and wood floors are welcoming, and the beautiful garden is the icing on the cake.

INFORMATION AND SERVICES

Before you go to the area, read up on the Côte-de-Beaupré area at **www.cotedebeaupre.com,** which offers useful information on restaurants, hotels, grocery stores, and events. Once you're on the ground, the Pavillon d'Accueil Récréotouristique de la Côte-de-Beaupré (5572 blvd. Ste-Anne, Boischatel, 418/822-3578; 10am-5pm Wed.-Sun. mid-May-mid-June, 9am-7pm daily mid-June-early Sept., 10am-5pm Wed.-Sun. early Sept.-early Oct.) can provide you with hands-on information.

The year-round **Île d'Orléans Tourist Office** (490 Côte du Pont, St-Pierre, 418/828-9411 or 866/941-9411, www.iledorleans.com, 8:30am-7:30pm daily July-Aug., 10am-5pm daily Sept.-June.) has a wealth of information and tips on hand.

GETTING THERE AND AROUND

Bus

Tours Voir Québec (800/267-8687, www.toursvoirquebec.com; 9am and 1pm daily June-Oct., 1pm daily Nov.-May, $173-310) offers a five-hour tour including wine, cider, and cheese tastings. This tour visits Chute Montmorency, Domaine Maizerets, and Île d'Orléans. Check website for dates and times.

Sainte-Anne-de-Beaupré can be reached by **Intercar** coach (320 Abraham Martin, 800/806-2167, www.intercar.ca), which leaves from Québec City's Gare du Palais bus terminal heading toward Baie Comeau one or two times a day (check the schedule online). A return ticket costs $16.80 and the journey takes 55 minutes.

Bike

Bike path **Corridor du Littoral** will take you right from Québec's Vieux-Port all the way to Chute Montmorency and even along the **Route de la Nouvelle France.** The Chemin Royal encircles the Île d'Orléans and is a great way to sightsee by bike.

Car

The simplest and quickest way to get around is to take Autoroute 440 east out of Québec City and watch for the signs; all of the sights are well marked out with the exits that accompany them. To get to Île d'Orléans, take the Pont Île d'Orléans to the island.

Charlevoix

Some of the most stunning views of the province can be found in Charlevoix, where people come to camp, hike, and to catch a glimpse of the whales.

Follow Route 138 north out of Québec City and you'll come across some of the most spectacular scenery you've ever seen. The impact of a meteorite 350 million years ago has shaped the face of the Charlevoix region and could be the cause of its mysterious seismic activity (rest assured—most earthquakes barely reach 2.0 on the Richter scale).

One of the first vacation destinations in Canada thanks to a couple of enterprising Scottish soldiers, Charlevoix's landscape is distinct in its variety. At times pastoral and hilly, the region's high cliffs and breathtaking fjords are adorned with tundra, while nearby, steep sand dunes rise unexpectedly along the coastline. These manifold landscapes translate into an area rich in biodiversity, where moose and caribou thrive alongside an astounding range of sea life. Where else can you sit on a sandy beach waiting to catch a glimpse of a pod of white beluga whales?

★ BAIE-SAINT-PAUL

One of the biggest towns in Charlevoix, Baie-Saint-Paul is known for its unique artist community, galleries, and off-beat boutiques. (It's also known as the birthplace of Cirque du Soleil, which now makes its home in Montréal.) Home to roughly 7,300 full-time inhabitants, the downtown core is quaint and full of shops and cafés. It's a lovely place to spend the afternoon strolling the streets no matter the season.

Sights

Musée d'Art Contemporain Baie-Saint-Paul (23 rue Ambroise-Fafard, 418/435-3681, www.macbsp.com; 10am-5pm daily summer, 11am-5pm Tues.-Sun. winter; $6 adult) honors the area's artistic heritage with a collection and temporary exhibits dedicated to contemporary works. Founded in 1992, the museum is located in what was once an old cinema and is a definite must on any itinerary.

Born in Switzerland in 1895, artist René Richard moved to Canada with his family as a child and was working as a fur trapper in northern Alberta by the time he was 18. By the 1940s he'd settled in Baie-Saint-Paul, where he painted some of his best-known landscapes. His century-old house, **Maison René-Richard** (58 rue St-Jean-Baptiste, 418/435-5571; 11am-5pm daily; free), has remained unchanged and is on the main street. Visitors get the chance to see both his home and his work in the adjoining gallery.

On the outskirts of town you'll find **Azulée** (54 chemin de la Pointe, 418/240-2620, www.moulindelaremy.com; 10am-5pm daily June-Canadian Thanksgiving; $5 adult, $3 child). Situated near the coast of Baie Saint-Paul, this quaint lavender farm offers guided visits of the fields and the mid-19th-century farmhouse. The views are spectacular, and you can pick up some

Train de Charlevoix

If you want to travel through the Charlevoix region in luxury, forgo the convertible and grab a seat on the **Train de Charlevoix** (844/737-3283, www.traindecharlevoix.com; June-Oct.). Inaugurated in 2012, the train chugs along a long-dormant track of railroad that follows the shore of the great St. Lawrence River all the way from Québec City to La Malbaie. The 125-kilometer-long train trip is an awe-inspiring journey, and it's all thanks to Daniel Gauthier, cofounder and former president of the Cirque du Soleil, and his project to entice tourists to explore the region and the town of Baie-Saint-Paul in particular.

Though the train journey's scenic surroundings make the landscape the star of the show, the train itself is gorgeous in its own right. With its high, arched ceilings, picture windows, and interactive displays, it immerses you in the surroundings. Guests can purchase local *terroir* products and snacks on board, as well as alcoholic and nonalcoholic beverages.

Trains for Baie-Saint-Paul (from $79 per person round-trip) and La Malbaie (from $128 per person round-trip) depart from the base of Chute Montmorency (with an option to take a connecting bus from Gare du Palais or Place d'Youville, located in the city proper), about a 20-minute drive outside of Québec City, between June and October. One to five trains run per day. Trains from Québec City (Chute Montmorency) to Baie-Saint-Paul take 2.25 hours one-way. Trains from Québec City (Chute Montmorency) to La Malbaie take just under 4 hours one-way. You can choose to do a day trip or stay overnight at a point along the route; check the website for accommodation packages.

It's definitely not fastest way to get to your destination—the train stops for short visits at each station—but it is perhaps the most memorable.

heaven-scented lavender goods in the boutique after you learn about the plant's cultivation.

Sustainability is the focus of **Habitat 07** (212 rue Ste-Anne, 418/435-5514, www.habitat07.org; 10am-6pm daily May-Aug., 10am-6pm Sat.-Sun. Sept.-mid-Oct.; $5 adult, $2 student), an ecofriendly house opened in 2007 and built to showcase the latest developments in new energy and recycling. The construction methods were inspired by ancient practices and used local, sustainable materials. The best part of the house, though, is the amazing view of the St. Lawrence River.

Restaurants

Baie-Saint-Paul has the best range of restaurants in the region. Fans of a good microbrew shouldn't miss **Le Saint-Pub** (2 rue Racine, 418/240-2332, www.saint-pub.com; 11:30am-10pm daily late May-Oct., 11:30am-8pm daily Nov.-late May; $25). This pub and bistro keeps things local and serves fresh fish, foie gras, and charcuterie. They also offer more regular pub-style dishes like poutine and nachos.

Relaxed dining can be found at **Joe Smoked Meat** (54 rue St-Jean-Baptiste, 418/240-4949, http://joesmokedmeat.com; 11am-9pm daily; $15),

Top: Musée d'Art Contemporain Baie-Saint-Paul. **Bottom:** Le Diapason, a bistro in Baie-Saint-Paul.

a family-owned business with locations in Québec City and Malbaie. Their specialty, as you may have guessed, is smoked meat, though they also served subs, pastas, and salads.

A French-born and trained chef puts his skills to work on local ingredients at the **Mouton Noir** (43 rue Ste-Anne, 418/240-3030, www.moutonnoirresto.com; 11:30am-10pm daily; $35). The emphasis is on modern French cuisine, and the menu includes everything from beef tartare to sweet potato gnocchi. Book ahead, and expect a crowd and lively atmosphere.

Located kitty-corner from the church, with a great *terrasse* view in the summer, **Le Diapason** (1 rue Ste-Anne, 418/435-2929, www.restolediapason.com; 5:30pm-9pm Mon., 11:30am-9pm Tues.-Sun.; $25) serves up classic dishes like escargots *à l'alsacienne,* braised beef cheek, and peppery duck. Their in-house special is the Alsatian dish *flammeküeche,* a thin-crust hand pie topped with *fromage blanc* and crème fraîche.

Hiking

PARC NATIONAL DES GRANDS-JARDINS

Once you're in the area you might as well take advantage of the nature that's available to you. West of Baie-Saint-Paul is the **Parc National des Grands-Jardins** (800/665-6527, www.sepaq.com/pq/grj), open year-round. This gorgeous national park has some of the most interesting vegetation, with a mix of both taiga and tundra. The landscape is vaguely arctic, with thick layers of lichen and black spruce forest. Home to a large caribou population, it offers many activities, including 34 kilometers of hiking trails in the summer, as well as kayaking and canoeing (rentals are available). In winter, visitors can use the 55 kilometers of cross-country ski trails and try their hand at ice fishing.

Skiing

★ LE MASSIF

One of the best hills in the province, **Le Massif** (455 QC-138, Petite-Rivière-Saint-François, 877/536-2774, www.lemassif.com; 8:30am-4pm daily mid-Dec.-mid-Apr., $64 adult day pass) is the area's largest ski mountain. Many high-ranking skiers come to train here, but even if you're more comfortable on the bunny runs, the views alone are worth the fees. It's on a cliff that looks out over the St. Lawrence, and there are times on these runs when you're sure the bottom is going to be on the shores. With 49 different trails of varying levels, it has something for everyone.

Hotels

Located south of Baie-Saint-Paul, **Les Sommets Charlevoix** (15 Chemin du Versant, Petite-Rivière-Saint-François, 877/469-0909, www.sommetscharlevoix.com; $235-675) rents chalets a quick drive from both Le Massif and Baie-Saint-Paul. A mix of rustic and luxurious, Les Sommets offers five-star concierge service—they'll sort out your ski tickets, have alcohol and groceries delivered to your chalet, provide a child-minding service, and set up local cultural activities for you. With a spa and sauna, outdoor pool, and skating in the winter, this is the perfect spot for active rest and relaxation.

The stone-clad, 30-room inn **Maison Otis** (23 rue St-Jean-Baptiste, 418/435-2255, www.maisonotis.com; $120-260) in Baie-Saint-Paul is a charming historical hotel that underwent significant renovations in late 2017, bringing it up from charming if dated to fully modern. With a floral country vibe, **Auberge La Muse** (39 rue St-Jean-Baptiste, 800/841-6839, www.lamuse.com; $120-400) is ideally located on a tree-lined street in the center of town, and the rooms are tastefully decorated.

For a modern, upscale experience, **Le Germain Charlevoix Hotel & Spa** (50 rue de la Ferme, 844/240-4700, www.legermainhotels.com, $255-305) in Baie-Saint-Paul is a design-award-winning, Scandinavian-looking hotel offering full spa services, including hot and cold pools and steam rooms, and seven different rustic-chic rooms.

Information and Services

Baie-Saint-Paul Tourist Office (6 rue St-Jean-Baptiste, 418/665-4454; 9am-5pm daily winter, 9am-7pm daily summer) is just off the highway on a hill overlooking the city below; it's a great view, but the turnoff is sharp. The website **www.tourisme-charlevoix.com** is a great online resource.

Getting There and Around

BUS

Intercar coaches (320 Abraham Martin, 888/861-4592, www.intercar.qc.ca) leave from Québec City's Gare du Palais bus terminal heading toward Baie Comeau twice a day during the week and once a day on the weekends. The same bus runs all along the Charlevoix coast. A round-trip ticket to Baie-Saint-Paul costs $43, and the ride takes one hour and 45 minutes. Pickup and drop-off is at a gas station (909 blvd. Monseigneur-de-Laval), which can be reached either by foot—it's about a 20-minute walk from downtown—or by taxi.

CAR

Take Autoroute 440 out of Québec City and continue past Côte-de-Beaupré on Route 138 all the way to Baie-Saint-Paul. Depending on traffic and weather conditions, the drive should take approximately 80 minutes.

TRAIN

The exclusive **Train de Charlevoix** (844/737-3283, www.traindecharlevoix.com; June-Oct.; $74 per person and up) offers stunning views, great food, and a totally unique way to get from Québec City to Baie-Saint-Paul. The train departs Québec City from the base of the Chute Montmorency on a regular basis (check the website for details), depositing travelers at a convenient location for exploring Baie-Saint-Paul.

Top: whale-watching near Tadoussac. **Bottom:** ski-jumping at Le Massif.

★ ISLE-AUX-COUDRES

Off the shores of Baie-Saint-Paul is Isle-aux-Coudres, one of the most picturesque islands in the St. Lawrence. Hop on the free ferry from Saint-Joseph-de-la-Rive just south of Baie-Saint-Paul and take the 20-minute ride out to the island.

Sights

Once on the island, it's easy to be transported to an earlier time. **Les Moulins de L'Isle-aux-Coudres** (36 chemin du Moulin, 418/760-1065, www.lesmoulinsdelisleauxcoudres.com; 10am-5pm daily mid-May-mid-Oct.; $8.70 adult, $4 child), a water mill and windmill that were built in 1825 and 1838, respectively, are a visceral link to the past. They're still in operation today, and you can tour these working mills and learn how buckwheat and wheat were once ground all over the region. Guided tours are available, but you're also welcome to explore all buildings and surroundings on your own.

With a parish that dates back to 1741, **Église de Saint-Louis de Isle-aux-Coudres** (1961 chemin des Coudriers, 418/438-2442) is one of the oldest religious sites on the island, built 1885-1886. It boasts hand-painted frescoes and impressive stonework. Mass is held on Sunday at 9:45am; call ahead for other hours.

No matter the season, stop in at **Cidrerie et Verger Pedneault** (3384 chemin des Coudriers, 418/438-2365, www.vergerspedneault.com; 8am-5pm daily). Opened in 1918, this family-run apple orchard also creates its own apple cider (alcoholic and non), jams, syrups, and honey. They offer apple-picking in the fall, and there's a hiking and biking trail that snakes around the premises and through the fields.

Restaurants

On Isle-aux-Coudres, many restaurants are located in hotels and are only open seasonally; it's best to check ahead if you're planning to travel between October and May.

Le Boustifaille (3031 chemin des Coudriers, 418/598-3061, www.hotelducapitaine.com; 8am-9pm daily; $11-25) is in the Hôtel du Capitaine and serves down-to-earth, simple food. In the summertime, the building also hosts La Roche à Veillon, a summer theater.

Located in Auberge la Fascine, **La Fascine** (1064 chemin des Coudriers, 418/438-1010, www.aubergelafascine.com; noon-close daily; $25) serves simple veggie and beef burgers, alongside some slightly more off-the-beaten-path fare, like horse steaks.

La Marée (444 chemin de la Baleine, 888/554-6003, www.hotelcapauxpierres.com; 7:30am-10:30am and 6pm-10pm daily May-Oct.; $25), housed in the Hotel Cap-Aux-Pierres, serves an American-style breakfast buffet and an upscale dinner service focusing on fresh, local ingredients. For a slightly less formal experience, check out the **Terrasse et Bar la Lucerne**

Parc National de la Jacques-Cartier

Less than a half-hour drive from downtown Québec City is **Parc National de la Jacques-Cartier** (103 chemin de la Parc National, Stoneham-et-Tewkesbury, 418/848-3169, ext. 6, www.sepaq.com/pq/jac). Situated in a valley with the same name, this park boasts both calm waters and rapids. Home of a 26-kilometer-long river, this is the perfect place to learn basic maneuvers. Those who haven't had the opportunity to learn how to canoe or kayak can do so here. They also have a number of mini-rafts, inflatable canoes, and inner tubes to rent for more relaxed water fun. Though the park is open year-round, equipment rental (canoe $16.75 per hour, kayak $15.25 per hour) is only available mid-May through mid-October. There are also bike trails for those who want to do some off-roading.

(444 chemin de la Baleine, 888/554-6003; 11:30am-7pm daily June-Sept.; $25), also in Hotel Cap-Aux-Pierres.

Recreation

Named Isle-aux-Coudres after the hazelnuts that Jacques Cartier found here, the 11-kilometer-long and 3-kilometer-wide island is easily explored by **bike. Vélo-Coudres** (2926 chemin des Coudriers, 418/432-2118, www.velocoudres.com; 9am-5pm daily May-June and Sept., 9am-6pm daily July-Aug., $10-60/hour) has different models available, including tandem, kids' bikes, and even quadricycles with room for up to four adults and two kids.

Hotels

Located on the northern tip of the island, **L'Hôtel Cap-aux-Pierres** (444 chemin la Baleine, 888/554-6003, www.hotelcapauxpierres.com; $105-155) has 46 rooms, tastefully decorated with wood floors, antique-style furniture, and a country feel. Each room has classic views of both the river and the garden. The hotel also has an outdoor pool.

Hôtel du Capitaine (3031 chemin des Coudriers, 418/438-2242, www.hotelducapitaine.com; $119 and up) is also on the northern tip, but closer to where the mainland ferry docks. The rooms have a country feel with their floral bedspreads and wooden furniture; the views of the river, however, are stunning, and you can opt to have a gourmet dinner included in the price. The breakfasts are complimentary.

Travelers on a budget might want to opt for the **Auberge la Fascine** (1064 chemin des Coudriers, 418/438-1010, www.aubergelafascine.com; $50-90), a cute, down-to-earth auberge with private bathrooms, mini fridges, and outdoor spaces featuring Muskoka chairs (known as Adirondack chairs in the United States).

Information and Services

Isle-Aux-Coudres Tourist Office (1024 chemin des Coudriers, 418/665-4454, 9am-5pm Sat.-Sun. mid-May-mid-Oct.) can be found on the main road, just a short walk from the quay. Open only during peak season, it closes during the off-season (typically after Canadian Thanksgiving). Read up on the island at **www.tourismeisleauxcoudres.com** before packing your bags.

Getting There and Around

BOAT

The only way to get to the island is by ferry. The ferry departs from Saint-Joseph-de-la-Rive and arrives at Saint-Bernard-sur-Mer on the west coast of the island. The trip takes about 20 minutes. It can take approximately 367 passengers and 55 vehicles. The boats are run by a government agency, **Traversiers** (877/787-7483, www.traversiers.com), and as such the service is free. Boats leave the mainland and the island about once an hour during peak season, but travelers should contact the company directly before making concrete plans. Once on the island, visitors are welcome to drive or ride a bike.

LA MALBAIE

If you want to continue exploring the region of Charlevoix, stay on the mainland and continue north from Baie-Saint-Paul on Route 362 until you arrive at La Malbaie, one of the oldest tourist spots in the region. Originally called Murray Bay, the area was first made popular by two Scottish officers who saw the potential in the area's beauty and made it the top resort choice from the 19th century right up until the 1950s.

Sights

MUSÉE DE CHARLEVOIX

Learn all you need to know about the region at **Musée de Charlevoix** (10 chemin du Havre, 418/665-4411, www.museedecharlevoix.qc.ca; 9am-5pm daily June-mid-Oct., 10am-5pm Mon.-Fri., 1pm-5pm Sat.-Sun. mid-Oct.-May; $8 adult, $6 senior and student, free for children). This charming museum offers exhibitions about the region's culture and history, including photographs of beluga whale-hunting, artifacts from Manoir Richelieu, and folk art from the 1930s and '40s.

CASINO DE CHARLEVOIX

In more recent times, one of the biggest draws to the region has been the **Casino de Charlevoix** (183 rue Richelieu, 800/665-2275, http://casinos.lotoquebec.com; hours vary by season; free). Opened in 1994, it has cherrywood paneling and granite floors, and is a step up from most casinos. Visitors must be at least 18 years old to enter. The casino is located on the same grounds as the luxury resort Fairmont Le Manoir Richelieu.

Restaurants

Run by two head chefs, **Vices Versa** (216 St-Etienne, 418/665-6869, www.vicesversa.com; 6pm-9pm Tues.-Sat.; $69 for three courses) is a unique take on fine dining. Customers are presented with two menus (one created by each chef) and must decide between the two. Choices include scallops on rye with smoked herring vs. scallops with lobster ravioli, or duck breast with duck-fat potatoes vs. duck confit terrine with foie gras. At the restaurant, it's all about pleasing the diner and the chefs' friendly rivalry. Situated on a busier street, it has a relaxed elegance that perfectly suits the flavors flowing from the kitchen.

Sometimes a little comfort food is the only way to go. **Pizzaria Du Poste** (448 rue St-Étienne, 418/665-4884, www.pizzariaduposte.ca, 11am-midnight daily June-Aug.; 11am-10pm Sun.-Tues., 11am-midnight Wed.-Sat. Sept.-May; $20) serves up Italian favorites like spaghetti, lasagna, and pizza in a convivial and sometimes raucous atmosphere. The pizza is thin-crusted and topped with the usual suspects and some that are more unexpected (shrimp and crab, anyone?). What's best about this place is the low-key atmosphere and the outdoor patio in the summer.

Hiking

★ PARC NATIONAL DES HAUTES-GORGES-DE-LA-RIVIÈRE-MALBAIE

Named after a series of valleys, **Parc National des Hautes-Gorges-de-la-Rivière-Malbaie** (418/439-1227, www.sepaq.com/pq/hgo; late May-Oct.) has steep sloping mountains that fall to meet Rivière Malbaie. With its unique mix of fauna, Hautes-Gorges is one of the most beautiful spots in eastern Canada. Not far west from La Malbaie, it offers a huge amount of outdoor activities, like boat cruises, fishing, cycling, and 33 kilometers of hiking. Swimming, canoeing, and kayaking can also be done here.

Golf

Murray Bay Golf Club (1013 chemin du Golf, 877/665-2494, www.golfmurraybay.com; $27-68) is one of the oldest courses in the country and the third oldest in North America. It first opened its links in 1876. Built high above the cliffs that look out over the St. Lawrence, it's a spectacular place to tee up and a must for any golfer visiting the area.

Hotels

In La Malbaie, one of the area's biggest draws is the romantic **Fairmont Le Manoir Richelieu** (181 rue Richelieu, 866/665-3703, www.fairmont.com; $160-350). Built in 1899, in a similar style as the Château Frontenac, it sits atop the Pointe-au-Pic overlooking the St. Lawrence River. Destroyed by fire and rebuilt in 1929, the hotel today is a luxury resort with an adjoining 18-hole golf course and an on-site spa, as well as five different restaurants. The rooms are elegant and tastefully decorated and aim for comfortable instead of sleek luxury.

Auberge des Peupliers (381 rue St-Raphael, 888/282-3743, www.aubergedespeupliers.com; $140-250) keeps things luxurious but at a more affordable price point. There's a contemporary edge to this hotel that others in the region lack, making it ideal for urbanites or those looking for a modern hotel in rustic settings.

If you're looking for a B&B, head to **Auberge Petite Plaisance** (310 rue St-Raphael, 866/500-4938, www.aubergepetiteplaisance.com; $90-150), a cute spot with a gorgeous wraparound veranda and delicious full breakfast offerings. The B&B is down-to-earth, affordable, and friendly.

Information and Services

La Malbaie Tourist Office (495 blvd. de Comporté, Route 362, 418/665-4454; 9am-5pm daily) is right on the water looking out over the river and has a nice park in front in which to take a break.

Getting There and Around

BUS

If traveling by public transport, hop on the **Intercar** coach (320 Abraham Martin, 888/861-4592, www.intercar.qc.ca), which leaves from Québec City's Gare du Palais bus terminal heading toward Baie Comeau once or twice a day (check website for details). The trip will take about 2.5 hours from Québec City and you'll be dropped off and picked up at Mikes la Malbaie (665 blvd. de Comporté) in the middle of the town. A round-trip ticket costs $62.

CAR

Follow Autoroute 440 out of Québec City and continue north on Route 138 all the way to La Malbaie. Depending on traffic and weather conditions, the drive should take approximately two hours.

★ TADOUSSAC

Tadoussac is the meeting point of the Saguenay and St. Lawrence Rivers. Before you can get to Tadoussac, however, you have to take a ferry across the convergence of these two mighty waterways. A free ferry will take you the short trip across the water to the historic town, one of the oldest places in Québec. It was France's first trading post and was established in 1600. Today the area's main draw is the rich marine life that thrives here, thanks to the warm St. Lawrence saltwater and the freshwater of the Saguenay.

Sights

Though the town itself is quite small, numbering only around 900 year-round residents, it's completely charming, the perfect place to stroll around. Visit **Chauvin Trading Post** (157 rue Bord de L'Eau, 418/235-4657; 10am-noon and 1pm-6pm daily late May-mid-June and early Sept.-late Oct., 10am-7pm daily mid-June-early Sept.; $5 adult, $3 senior, $2.50 student

Saguenay Fjord

Before you arrive in Tadoussac, a charming town three hours north of Québec City, you come to a dead stop—it's here that the cliffs widen to reveal the banks of the Saguenay River and the majestic fjord beyond, and you need to take a ferry to bridge the gap.

The Saguenay Fjord is a rare natural wonder. One of the most southerly fjords in the world, it was created by the weight of a glacier turning a crevasse into a wide, calm river approximately 200 million years ago.

Once a hotbed of activity for the logging industry, the region's forests were critically depleted by the 1920s. To preserve the fjord, the government began buying up land, eventually turning it into a national park in the 1980s. The **Parc National du Fjord-du-Saguenay** (91 rue Notre-Dame, Rivière-Éternité, 418/272-1556, www.sepaq.com/pq/sag; $8.50 adults, children and youth under 18 free), open year-round, has since become one of the most popular in the province, with close to a million visitors in 2010. Activities in the park include everything from skiing to hiking and camping, but it's the kayaking adventures offered by the park, which allow you to explore the fjord firsthand, that are the most exciting.

The fjord is also home to a number of species, including four species of whales: the blue whale, the fin whale, the minke, and the beluga.

and child). This may just be a reconstruction, but it's still cool to visit a reasonable facsimile of the first trading post in Québec, and the exhibitions, though brief, are informative.

About five kilometers northeast of the town are sand dunes, an incongruous natural phenomenon in the region. **La Maison des Dunes** (750 chemin du Moulin-à-Baude, 418/235-4238; 10am-5pm Sat.-Sun. mid-June-early Sept., 1:30pm-8pm Fri.-Sun. early Sept.-mid-Oct.; free) is a restored house that's been turned into an interpretation center that explains exactly how the sand dunes came about.

After the French arrived in 1600, the Jesuit monks quickly followed. The **Petite Chapelle de Tadoussac** (108 rue Bord de L'Eau, 418/235-4324; 9am-7pm daily June-Oct.; free) was constructed in 1747 and is the oldest wooden church still in existence in North America. In addition to offering great views of the river, it's home to religious artifacts. It's a bit of untouched history in the region.

Restaurants

In Tadoussac most of the restaurants are only open May-October, something to keep in mind if you're traveling north in winter. If you're visiting in summer, there's a lot more choice but it isn't always varied. One of your best bets for a light breakfast, lunch, or dinner is **Café Bohême** (239 rue des Pionniers, 418/235-1180, www.lecafeboheme.com; 8am-10pm daily May-June and Sept.-Oct., 7am-11pm daily July-Aug.; $20). Serving different types of fair-trade coffee, they also have a selection of desserts (try the brownie) and other treats as well as a range of soups, sandwiches, and salads. On the second floor, they also have a small book exchange library, and you can pick up some gourmet Charlevoix products.

For something more upscale, there is the **Restaurant le William** (165 rue Bord-de-l'Eau, 418/235-4421, www.hoteltadoussac.com; 5pm-10pm daily; $83 tasting menu) in the Hôtel Tadoussac, which offers a six-course tasting menu and views over the Bay of Tadoussac and the St. Lawrence.

Recreation

Between mid-May and mid-October tourists come from all over the world to see the **whales** that flock to the region; approximately 10 different species can be found every year, including humpback, finback, blue whales, and white belugas. The best places to catch a glimpse of these majestic creatures are the **Parc Marin du Saguenay-Saint-Laurent** (182 rue de l'Église, 888/773-8888, www.parcmarin.qc.ca) and **Parc National du Fjord-du-Saguenay** (91 rue Notre-Dame, Rivière-Éternité, 418/272-1556, www.sepaq.com/pq/sag). Both parks offer different ways to see the whales, including boat excursions and sea kayaking. Interpretation centers are open along the trails, and they both offer stunning views of the fjords and the rivers. The parks are open year-round; admission, which gives you access to both parks, is $8.50 adults, children and youth under 18 free.

Independent companies offer up-close and personal **whale tours.** The largest game in town is **Croisières AML** (Baie du Tadoussac, 866/856-6668, www.croisieresaml.com; May-Sept.; $65-135), which offers tours of varying lengths—including tours that offer transportation up to Tadoussac from Québec City. Most of the tours take place on larger boats with food facilities and naturalists who'll walk you through the action; tours on Zodiacs (sleek, low boats) let you get even closer to the animals. Passengers are given life jackets and waterproof overalls but you will likely get wet anyhow as you bump along the waves. Departure times vary depending on the day of the week, the month, and the type of tour; it's best to plan ahead, especially during the busy season.

For the brave and experienced, **kayak trips** are also available through **Mer et Monde Ecotours** (866/637-6663, www.meretmonde.ca; May-Sept.; $56-125), whose three- to eight-hour tours start at the bay of Tadoussac, just past the lawn of the Hôtel Tadoussac.

Hotels

Sitting on the Baie de Tadoussac, **Hôtel Tadoussac** (165 rue Bord-de-l'Eau, 800/561-0718, www.hoteltadoussac.com; May-Oct.; $129-149) stands out on the horizon with its red copper roof and white clapboard siding. Opened in 1864, it's one of the oldest hotels in the region and maintains its historical feel (it has no air-conditioning, but then again you don't really need it). The rooms have been modernized and have a nice, airy quality about them. The **Petite Chapelle de Tadoussac** is on the property. Built by Jesuit missionaries, it is the oldest wooden church in North America and still has some of its original artifacts.

Information and Services

Before you go, check out **www.tourisme-charlevoix.com** for all the necessary tips and information.

The **Tadoussac Tourist Office** (197 rue des Pionniers, 418/235-4744, www.tadoussac.com; 9am-5pm Mon.-Sat. May-late Oct.) is in the center of town and hard to miss. It has loads of information on the region as well as a few historical exhibits to give you more of an idea about the place, its culture, and history.

Getting There and Around

BUS

Intercar coaches (320 Abraham Martin, 888/861-4592, www.intercar.qc.ca) leave from Québec City's Gare du Palais bus terminal heading north once a day. The same bus runs all along the Charlevoix coast. A round-trip ticket to Tadoussac costs $98 and the ride takes a little over 4.5 hours, depending on traffic and weather. The bus pickup and drop-off is at Accommodation JB (443 rue du Bateau-Passeur) in the center of the town.

CAR

From Québec City take Autoroute 440 and then Route 138 all along the coast to Tadoussac. The drive should take a little over three hours depending on the weather and traffic conditions.

Background

The Landscape

GEOGRAPHY

Québec is Canada's largest province. It covers an area of 1,540,681 square kilometers, basically the size of France, Germany, Belgium, Spain, Portugal, and a couple Switzerlands put together, all in all an enormous territory. For the most part, it is filled with boundless forests and innumerable lakes (some say more than 400,000), vestiges of the huge Sea of Champlain that flooded the area 10,000 years ago.

Québec's geography can be divided into three main regions. The Canadian Shield goes from the extreme north down to the plain of the St. Lawrence River and includes the Laurentian Mountains, said to be the oldest mountain range in the world. At the south of that plain, the Appalachians turn the landscape into a green and hilly area characteristic of the Eastern Townships region (southeast of Montréal) and extend down to the United States. A rift valley between these two antediluvian geological formations, the St. Lawrence is a 1,200-kilometer-long river that takes its source from the Great Lakes and ends up in the world's largest estuary. The majority of Québec's residents live along the banks of the river, and it's also the center of Québec's development. Looking out over the landscape from the window of a plane, you can see (along with the sprawling cities of Montréal and Québec) the rural landscape divided into narrow rectangular tracts of land extending from the river: These patterns denote the seigneurial land system, designed to allow each parcel access to water; they date back to the settlement of 17th-century Nouvelle France (New France).

Québec City, with a population of over half a million, thrives on the north bank of the St. Lawrence near its meeting point with the St. Charles River and not far from the foothills of the Laurentian Mountains. Built on top and around the 98-meter-high Cap Diamant, it overlooks the dramatic narrowing of the river that takes place in the St. Lawrence after Île d'Orléans. It's from this narrowing that the city gets its name, taken from the Algonquin word *kebec,* which means "where the river narrows."

This particular position made it a logical commercial port as well as a strategic military point. The ramparts surrounding Vieux-Québec's Upper Town, the only fortified city left in North America, have made it an architectural jewel and helped the city earn the name the "Gibraltar of North America." Near the southern edge of Cap Diamant, the Plains of Abraham (Québec's version of Central Park) extend along the cliffs. It was on these rolling hills that North America's fate was sealed in the haze of a battle between the British and the French in 1759.

One of the main physical features of the city is its two-level construction.

Previous: Vieux-Québec's Lower Town; monument to faith in Place d'Armes in Upper Town.

Cap Diamant and its cliffs break the urban landscape in two, prompting significant opposition between Haute-Ville (Upper Town) and Basse-Ville (Lower Town). This opposition is as significant sociologically as it is topographically. Thus, Upper Town (with the exception of Faubourg Saint-Jean-Baptiste) is historically the home of the ruling bourgeoisie, while Lower Town (Limoilou, Saint-Roch, Saint-Sauveur), which developed along the shores of the St. Lawrence and St. Charles Rivers, was the home of seamen, dock workers, and factory workers. This antagonism is in flux nowadays, as exemplified by Nouvo Saint-Roch's gentrification. Motivated by the city's 400th anniversary's celebrations in 2008, much urban redevelopment has been done, particularly along the banks of the rivers, making Québec City one of the most likable cities in the world.

CLIMATE

"Mon pays ce n'est pas un pays, c'est l'hiver" (My country is not a country, it's winter) sang Québec's premier *chansonnier* (singer-songwriter), Gilles Vigneault. Truer words have never been spoken, especially regarding the six months during which winter takes over, changing the landscape and affecting the mood of its resigned inhabitants. Yes, wintertime temperatures have an average of -10°C and can drop down to -30°C. However, the winters aren't as harsh, cold, and snowy as they used to be, thanks to global warming. But the freezing wind, blowing *poudreuse* (drifting snow) everywhere like a tempest in the desert, is probably the toughest thing about being here in the winter. When the temperatures dip to bone-chilling proportions, make sure to cover up everything from your nose to your toes or you could end up with frostbite.

Approximately three meters of snow fall every winter, but sometimes there's more. Snowstorms are frequent and can last up to a day if not more. Snow removal can be interesting to watch if you're a tourist and have never seen it before. The sidewalk and road snowplows can also be deadly, so be careful, especially when walking at night.

Despite being harsh and long, winters in Québec are also sunny, with a bright luminosity that can sometimes be blinding. Because of the length of the season, stoical locals have adopted an "if you can't beat 'em join 'em" attitude in order to survive, and you'll be surprised to see just how active Quebeckers can be in winter, putting on their skates and snowshoes after every snowstorm, sometimes going to work on cross-country skis and pulling their kids in toboggans along the sidewalks.

Of course, Québec isn't just about winter, and people are often surprised to see just how hot and humid the summers are, with temperatures often reaching 35°C. After having complained about the cold all winter, locals curse the heat and turn their air-conditioners on full blast.

Autumn and spring are shorter in Québec, but in many ways they are the most impressive seasons. In spring, the snow melts away, revealing new blossoms, while autumn has a particular beauty as the trees change to a rainbow of colors before shedding their leaves.

PLANTS AND ANIMALS

The best place to explore Québec's rich and diverse fauna and flora is in the national parks. National parks offer interpretive materials and guides to help you understand just exactly what it is you're surrounded by.

There's not much chance to run into a moose or a black bear while getting a pint of milk at the *dép* (corner store). But, the city has Parc des Plaines d'Abraham, with protected fauna and flora, where you might see animals that can be exotic for some: red and gray squirrels, chipmunks, and raccoons.

Québec City is remarkably green for its size, with trees lining just about every side street. Originally part of the Laurentian forest ecosystem, the vegetation has changed over time due to urbanization.

History

EARLY INHABITANTS

Long before its European takeover, the North American continent was home to indigenous people for thousands of years. Historians date the population back to at least 12,000 years ago—though it may date back much further. One theory posits that hunting tribes crossed the Bering Strait in pursuit of game from Siberia. Those tribes then scattered all over the land, developing diverse ways of life as they adapted to different environments. By the time explorers arrived, the area that would eventually become known as the St. Lawrence Valley was populated by the nomadic Algonquin and sedentary Iroquoian peoples who lived off game, fish, and crops, and were particularly well adapted to their environment.

EUROPEAN ARRIVAL

When it comes to the "discovery" of Canada, French explorer Jacques Cartier's name usually pops up. But the truth is that by the time he finally made it to Québec in 1534, Newfoundland's coastline had been periodically cruised by explorers and fishermen from different nations—the Vikings had sailed its coast and even put down a few roots 500 years before.

What Jacques Cartier did that other Europeans didn't was explore the interior of the river, a river that he named in honor of the saint on the calendar the day he reached it: Saint-Lawrence. Sent by the king of France, Francis I, with the mandate of finding gold and—the typical request of the day—a passage to Asia, the sailor explored the region thoroughly, visiting Iroquoian villages Stadacona (Québec) and, farther upstream, Hochelaga, in present-day Montréal. After many voyages, he found neither gold nor Asia, bringing home instead a bunch of made-up stories told by fabulist natives and a handful of rocks he thought were diamonds (a popular French saying of the time was "*faux comme un diamant du Canada*" (fake as a Canadian diamond). Deemed by the French to be inhospitable and dull,

Canada's Indigenous Peoples Today

Today, Canada is undergoing a process of truth and reconciliation with First Nations, Métis, and Inuit peoples. (The Métis are a post-contact indigenous people; their culture came about through a mix of mostly Cree, French, and Scottish traditions and new traditions in the Prairies region.) The idea is to make amends for historical and ongoing colonial policies—many violent—that had negative and lasting impacts on indigenous peoples.

Indigenous peoples, seeking self-determination and nation-to-nation relationships, are also leading cultural and linguistic renaissances in their communities across the country. When you visit, keep an eye out for gorgeous indigenous art—sculpture, painting, beadwork—but do a little research to ensure that you're purchasing an item that is made by an indigenous person and will support their indigenous culture (there are a lot of commercial knock-offs out there!).

what we know today as Canada remained unvisited and almost forgotten by Cartier's nation for half a century.

NOUVELLE FRANCE (NEW FRANCE)

Two things rekindled the French interest in this part of the world: the fur trade and an appetite for colonial expansion. In addition to these two motives, the Catholic Church saw an opportunity to spread the gospel to the indigenous population and sent missionaries along on the expedition. Seeing promise in the new European fashion of fur hats and coats, trading companies quickly formed, including the Compagnie des Cent-Associés, which set up outposts around Québec where the French newcomers and First Nations peoples could trade.

In 1608, Samuel de Champlain set up the first permanent European trading post in an abandoned Iroquoian village that Jacques Cartier had visited 80 years before, building a wooden fort he called l'Abitation de Québec (*kebec* in Algonquin means "where the river narrows"). That first winter, most of the settlers died of scurvy and harsh weather, but the colony continued even though it faced numerous difficulties and was slow to grow. In 1635 (the year Samuel de Champlain, the Father of New France, died), the population was slightly more than 300 settlers, a fair number of them Catholic missionaries. Some of these missionaries organized the Société Notre-Dame de Montréal and, in 1642, decided to establish an evangelizing mission near the deserted village of Hochelaga. Called Ville-Marie, it would eventually become Montréal.

While colonists cleared forests and cultivated the land, the thriving fur trade attracted a different kind of young explorer, one daring enough to go farther and farther into the continent seeking bearskins, mink furs, and, above all, the popular and coveted beaver pelts. Called *coureurs des bois* (wood runners, or woodsmen), these adventurers are legendary figures in

Québec, since they represent a life of freedom and a particular connection with nature that characterized the colonization of the continent. These *coureurs* also paved the way for the explorers and voyageurs to whom we owe the exploration of the regions of the Great Lakes and the Mississippi Valley, much of which they claimed for the French. These explorers left their mark on places all over the United States, including Detroit, St. Louis, and Baton Rouge.

The commercial relations brought on by the trade helped the French secure alliances with the Hurons, who in exchange for the pelts received copper and iron utensils, alcohol, and rifles. This alliance put the French colony in the middle of a bloody war when the English-backed Iroquois Five Nations launched an offensive campaign to wipe out the Hurons, their long-time enemies. The war lasted 25 years, seriously affecting both the First Nations and the French colony.

TOWARD DEFEAT

The conflicting commercial and political interests of the French and English caused a succession of intercolonial wars. In 1713, following a military defeat in Europe, the Treaty of Utrecht resulted in France relinquishing control of Newfoundland, Acadia, and Hudson Bay, something that considerably hurt New France's fur trade and jeopardized its colony. This date marks the beginning of the end for New France, even if it took another 50 years for the British to secure power, a takeover that seemed inevitable considering the difference in population. Indeed, on the eve of the final battle, there were 60,000 French living in a huge territory, surrounded by two million British colonists living in the narrow strip of the 13 colonies.

The final showdown happened on September 13, 1759, on an open field by Cap Diamant, now called the Plains of Abraham, in present-day Québec City. After a two-month-long siege, the French army, led by General Montcalm, was attacked by surprise early in the morning. General Wolfe and the British army used a dried-up old creek to climb the cliff, something everyone thought was impossible. The Battle of the Plains of Abraham, which sealed the fate of French North America, was bloody, lasted barely 20 minutes, and cost the lives of both generals. One year after, Montréal capitulated and thus France lost all of its colonies in North America, leaving behind a small population of deeply rooted French Catholics in an ocean of British Protestants.

BRITISH REGIME

Though at first they tried to assimilate the French minority by imposing British Common Law and having them swear an oath to the British king, the victors decided that it was wiser to accommodate the French, wanting to secure their allegiance as social unrest and rebellion smoldered in the south. To cement the support of the French-Canadians, England wrote up the Act of Québec in 1774, recognizing both the French language and French civil law, and granting them freedom of religion. These concessions

Coming North: United Empire Loyalists

When things started looking really bad for the British during the American Revolution, colonists who wanted to remain loyal to the British crown were offered free land (no matter that much of it was indigenous territory, not really England's to give) and safe passage to other—non-rebelling—parts of the British colonies.

Called United Empire Loyalists because of their unyielding devotion to King George III, many chose to escape north, settling in the regions of southern Ontario and Québec. So many immigrated to the province, close to 50,000, that it sent the Québécois into a breeding frenzy and kicked off the *revanche des berceaux,* the "revenge of the cradle."

By 1791 so many loyalists had arrived in the country that the government signed the Constitutional Act, dividing the province in two: Upper Canada, which would eventually become Ontario, and Lower Canada, the province of Québec.

Though many Loyalists and descendants of Loyalists eventually moved out of the province, their influence can still be seen in the Eastern Townships, where covered bridges, clapboard houses, and Victorian gingerbread moldings are the norm.

succeeded in preventing the French-Canadians from joining the rebels in the south who started the American Revolution a year later.

At the end of that war, in 1783, 50,000 United Empire Loyalists (British Loyalists) had fled the United States for the province of Québec, many of them settling into the Eastern Townships region, a hilly area southeast of Montréal. To accommodate these Loyalists, who were an English minority in a French-speaking majority, a new Constitutional Act was signed in 1791, dividing the province in two: Upper Canada (which would eventually become Ontario) and Lower Canada (the province of Québec). The names Upper and Lower Canada were given according to their location on the St. Lawrence River.

The 19th century was marked by the power struggles between the Francophones and the Anglophones in Lower Canada. The elected French-Canadian representatives were constantly at odds with the colonial British executive and legislative powers. Over the years, the nationalist and reformist Parti Canadien denounced the untenable situation, ending up in an armed insurrection. The Patriots War (Guerre des Patriotes) of 1837-1838 was immediately crushed, and an emissary was sent from London to study the problems of this wayward colony. The solution proposed by Lord Durham was radical: Make every effort to assimilate French-Canadians. This was the impetus behind the Union Act, laid down by the British government in 1840. Along with unifying Upper and Lower Canada and giving them an equal political power—despite the fact that Lower Canada was much more populated—it also made English the only official language, although the vast majority were French-speaking. These new laws and the constant arrival of English-speaking immigrants prompted a major exodus of Francophones, many of whom emigrated to the United States.

CONFEDERATION

The troubled politics of the subsequent years coupled with a dire economic situation prompted leaders of Upper and Lower Canada to unify. The British North America Act, signed in 1867, is the constitutional act that solidified Canada as an independent nation that would eventually stretch from the Atlantic to the Pacific.

It also created the two-level structure of government, in which power is split between the federal and provincial levels. Even though Québec's minority status was deepened by it, the new structure granted the province jurisdiction over education, civil law, and culture, among other things. Québec maintained a central importance in the evolution of the country, and before long a French-Canadian, Wilfrid Laurier, became prime minister of Canada. Elected in 1896, he was the first of many Québécois, including Pierre Elliot Trudeau and Jean Chrétien, who would lead the country—most recently, Justin Trudeau was elected prime minister.

Faced with a prodigious period of economic growth at the beginning of the 20th century, Prime Minister Laurier declared it "Canada's century." The prediction fell short, though, when the Great Depression disrupted economic and social progress in Québec for many years. World War II finally put an end to the economic doldrums, and Québec came out of the war economically stronger than ever before and ready for social change, as the anarchist manifest *Refus Global* (Total Refusal), signed by artists and writers, made clear.

Despite this exciting new energy and mind-set, the province would remain under the spell of Maurice Duplessis and his conservative party (Union Nationale) for another 15 years. In spite of its considerable economic growth, this period is often referred to as "La Grande Noirceur" (The Great Darkness), the last obstacle before real transformation.

THE QUIET REVOLUTION AND CONTEMPORARY TIMES

After the death of Maurice Duplessis in 1959, Québec was ripe for change, and the Liberal Party government of Jean Lesage was elected the year after, kicking off what would be dubbed the Révolution Tranquille (Quiet Revolution), a wide range of bold economic and social reforms. The most important result of these reforms is the secularization of society, putting an end to the centuries-long overarching power of the church in every aspect of Québécois society. Education, health care, and social services were no longer under the control of the church as the state began to take over.

The most ambitious economic project of the time, the nationalization of the province's electric companies under Hydro Quebec is a powerful symbol of that new ambition. The Quiet Revolution also witnessed the rise of nationalism. Jean Lesage's Liberal government election slogan, *maîtres*

Top: the icy St. Lawrence River. **Bottom:** Québec's fortifications protected New France from English incursions.

chez nous (masters in our own home), meant to put a stop to the unbridled selling of the province's natural resources to foreign business interests.

Montréal hosted two major international events that still define its identity: the 1967 World's Fair (Exposition Universelle—Terre des Hommes) and the Summer Olympic Games in 1976. The sentiment of empowerment at the time exacerbated enthusiasm for the idea of a stronger autonomy within the Canadian federation, and more and more people became attracted by the idea of building a new country instead, some groups even falling into extremism. Thus, the Front de Liberation du Québec (FLQ), founded in 1963, used terrorist tactics against the Québec and national governments and businesses with the aim of establishing a socialist independent country.

In 1970, during the October crisis, when the FLQ kidnapped Québec Labour Minister Pierre Laporte and eventually killed him, Pierre Elliot Trudeau, then Canadian prime minister, launched the War Measures Act against Québec dissidents, putting the country under martial law to much public controversy. After that, the FLQ declined drastically and eventually disappeared.

Despite these radical actions and a certain support the FLQ gained with the public, the majority of pro-sovereigntists preferred moderate nationalism. In 1967, René Lévesque, a rising star of the Liberal government, quit the party and founded the Parti Québécois (PQ). Soon after, in 1976, a stunning and unexpected victory brought the PQ to power, putting the question of sovereignty at the forefront of political and social life of Québec society for decades. Bill 101 in 1977 made French the only official language of Québec. In 1980 Lévesque's government launched a referendum on the issue of independence, losing when the "no" side won with 60 percent of the vote. In time, the tensions with the federal government became aggravated, mostly over constitutional matters and Québec's refusal to ratify the repatriated Canadian constitution in 1982.

In 1995, a second referendum campaign was launched. This time the results were extremely close, and Canada held its breath: 49.4 percent of Quebeckers voted "yes" and 50.6 percent voted "no," underlining the deep division of the population over the issue.

However, the national question has faded in importance over the last 20 years, with public attention drifting toward other public matters like the environment and economy. In 2003, the PQ was ousted from power after 10 years, and the Québec Liberal Party, resolutely federalist, was elected. Led by Premier Jean Charest, they were voted in for a third term in 2009. Thanks to political unrest related to the rising costs of tuition, the PQ regained political power with a minority government in the autumn 2012 election. They lost to the Liberals again in 2014, in large part due to a bill the PQ introduced in 2013 called the Charter of Values, which would have, among other things, limited the wearing of "conspicuous" religious symbols by state personnel—small crosses would have been fine, but Jewish workers would not have been able to wear kippot, and Muslim women would not have been able to wear the hijab. The bill was met with some support as well as a strong backlash, and the Liberals took power in the next election.

Contemporary Québec is a province in flux: Multicultural and multilinguistic, it is influenced by particularly French conceptions of secularism and free speech, as well as values that underscore the importance of a pluralistic society. Particularly for Francophone Québécois, it is increasingly important to find a balance between supporting and ensuring the strength and longevity of Francophone culture and the French language, while ensuring that newcomers to the province can thrive and be culturally recognized and supported here. Over the past generation, major gains have been made in cities like Montréal, where traditionally Anglophone Montréalers have embraced learning French, and French has increasingly become the language of business—this shift in power has allowed for a positive shift in cultural commingling. Of course, there are still tensions, and much work to be done, but visitors to the province will notice mostly the citizens' warmth and cultural vibrancy.

Government and Economy

POLITICS

Canada's political system is modeled after the British parliamentary system it historically inherited. Central in the government organization is the House of Commons, sitting in Ottawa, a democratically elected body consisting of 338 members known as Members of Parliament (MPs). Each MP in the House of Commons is elected by simple plurality in an electoral district, also known as a riding. Elections are called within four years of the previous election or when the government loses a confidence vote.

The leader of the party that won the most seats generally becomes the new prime minister and forms the new government. Canada being a federation, this political structure is reproduced for every province. Therefore, each has its own parliament. In Québec, the provincial government is called the Assemblée Nationale, and its 125 elected members sit in Québec City, the province's capital. The Canadian Constitution divides the power between federal and provincial governments. For example, defense, postal services, and international relations are under federal jurisdiction, while education, health, and natural resources are under provincial jurisdiction. Since the Constitution is not always clear about these divided powers, constitutional conflicts arise, a situation that has been particularly true between Québec and the federal government.

Canada is also a constitutional monarchy. People are often surprised to know that there is a queen in Canada: Queen Elizabeth II of England is the Canadian head of state. Though her role is mostly formal and symbolic, she does have a representative in Canada acting on her behalf:

the governor general. She is represented by the lieutenant-governor in the provinces.

Though Canada's first-past-the-post governmental structure favors a two-party system, in Canada's case, five parties make up the federal government: the right-leaning Conservative Party, centrist Liberal Party, left-leaning NDP (New Democratic Party), the Bloc Québécois (the Québec sovereigntist party), and the Green Party (environmentalists who are relatively new on the scene and usually don't hold many seats). In major political battles, the Conservatives and Liberals are generally the front-runners, but the NDP and Bloc Québécois are instrumental to how government is run and what bills are passed in the House of Commons.

From 2006 to 2015, the Conservative party, under the leadership of Stephen Harper, formed the federal government, ruling alternately with a majority rule and a minority rule. In 2015, facing growing public criticism over issues like nonrenewable energy, press freedom, and senator expense scandals, the Harper Conservatives with ousted in favor of the Liberal Party under the leadership of Justin Trudeau, whose father, Pierre Elliott Trudeau, served as the prime minister of Canada from 1968 to 1979 and again from 1980 to 1984. The Liberals, who have a majority government, were elected on promises to develop renewable energy strategies, work on reconciliation with indigenous peoples in Canada, and change the electoral system from first-past-the-post to some form of proportional representation. (So far on shaky ground in terms of *keeping* those promises, it's anyone's guess as to what will take place next election year.)

On the provincial stage, two parties have been exchanging power for half a century: the centrist, federalist Québec Liberal Party, and the sovereigntist Parti Québécois founded by René Lévesque. In the 1980s and '90s, the Parti Québécois (PQ) became the center of international attention when it organized two referendums on Québec sovereignty. The consecutive defeats of the PQ in these referendums and in recent elections have laid the sovereigntist question aside for the time being, and the Liberals are currently in power.

ECONOMY

Since the beginning, Québec's natural resources have been the major asset in the province's economy. Vast forests, mining resources, rich agricultural land, and a huge potential for hydroelectricity—because of all the lakes—make this province, like much of Canada, good for a primary, resource-based economy. Historically everything began with the fur trade, kicking off the European colonization of the territory and sustaining it for over a century. In the 19th and most of the 20th centuries, wood, pulp, and paper industries took the lead and are still, along with the mining sector and hydroelectricity production, the most important sectors of Québec's economy.

The government plays an important role in the economy and is the largest employer in the province. Despite the trend toward more privatization, this strong state involvement reaches a certain consensus in the population and is considered essential due to the small size of its economy. Government-owned Hydro Québec, the world's leader in hydroelectricity, remains a national pride, and dams and development projects in the north are thoroughly followed by the population. Another economic national jewel is aerospace and railway maker Bombardier, a world-class company started in 1942 by Joseph Bombardier, the inventor of the snowmobile.

Québec City has discreetly developed into a very successful city, with one of the lowest unemployment rates in Canada at 4 percent. Most jobs in Québec City are found in public administration, services, and tourism, with a large proportion of civil servants, because it is the seat of the entire provincial political apparatus.

The past decade has seen a particularly sound growth rate and many urban development projects, probably prompted by the enthusiasm occasioned by the city's 400th anniversary. The result of this growth meant that Québec City virtually averted the economic crisis of 2008 and has continued to grow since then.

People and Culture

INDIGENOUS PEOPLES

Québec's first inhabitants were indigenous peoples. Ten different First Nations tribes, as well as the Inuit in the northern part of what is now Québec, have made their homes here for tens of thousands of years. Today, after centuries of harsh colonial policies, indigenous peoples represent a small but growing part of the population. Three quarters of indigenous peoples in Québec live on reserves throughout the province: The Mohawk reserves Kahnawake and Kanesatake in the Montréal region and the Wendat-Huron reserve Wendake north of Québec City are some of the bigger ones. Though some indigenous peoples live in areas where they can hunt and fish, many reserves preclude following a traditional way of life, and the federal government has not honored commitments to ensure their livelihood—or sometimes even provide basics like access to food and clean drinking water.

One of the most important political events of the past decades was the Oka Crisis: For two months in the summer of 1990, Mohawks barricaded one of the main bridges into Montréal, protesting land claims and issues of self-government. The incident forced native issues to the forefront, and in recent years nation to nation agreements have granted indigenous peoples more autonomy—though there is still much work to be done if Canada is to honor its treaties and work in good faith with indigenous peoples.

FRANCOPHONES

The vast majority of the Québécois people are descendants of the settlers who arrived between 1608 and 1759. From the 60,000 French-Canadians in 1759 there are now seven million living in Canada. Part of the reason Québec has such a strong cultural and social heritage is because of the population's demographics. In the late 18th century with the arrival of the United Empire Loyalists, the French-Canadians became nervous at the idea of being overpopulated by the English-speaking contingent. One response to this immigration was something that would later be called the *revanche des berceaux* (revenge of the cradle), which saw the families of French-Canadians growing larger by the year. Of course, the province's Catholic background helped, and throughout the years Québécois families were typically large and women had an average of 8 children (Céline Dion is from a family of 14 kids). In the 1970s, however, the birthrate dropped considerably, and it remains one of the lowest in the world.

Though today the province is experiencing a baby boom, it is a mere blip compared to the numbers in the mid-20th century. Much of the growth to the province's Francophone population now comes from immigration.

ANGLOPHONES

The first Anglophone immigrants arrived after the British conquest in 1759. Most of them were well-to-do Protestant merchants, forever forging the stereotype of the rich Anglophone. However, this wasn't always the case; one of the most important groups of immigrants was the working-class Irish, who arrived in the province as early as the founding of New France. The biggest wave of Irish immigrants came 1815-1860, driven from Ireland by the potato famine. They came to the province by the boatload, disembarking at Grosse-Île, an island off the shores of Québec City that was set up as a reception center. During the summer of 1847, thousands died during a typhus epidemic, and the orphaned children were adopted by Québec families. It is estimated that a staggering 45 percent of Quebeckers have Irish ancestry, even if most of them don't know it. In Québec City many immigrant families were relegated to the slum-like dwellings in Petite Champlain.

The arrival of the United Empire Loyalists between 1783 and the beginning of the 19th century shaped not only the Eastern Townships, where most of them settled, but also the future of the country. They fled the United States in such great numbers as to facilitate the division of the province into Upper and Lower Canada. The 19th century also saw the largest number of immigrants from the British Isles, many of whom would put down roots in Montréal and, in the case of the Scots, found McGill University.

In the 1970s, after the rise to power of the PQ and the October Crisis in particular, many English speakers left Québec, often settling in Ontario. Nowadays, they make up only 10 percent of the total population of the province and live mostly in Montréal. Of the English-speakers who did stay, the vast majority are now bilingual.

QUEBECKERS OF OTHER ETHNIC ORIGINS

Immigration from countries other than Britain and France began in earnest in the 20th century. Canada's growing ethnic diversity is particularly obvious in Montréal, whose history has been defined by successive waves of immigrants. After World War II, the majority of immigrants arrived from Italy, Greece, and Portugal, communities that continue to have a stronghold in Montréal neighborhoods like the Mile End and Little Italy. For the most part, these immigrants aligned themselves with the Anglophone community, raising Québec's perennial concerns over French language subsistence. In 1977, the Parti Québécois passed Bill 101—among other things, the children of newcomers were required to attend French schools. Immigration demographics began to change in the latter part of the century, and the 1970s and '80s saw exiles from Vietnam and Haiti join the ranks, followed more recently by North African, Middle Eastern, Chinese, and Central European immigrants. Many immigrants now arrive speaking French, and the government funds programs for those who don't so that they may, with financial support, acquire French proficiency.

Québec also has a large Jewish community, whose roots can be traced all the way back to the British conquest, while a large Hassidic community can be found in the Mile End and Outremont, two popular neighborhoods in Montréal.

LGBTQ COMMUNITY

The first recorded gay establishment in North America, Moise Tellier's apples and cake shop, opened in Montréal in 1869. At that time, homosexuality was illegal in Canada, and punishable by death. It wasn't until 1969 that the federal government, under Pierre Elliot Trudeau, decriminalized homosexuality. In the 1970s, '80s, and '90s, LGBTQ rights were slowly recognized and added to charters of rights and freedoms provincially and federally across Canada; in 2005, same-sex couples gained the right to marry in Canada.

Though Québec City doesn't have a gay village (most larger Canadian cities do, including Montréal, Toronto, and Vancouver), there is a good concentration of LGBTQ and LGBTQ-friendly bars and restaurants along rue St-Jean, just outside the fortified city in the Saint-Jean-Baptiste neighborhood. LGBTQ and LGBTQ-friendly accommodations—often, B&Bs—also dot the city.

Québec City hosts an annual pride celebration every Labor Day weekend; decorations go up all over rue St-Jean, and Place d'Youville turns into a street party.

RELIGION

There is no denying the influence of the Catholic Church on the history of Québec, and almost every street corner features a three-story-high cathedral, though today many of them have been converted into condos.

Jewish Québec

King Louis XIV of France might have banned Jews from entering the colony of Nouvelle France, but Québec's Jewish roots can still be traced for centuries.

The first Jewish people to settle in Québec were members of the British army who arrived after the initial conquest. Several are thought to have been a part of General Jeffery Amherst's battalion, four of which were officers. Of those officers at least one, Aaron Hart, remained in Canada, settling in Trois-Rivières and eventually becoming a wealthy landowner. One of his sons, Ezekiel Hart, later became the first Jew to be elected to public office in the British Empire.

Though the Jewish community in Montréal numbered little more than 200, the Spanish and Portuguese Synagogue of Montréal opened its doors in 1768 and became the first non-Catholic house of worship in the province. In Québec City the first known Jewish inhabitant was Abraham Jacob Franks, who settled in the city in 1767, but it wasn't until 1892 that the Jewish population in Québec City had enough members to warrant a proper synagogue. In the interim, however, they had founded a number of institutions, including the Québec Hebrew Sick Benefit Association, the Québec Hebrew Relief Association for Immigrants, and the Québec Zionist Society. By 1905, Québec City's Jewish population numbered 350.

As anti-Semitism mounted in Europe, over 155,000 Jews resettled in Canada, many of them in Montréal, where they became storekeepers, tradespeople, and workers in the city's numerous garment factories. The history of one of the city's greatest streets, boulevard St-Laurent, can be traced back to the immigrant families who worked and lived along the Main or in the factories nearby. Jewish businesses left an indelible mark on the city, and many of Montréal's most recognizable symbols—the smoked-meat sandwich, the bagel—come from that strong Jewish lineage.

At the end of World War II approximately 40,000 Holocaust survivors came to Canada, and in 1947, the Workmen's Circle and Jewish Labour Committee started the Tailors Project, aimed at bringing Jewish refugees to Montréal in the needle trades. Jewish immigration continued to expand in Québec, especially in the 1950s when North African Jews fled the continent, settling in Québec City and Montréal where their French language would be an asset.

Though Québec City still has a Jewish community, the majority of the province's Jewish population lives in Montréal, in areas such as Hamstead, Côte-St-Luc, and Outremont, with a large Hassidic community in the Mile End.

Instrumental in the founding of the nation and throughout most of its history, the Catholic Church only really began to lose its prominence in the 1960s and '70s. For the most part, Francophones remain Catholic (though most are non-practicing) and Anglophones are Protestant, but there are also diverse religions encompassing Muslims, Jews, Hindus, and Sikhs.

LANGUAGE

Language is arguably the most important for Québécois Francophones since it's really what makes them both distinct and recognizable. Francophones, particularly older generations, can be very touchy about how other people view their language, be it toward other Francophones who consider *joual* (colloquial Canadian French) a mere dialect, or toward people who obstinately refuse to make any efforts to speak French. Don't be afraid, though; people are usually not hard to please, and using a mere *bonjour* (hello) or *merci* (thank you) will demonstrate an awareness that you realize you're visiting a French-speaking province. Francophones who speak English will often switch to English if they see you struggling.

In order to understand linguistic tensions in Québec, you have to understand the history. After the British conquest in 1759, even though language, religion, and other rights were granted to the French community, they were barred from political and economic power for a long time. This linguistic exclusionism, in which access to the upper levels of business and power was barred to the French-Canadians, lasted well into the 20th century. In fact, until the 1970s English-speakers were the minority that ran many of the businesses and held positions of power in the province.

The Quiet Revolution in the 1960s, however, helped to change all that as it fostered nationalist sentiment, which reached a peak when the Parti Québécois was elected in 1976. In 1977, Bill 101 was passed, asserting the primacy of French on public signs across the province, and apostrophes were removed from store fronts in the 1980s to comply with French usage. English is allowed on signage as long as it's half the size of the French lettering. Despite the debate that surrounded the bill when it was first implemented, many believe it has helped to preserve the language.

Anyone with a good ear will likely be able to tell that there's a big difference between the French spoken here and the French in France. The French here is said to be its own evolved version of the French spoken in the 17th and 18th centuries in France, partially preserved due to its geographical isolation. The language spoken in everyday life is full of funny expressions and syntax. Depending on where you are in the province, some accents may be harder to understand than those in the cities.

Unlike in France, where they've integrated English terms like "weekend" into regular usage, Québec—surrounded by Anglos and Anglo culture—is much more ardent about the preservation of the language. That's not to say English words aren't in common usage in Québec; there is simply a heightened awareness of them. The Office Québécoise de la Langue Française is an institution whose mandate is to translate new words, typically those related to IT or technology, into a French equivalent. For example, in Québec, email is *courriel,* the French contraction of electronic mail, and Québec's stop signs are also written in French, with the word *arrêt* at their center, though even in France the signs read "stop."

MUSIC

Without a doubt the province's best-known recording artist is Céline Dion. Born in the small town of Charlemagne 30 kilometers from Montréal, she was a mega-star in Québec and France when she was just a teenager and well before she started singing in English. Although she was criticized at first by her Francophone fan base for "selling out," her worldwide success is now a huge source of pride for the province, and fans now love (and buy) her English albums just as much as her French ones.

The province's second biggest export, music-wise, is Montréal's Arcade Fire, who took over the airwaves in 2004 with their infectious indie rock anthems and haven't looked back. Despite their rock star status—they've shared the stage with everyone from David Byrne to David Bowie—they remain active in the community, and many of the group's members play in other Montréal bands. Their success in the early 2000s was also part of a bigger Montréal indie rock explosion, with bands like The Dears, Wolfe Parade, and the Unicorns, among others. The scene has continued to grow since then and is constantly evolving. Francophone bands like Malajube, Radio Radio, and Karkwa—who won the 2010 Polaris Music Prize, Canada's largest for an "indie" band—have been gaining fans across the language divide. Godspeed You! Black Emperor and Cœur de Pirate are two other favorite acts from the province, beloved for their craft and creativity.

Poet and singer/songwriter Leonard Cohen, who died in 2016, was one of Montréal's most-loved inhabitants, and many of his melancholy and soulful compositions were inspired by the city, including the song *So Long Maryanne.* Grammy Award-winning artist Rufus Wainwright is also from Montréal, though he now resides in New York. Mixing symphonic sounds with a pop mentality, his sweeping compositions are utterly unique and catchy. His sister, Martha Wainwright, also a musician, is somewhat less experimental in her style, but continues to push the boundaries of pop. On one of her albums *(Sans Fusils, Ni Souliers, à Paris)* she sings the songs of Edith Piaf. Of course, it helps when you have good genes, and the Wainwrights have them in spades: Their father is American folk singer Loudon Wainwright III, and their mother is Kate McGarrigle; Kate and her sister Anna are two of the biggest folk singers in the province. Since the 1960s, the McGarrigle sisters have sung and written in both French and English.

It wasn't until the 1960s that modern music really started to hit its stride in the province. Québec held a festival of experimental music in 1961, and by the mid-1960s, the symphony was starting to attract a larger audience. It was also the heyday of folk singers or *chansonniers* like Félix Leclerc and Gilles Vigneault. Leclerc in particular had been singing and writing for a long time, even finding success in Paris, before returning to find the same success at home. Singing about themes like nature and celebrations has made him one of the most revered musicians in the province.

CINEMA

After being under religious censorship during the first half of the 20th century, Québec cinema really kicked off in the 1960s, when a generation of directors formed the National Film Board (NFB). This film board gave them a platform, and they started to make movies mostly about the Québécois identity. Part of the enthusiastic social transformations that were happening in arts in this period, they shot documentaries and features that gained international recognition, despite their local flavor. Experiments in documentary film led to the Direct Cinema genre, which included Pierre Perreault's *Pour la Suite du Monde,* a vivid documentary about the ancestral beluga hunt in Isle-aux-Coudres, and Michel Brault's *Les Orders,* a rendition of the October crisis of 1971.

In the 1970s, a number of feature films gained wide critical acclaim and today are seen as part of a golden age in Québec cinema. Among these are *La Vraie Vie de Bernadette* by Gilles Carle (1972), *J.A. Martin Photographe* by Jean Beaudin (1977), and Frank Mankiewicz's *Les Bons Débarras* (1979). Most important of all is Claude Jutra's 1971 movie *Mon Oncle Antoine,* a coming-of-age story set in the rural Québec of the 1940s, which is considered to be the greatest Canadian film.

The Québec film industry is seen as the strongest in the country, and Québec films regularly win top accolades at the Genie Awards, which are the Canadian film industry awards. Québec's French cinema has a stronger character than its English counterpart, which often struggles to differentiate itself from American cinema.

With movies like *Le Déclin de l'Empire Américain* (1986) and *Jésus de Montréal* (1988), Denys Arcand is probably the best-known Québécois director. *Les Invasions Barbares* (2003), a poignant critique of the aging generation of the Quiet Revolution, won the Oscar for Best Foreign Film and was Best Screenplay at Cannes. Other stand-out directors have been scooped up by Hollywood, including Jean-Marc Vallée, who directed *Dallas Buyers Club,* and Denis Villeneuve, who directed *Prisoners.* Xavier Dolan has been recognized at the Cannes Film Festival for his films *J'ai Tué Ma Mère, Les Amours Imaginaries, (Heartbeats), Lawrence, Anyways and It's Only the End of the World,* and has set the course for a new generation of filmmakers.

LITERATURE

After Paris, Montréal has the most French-language writers in the world, many of whom have been translated into English. Playwright and author Michel Tremblay wrote *Chroniques du Plateau,* which has made him one of the most prolific and well-recognized authors in the province. His stories about working-class French-Canadians in the 1960s, written almost entirely in *joual* (colloquial Canadian French), defined the writing of his generation. Other writers include Hubert Aquin, Dany Laferrière, Marie-Claire

Blais, and Anne Hébert, whose *Kamouraska* looks at treachery and love in 19th-century Québec. Gabrielle Roy's *The Tin Flute* tells the tale of a young woman in working-class Verdun during the Depression.

Notable Québec City writers include Claire Martin, who won a Governor-General's award for her 1966 book *La Joue Droite*, a feminist book recounting the narrator's years at a convent; Octave Crémazie, a French-Canadian poet and bookseller known for his patriotic Québécois verse; and Neil Bissoondath, a Trinidadian-Canadian writer and critic of race relations and the multicultural system in Canada.

VISUAL ARTS

Early Québec art can be divided into two subject matters: landscapes and religion. The province's first painters were Catholic missionaries who used paintings and engravings to convert indigenous peoples. Since many of the works were by priests and nuns, they have a particularly naïve quality, a trend that continues in Québécois art. The first great Québécois painters emerged in the 19th century and included Théophile Hamel, known for portraits of explorers; Dutch-born Cornelius Krieghoff, who depicted settlers and images of the wilderness; and Ozias Leduc, whose portrait *Boy with Bread* is one of the defining images of Québécois art.

Work continued to be defined by snowy city-scapes and bucolic farmland until the modern era of Canadian painting was ushered in by Paul-Émile Bourduas, John Lyman, and Alfred Pellan in the 1940s. Bourduas was the most prolific and outspoken of all three and developed a radical style of surrealism that came to be identified with a group called the Automatistes.

In 1948 Bourduas published the manifesto *Refus Global* (Global Refusal), rejecting traditional social, artistic, and psychological norms of Québécois society and the religious and bucolic art that defined it. The manifesto called instead for an untamed liberation of creativity and championed abstract art.

Canadian art and Québec's artistic community were never the same again. Automatiste artist Jean-Paul Riopelle would soon emerge as the movement's newest driving force, and his abstract works, called "grand mosaics," would become world-renowned.

The 1960s and '70s were defined by artists like Claude Tousignant and Guido Molinari, whose abstract works used hypnotic geometric shapes and unusual color combinations to almost psychedelic proportions.

Some of Québec's biggest contemporary artists include David Altmejd, known for mixed-media pieces that incorporate various materials—everything from a decapitated werewolf head to shards of broken mirrors—into something cohesive and anthropomorphic. Valérie Blass also plays with a mix of materials and human yet non-human forms. Adnad Hannah's film and photographic works play with traditional art history. Melanie Authier, born in Montréal, is an abstract painter whose playful, colorful style evokes Turner-like landscapes and weather events. Two of the province's biggest

Architecture in Québec

When settlers first arrived in Québec their main concern was with security; with that in mind all of the first towns started out as fortified enclosures. These were made of wood or stone and designed in the five-pointed Vauban style. By the end of the French regime, New France closely resembled provincial towns in the old country, with hospitals, convents, colleges, and churches whose steeples peeked out over the walls.

Early-1700s inhabitants had trouble adapting their homes to the cold weather, and many froze to death before the colony got it right. The design was altered and structures were made of rubble stone instead of wood, with small casement windows that were few and far between. The number of rooms in the house matched the number of chimneys. In 1721, wooden houses with mansard roofs were banned after a devastating fire, and stone firewalls and attic floors covered in terracotta tiles became the standard.

Although the British conquest took place in 1759, it wasn't until the 1780s that English influence could be seen in architecture around the province. A few high-ranking officials started building homes in the popular Palladian and Regency styles, with open-air porticoes and Italian columns. The Regency balconies and windows allowed for a perfect mix between inside and out, while also stopping the snow from blocking windows and doors in winter. Roofs became less slanted, so the snow no longer fell directly on your head as you closed the door on your way out. All buildings during this period, commercial or residential, resembled country homes. You can still get a sense of this today on rue St-Jean in Québec City. Commercial buildings were set up to look like homes in part because the Catholic Church disapproved of the expansion of commerce.

Four generations of the Baillairgé family—noted for their architectural skills as well as carpentry, sculpture, and painting—left their mark on Québec City. Jean Baillairgé (1726-1805), a pious man who fought against American invasion in 1775-1776, is best known for his contributions to the steeple and interior effects at the Basilique-Cathédrale Notre-Dame in Québec City. His son François (1759-1830) studied in Paris at the Académie royale de peinture et de sculpture and continued in his father's footsteps, designing the interiors for many of the churches in the Québec City region and contributing the tabernacle for the Basilique-Cathédrale Notre-Dame. François's son Thomas (1791-1859) incorporated Renaissance sensibilities with English and French neoclassicism; Thomas designed both church interiors and facades, notably (you'll see a pattern!) the facade for the Basilique-Cathédrale Notre-Dame. Charles Baillairgé (1826-1906), Thomas's son, continued the family tradition into its fourth generation. His work can be seen at the Charles-Baillairgé building at the Musée National des Beaux-Arts du Québec—originally designed as a prison, it was incorporated into the museum in 1991.

artists are collectives: The work of BGL plays with conventional objects or pop culture icons in unconventional ways—a melted Darth Vader, or a motorcycle covered with snow in the middle of a gallery floor. Cooke et Sasseville play with similar ideas, and one of their works involves a giant flamingo laying its head down on train tracks.

DANCE AND THEATER

The established Québécois culture and the province's bohemian disposition help nurture a particularly diverse arts scene in both languages.

French theater is some of the best in the world, while English theater struggles to keep the pace. The country's top performing arts educational institution, the National Theatre School of Canada, is found in the Plateau in Montréal, attracting Canada's most promising playwrights and stage actors in either language.

An innovative contemporary dance scene in the province has fostered internationally recognized companies like La La La Human Steps, O Vertigo, and Fondation Jean-Pierre Perreault, as well as the careers of dancers and choreographers Margie Gillis, Marie Chouinard, and Benoît Lachambre. Québec supports two classical ballet companies, Les Grands Ballets Canadiens de Montréal and Le Ballet de Québec.

THE CIRCUS

Cirque du Soleil is undoubtedly the most famous Québécois circus, founded in Baie-Saint-Paul in the early 1980s by a group of street performers. These stilt-walkers, jugglers, and fire-eaters banded together to create a performance platform, since the circus tradition didn't exist in the province at the time. In the years since then, they've become part of a rich circus culture they helped to create. Two schools dedicated to the circus arts are located in Montréal: the National Circus School, established in 1981, and Tohu, established in 2004.

Cirque Éloize, established in 1993, is another professional company situated in Montréal that is quickly following in the footsteps of Cirque du Soleil when it comes to pushing boundaries and innovation. They bring an edginess and dance sensibility to their shows, which can be seen throughout the world. This dedication to circus arts also means that the province has some of the best street performers in the world, who are especially visible during festival season.

Essentials

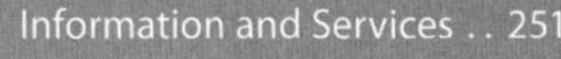

Transportation

GETTING THERE

By Air

Major airlines fly directly into Québec City's teeny-tiny **Aéroport International Jean-Lesage de Québec** (418/640-3300, www.aeroport-dequebec.com). Most air traffic comes from Montréal, though there are a few direct flights from within Canada as well as some international flights, mostly from France and from a few major U.S. cities, including Chicago, Philadelphia, Newark, and New York City.

The airport is about 15 kilometers from downtown; the best way to get to downtown is by taxi, which will set you back about $35. Public bus route 78 connects downtown with terminus Les Saules at the airport during the early morning and late afternoon only; the fare for the airport bus is $3.50, but it is best to plan ahead, as the bus does not run frequently.

By Rail

Train passengers arrive in Québec City at the **Gare du Palais** (450 rue de la Gare du Palais, 888/842-7245) in Vieux-Québec's Lower Town. Depending on where you're staying and the amount of baggage you're carrying, it might be wise to take a taxi. City buses are also available just outside the terminal to Upper Town, including bus 800, which will take you through Saint-Jean-Baptiste and up to La Grande-Allée, Parliament, and the Plains area. A single ride costs $3.

By Bus

Buses to Québec arrive at the same place as the trains at the **Gare du Palais** (320 rue Abraham Martin, 888/842-7245), near the Vieux-Port. (The building has separate wings for train travel and bus travel.) Most hotels will be a short cab ride or uphill walk away.

By Car

Québec City can be reached by Autoroute 20 in the south and Autoroute 40 in the north. The drive from Montréal will take approximately 2.5 hours, and though the drive along Route 40 is more scenic, it's also a little bit longer. From Toronto, Route 401 connects with Route 20, as do I-87 in New York and I-89 and I-91 in Vermont. If arriving on Route 20, follow the signs for Pont Pierre-Laporte, and once you've crossed the bridge, turn right onto boulevard Laurier, which becomes La Grande-Allée. Route 40 turns into boulevard Charest as you approach the city.

Previous: the Gare du Palais in Lower Town; the Québec flag, flying over the St. Lawrence River.

Traveling to Montréal

BY AIR

Short-haul 50-minute flights depart from Québec City several times a day on **Air Canada** (888/247-2262, www.aircanada.com), though by the time you go to the airport, check in, and collect your baggage afterwards, it might be just as fast to drive.

BY RAIL

The train is a fast and fairly efficient way to travel, though the costs can sometimes be prohibitive. **VIA Rail** (888/842-7245, www.viarail.ca) runs the only service between the two cities and offers several daily departures from both Montréal's **Gare Centrale** (895 rue de la Gauchetière W., 514/989-2626) and Québec City's **Gare du Palais** (450 rue de la Gare du Palais, 888/842-7245). Train times run anywhere from 3.25 to 3.75 hours, and a regular one-way ticket costs $63 before taxes, though regular Tuesday seat sales can bring the price as low as $33 if you are booking in advance.

BY BUS

Both cities are served by the **Orléans Express** (888/999-3977, www.orleansexpress.com), with hourly departures from both Montréal's **Gare d'Autocars** (505 blvd. de Maisonneuve E., 514/842-2281, www.stationcentrale.com) and Québec's **Gare du Palais** (320 rue Abraham Martin, 888/842-7245). A round-trip ticket costs approximately $80 and the ride can take anywhere from three to five hours.

BY CAR

Driving is often the quickest and easiest way to get to Montréal from Québec City. The drive can last anywhere from 2.5 to 4 hours depending on traffic. Take Autoroute 20 or Route 40 and head west. Heading into Montréal on Route 20, follow the signs for Pont Jacques-Cartier, which will take you straight into the heart of the Plateau. From Route 40, exit on any number of southbound streets, including Papineau, St-Denis, and St-Laurent.

Taking the 40 instead of the 20 will add approximately 20 minutes onto your trip, but it's more scenic and you have the option of stopping off at Trois-Rivières at about the halfway point.

GETTING AROUND

Public Transportation

Québec City buses (www.rtcquebec.ca) are fast and efficient, with six major bus lines, called **Métrobus,** that run frequently and cover all the major areas of the city—some will even take you as far out as Chute Montmorency. A single bus ticket costs $3 and also acts as a transfer if you're transferring lines; if you don't have a ticket the bus accepts exact change. A one-day unlimited pass will set you back $8.50, and unlimited weekend passes and five-day passes are available for $15.50 and $29, respectively.

Driving

Driving in Québec City is not ideal, especially if you're heading into Vieux-Québec's Upper and Lower Towns. The small, winding streets make them difficult to navigate, especially if you're not used to that type of driving. In the summer, many of the streets are blocked off to accommodate pedestrians, mainly during the day and into the night. In the winter, these same streets are covered in ice and snow. Though there is light traffic in general in Québec City, parking is still a problem, especially on streets with slopes of 45 degrees. The city has very few underground parking lots.

The speed limit on Canadian highways is 100 kilometers per hour (kph), and it's 50 kph on city streets unless otherwise noted. U.S. citizens don't need an international license and neither do drivers from England or France. If your driver's license is in a language other than English or French, you need an International Driver's Permit; see the Québec government website (www.saaq.gouv.qc.ca) for more information. Members of AAA (American Automobile Association, www.aaa.com) are covered under the Canadian equivalent CAA (www.caa.ca). Gasoline is more expensive than in the United States, so fill up before crossing the border.

RENTAL CARS

Many of the large rental companies (Avis, Budget, Discount, Enterprise) are available in Québec City. The minimum age to rent a vehicle is 25, and rates run the gamut from $34 to $80 per day depending on time of year.

Taxis

Québec City has a ton of taxi companies. Try **Taxi Coop Québec** (418/525-5191). The initial charge is $3.45, each kilometer adds $1.70, and each minute of waiting is $0.63. Tip is usually 10-15 percent. Some drivers know the city well, others not so much, so make sure you have your destination with the cross street written down to show the driver, especially if it's a word you're unsure how to pronounce.

Bicycling

Biking in Québec City can be tough, as there are some seriously steep hills that aren't fun to ascend (and may be slightly nail-biting to descend). That being said, if you're planning on staying exclusively, or at least mostly, in Lower Town or Upper Town, then renting a bike is a great way to get around—and even if you want to switch between the two, you can always walk your bike up the hills. In Lower Town, the Corridor du Littoral will allow you to ride along the river and the Vieux-Port; this bike path and a few others connect Québec City with spots like Île d'Orléans. These paths are safe and very popular with cyclists in the summer and fall.

Visas and Officialdom

PASSPORTS AND VISAS

All visitors must have a valid passport or other accepted secure documents to enter the country, even those entering from the United States by road or train. Citizens of the United States, Australia, New Zealand, Israel, Japan, and most western European countries don't need visas to enter Canada for stays up to 180 days. U.S. permanent residents are also exempt. Travelers who travel regularly between Canada and the United States can consider getting a Nexus membership; details are available online (www.cbsa-asfc.gc.ca/prog/nexus).

Nationals from South Africa, China, and about 150 other countries must apply for a temporary resident visa, or visitor visa, in their home country. Full details can be found at **Citizen and Immigration Canada** (888/242-2100 within Canada, www.cic.gc.ca). Single-entry visitor visas are valid for six months and cost $100; multiple-entry visas last for up to 10 years, as long as a single stay doesn't last for longer than six months, and cost $100. A separate visa is required if you intend to work in Canada.

CUSTOMS

Depending on how long your stay in Canada is, you're allowed to take various amounts of goods back home without paying any duty or import tax. There is a limit on the amount of tobacco and liquor you can bring back duty-free, and some countries have a limit on perfumes. For exact amounts, check with the customs department in your home country. Also check the **Canadian Border Services Agency** (505/636-5064, www.cbsa-asfc.gc.ca) for details on bringing in and taking home goods.

There are very strict rules on bringing plants, flowers, food, and other vegetation into the country, so it's not advisable to bring them. If you're 18 years or older, you're allowed to bring into the country 50 cigars or 200 cigarettes, as well as 1.14 liters of liquor, 1.5 liters of wine, or 24 cans or bottles of beer. If you bring more, you'll face a hefty fine. Those traveling with their pets should check with the Canadian Food Inspection Agency (www.inspection.gc.ca) to see what is required. If you're traveling from the United States with your cat or dog, for example, you'll need a rabies vaccination certificate that meets certain requirements, and you will need to pay inspection fees.

Blasphemy the Québécois Way

In Québec, swearing is its own language. Instead of being derived from naughty sexual innuendo, swear words generally come from Catholicism and its practices. Originating in the early 19th century, many of the swear words or *sacres* developed out of a frustration at the church that seemingly controlled everything. The church is much less influential since the Quiet Revolution of the 1960s, and though the swear words are still in use, they are no longer as powerful and have become part of common language. Even English-speakers get into the habit, especially when talking with Québécois friends.

Among the most popular *sacres* and the ones you'll likely hear the most are *crisse* (Christ), *tabarnak* (from tabernacle), *ostie* (from host), and *sacrement* (from sacrament). Like all good swear words, however, they work best when used together, as in *crisse d'ostie de tabarnak,* which defies translation.

Another word you might hear is *fucké,* which, weirdly enough, has nothing to do with the English pejorative; instead it means strange or bizarre, as in *"ce film était vraiment fucké,"* or "that film was really weird."

Conduct and Customs

MOVING DAY

While the rest of the country celebrates Canada Day, the nation's national holiday, on July 1, Québécois move. It is the unofficial moving day for renters across the province—this is the day most leases change hands—and it is usually a hot, sweaty day with cars, vans, trucks, SUVs, and even bikes loaded to the hilt and headed for new digs. It's also not uncommon to see people simply schlepping their belongings by foot.

Don't even think about renting a car on July 1, as there won't be any left. A thrifter's paradise, the aftermath of the move leaves sidewalks and alleyways littered with discarded belongings and unwanted junk, which may turn out to be your treasure.

ALCOHOL

As in most Canadian provinces, if you're looking for good wine or spirits, you have to get it at the **SAQ** (Société des Alcools de Québec, www.saq.ca), the store run by the provincial liquor board. Found all over the city, they carry a wide selection of wine and spirits and a small selection of imported beer. Québec differs from most other provinces in that beer and wine can also be purchased in your local grocery and corner stores.

The selection of wine and beer varies from store to store; both the *dépanneur* (corner store) and the grocery store carry generally lower-quality wine than you'll find at the SAQ (Montréalers commonly use the term "*dép* wine" to denote overpriced cheap-quality wine—though that's not always the case). If you're looking for beer, however, a *dép* is your best bet. If you don't find the brand you're looking for, just step into the fridge yourself; it might look like just another display case, but step through the camouflaged door and you're in beerville. Drinking age in Québec is 18, and stores stop selling alcohol at 11pm.

TIPPING

Tips and service charges aren't covered in the bill; instead a 15 percent tip should be added to the total bill at restaurants and bars at which you run a tab. When you order a drink at a bar, you're usually expected to pay when the drink is brought to you; a $1-2 tip for drinks is the standard. Tip the same for valet parking attendants, bellhops at the hotel, and coat-check attendants. Housekeeping staff should be tipped $3-5.

SMOKING

Smoking is illegal in bars, cafés, clubs, and restaurants and not permitted in enclosed public spaces. Outdoors on the sidewalk or on a restaurant's or bar's patio is fair game. Some hotels, however, still have smoking and nonsmoking options, though it's becoming rarer. There are a few cigar bars, including Société Cigare in Québec City, where smoking indoors is allowed due to specialized ventilation systems. You must be 18 years or older to buy tobacco in Québec.

Travel Tips

TRAVELING WITH CHILDREN

The plentiful kid-friendly activities in Québec City will tucker any kid out by the end of the day. Top choices include ice-skating and tobogganing in winter, and wading pools and bike rides along the canal in summer. Public parks with playgrounds can be found throughout the city and are perfect for blowing off some steam. However, some of the sleeker, cooler boutique hotels might not be the most fun for the kids. Children are also given half-price or free entry to most museums and attractions; some venues offer family rates. Hotels can often recommend babysitting services if none are available in-house.

WOMEN TRAVELERS

Québec is a relatively safe city, and women should feel at ease traveling alone. Still, the usual rules apply: Women should avoid walking alone on quiet streets and dimly lit areas late at night. Violence is far less prevalent here than in the United States, but if you are attacked or sexually assaulted call 911 or the **Sexual Assault Center** (418/522-2120).

LGBTQ TRAVELERS

Québec is one of the top destinations for gay travelers. In 1977 Québec became the second political entity (after Holland) to include a nondiscrimination clause on the basis of sexual orientation in its charter of rights. Gay marriage is legal in Québec, and attitudes toward homosexuality in the province are open and tolerant.

Though there are a number of LGBTQ publications, monthly magazine ***Fugues*** (www.fugues.com) is the most comprehensive and has information on everything from hotels to saunas and upcoming gay events.

ACCESS FOR TRAVELERS WITH DISABILITIES

Most public buildings, including tourist offices, museums, and sights, are wheelchair accessible. Québec City is quite hilly, and it can be challenging to get around for travelers with mobility issues. The funicular provides one method to connect Vieux-Québec's Lower Town with its Upper Town; public buses provide an alternative option. Either way, it is best to plan ahead.

Access to Travel (www.accesstotravel.gc.ca) is a guide to accessible transportation across the country.

Kéroul (514/252-3104, www.keroul.qc.ca) specializes in tourism for people with disabilities. The association publishes *Québec for All magazine,* which lists 1,000-plus hotels, restaurants, museums, and theaters that are accessible. Kéroul's *The Accessible Road,* an online tool, offers information on everything from the most accessible top sights to how to get a handicapped parking sticker.

Health and Safety

HOSPITALS AND CLINICS

Canadians have free health care, but it's not free for visitors, so get travel insurance before you leave your home country. Emergency room waits can be lengthy, and if you're not a Canadian citizen, the treatment could be pricey (though not compared to U.S. hospitals).

For emergency treatment in Québec City, head to the **Chu de Québec Université Laval** (2705 blvd. Laurier, 418/654-2114).

For minor maladies in Québec City, the closest clinic can be found by checking online at www.csssvc.qc.ca. Though the clinics will be glad to help you, it's best to bring cash as they don't always take debit or credit.

If you're feeling unwell and just want some advice, call the health hotline (811) from any landline to speak with a nurse 24 hours a day.

Winter Essentials

If you want to fit in among the locals during winter's deep freeze you need two things: a parka and a pair of Sorel boots.

- **Parka:** When it comes to parkas, there are two schools: The younger generation goes for a selection from Canada Goose, while many mature Québécois opt for the Kanuk. Both are made in Canada and offer that important balance of warmth without too much puffiness. When buying a parka, the goal is to avoid the "Michelin Man" look; don't buy white and stay away from anything that has a ringed effect. Make sure it's got a fur- or faux fur-trimmed hood and covers your bum—good coverage is essential, especially if you're going to be taking advantage of the city's many winter slides.

- **Boots:** Made with a heavy insulated rubber sole and sturdy leather, Sorel winter boots have been a Canadian staple since 1959. Introduced by Ontario-based Kaufman Footwear, the boots were originally made in Canada, but the brand was bought by Columbia Sports in 2000. Though the boots are no longer Canadian owned and made, there is still a strong connection to their Canadian heritage. The ingenious construction of a thermal, waterproof sole paired with a more stylish upper is ideal for city life when you're often walking through freezing gray slush.

- **Fur:** Another popular winter material in Québec is fur, and it's not unusual to see both men and women covered in fur from head to toe. If you find fur offensive, try to suppress your inner activist and instead take a deep breath—see that? Your nose is now completely frozen. Fur in Québec is less about style and more about survival and heritage, and many of the furs have been passed down through family members.

PHARMACIES

In Québec City, the largest pharmacy is **Jean Coutu** (110 blvd. René-Lévesque, 418/522-1235, www.jeancoutu.com, 9am-9pm Mon.-Sat., 10am-9pm Sun.), near avenue Cartier.

EMERGENCY SERVICES

The fire department, police, and ambulance can all be reached by dialing **911.** When in doubt, you can reach the operator by dialing **0.** There's also the **Poison Center** (800/463-5060) if you're worried about something you've ingested.

CRIME AND HARASSMENT

Québec City is relatively safe and violent crime is rare. Tourists are more likely to be the targets of thieves, like pickpockets at crowded bars, markets, and bus stations. Cars with out-of-province license plates are also targets, so make sure not to leave anything of value in the car and to remove your car registration and identification papers.

Information and Services

MONEY

Prices quoted in this guide are in Canadian dollars. Canadian coins come in 5-cent (nickel), 10-cent (dime), 25-cent (quarter), $1 (loonie), and $2 (toonie) pieces. Paper money comes in $5 (blue), $10 (purple), $20 (green), $50 (red), and $100 (brown). In 2013, the government phased out the penny, so most companies round up their prices to the closest 5 cents. The Canadian dollar's value is sometimes much lower than the American dollar and sometimes trades at a few cents off par; www.xe.com has the most current rates.

ATMs

ATMs are all round the city, not just in banks. Though if you're getting money out from a foreign account, the safest way is to get it from a proper bank machine, to avoid fraud. Most banks charge you an additional fee (along with the original transaction fee) when you withdraw a currency different from that of your home country. Check your daily withdrawal limit so you don't get caught short.

Changing Money

Counters dedicated solely to exchanging money are becoming rarer. It's much simpler just to head to the bank. Foreign-exchange desks can also be found at the main tourist office and at the airport. Try **Transchange International** (43 rue de Baude, 418/694-6906).

Credit Cards

Major international credit cards are accepted at most stores, hotels, and restaurants. Carrying a credit card means you don't have the worry of carrying cash, and it also gives you excellent exchange rates. Visa and MasterCard are the most widely accepted, though certain places also accept American Express and, more rarely, Diners Club.

MAPS AND TOURIST INFORMATION

Airports have information offices open year-round. For Québec province info about Montréal, Québec City, and environs, visit **Québec Original** (www.quebecoriginal.com).

The major tourism office in Québec City is in Vieux-Québec's Upper Town: **Centre Infotouriste** (12 rue Ste-Anne, 800/363-7777, 9am-6pm daily mid-June-late Aug., 9am-5pm daily Sept.-mid-June). This center offers maps and lots of information about the city, the surrounding area, and the province, and tourism agents can help you book everything from accommodations to guided tours.

COMMUNICATIONS AND MEDIA

Phones

Thanks to the massive popularity of cell phones, public pay phones are becoming almost impossible to find, but if you do manage to find one, a single local call will set you back $0.50. Though many are coin operated, some also accept phone cards and credit cards. Québec City's area code is **418.** When dialing local numbers, you must include the area code.

Toll-free numbers begin with **800, 866,** or **888** and must be preceded by a 1. Most of these numbers work in both Canada and the United States, but some may only work in a specified province. Dialing **0** for the operator or **911** for emergency services is free of charge from landlines and public phones, but calling **411** for directory assistance will cost you.

CELL PHONES

Tribrand model cell phones working on GSM 1900 and other frequencies are the only foreign cell phones that will work in Canada, and you will probably need to purchase a local SIM card—but check with your phone service provider for details. If your phone doesn't work, it might be worth picking up an inexpensive phone at an electronics store and getting a pay-as-you-go plan. Travelers from the United States will likely have service, though roaming charges will probably apply; check with your provider for details.

MOBILE APPS

Québec City's tourism board has created apps for both Android and iPhone, and their website is also mobile-friendly. Head to www.quebecregion.com to check them out before downloading from the appropriate app store.

Internet Services

Numerous cafés offer free Wi-Fi. Visit www.zapquebec.org for free Wi-Fi in Québec. If you left your computer at home and can't check your email on your phone or at your hotel, your best bets are the local libraries.

In Québec City, a couple of libraries offer free Internet access to visitors. **Bibliothèque Clair-Martin** (755 rue St-Jean, 418/641-6798 10am-5pm, Mon.-Tues. and Fri.-Sun., 1pm-8pm Wed.-Thurs.), in the Faubourg Saint-Jean-Baptiste, offers an hour of free access, and **Bibliothèque Gabrielle-Roy** (350 rue St-Joseph E., 418/641-6789, 8am-9pm Mon.-Fri., 9am-5pm Sat.-Sun.) in Saint-Roch offers two hours of free access.

Many hotels, though not all, offer free Wi-Fi access, and the majority also have public computers.

Mail Services

Québec City's main post office (5 rue du Fort, www.canadapost.ca, 8am-7:30pm Mon.-Fri., 9:30am-5pm Sat.) is in Vieux-Québec's Upper Town. Stamps can also be purchased at newsstands, convenience stores, and tourist shops. Standard first-class airmail postage for letters and postcards costs $0.65 to Canadian destinations and $1.10 to the United States. Other destinations cost $1.85.

Newspapers and Periodicals

The Globe & Mail (www.globeandmail.com) and the ***National Post*** (www.nationalpost.com) are the country's two national papers, and while both cover national and international events as well as the arts, the *Globe* leans more to the center-left and the *Post* to the right.

For French readers there's the federalist ***La Presse*** and separatist-leaning ***Le Devoir,*** both of which cover the news and art of the entire province, not just the Francophone community (though that's a large part of it). In Québec there's ***Le Soleil,*** a great little paper with a focus on events in the capital. There's also the Francophone alternative weekly ***Voir*** (www.voir.ca), great for getting the latest scoop on what's going on in town or for scoping out their restaurant reviews.

L'actualité is the Québec monthly news magazine, and ***The Walrus*** and ***Maclean's*** are Canada's best-known national general interest magazines.

Television

The main public-radio and television stations are run by the Canadian Broadcasting Corporation. The CBC is the English-language component and Radio-Canada is the French-language component; both are revered for their long broadcast history. The other major English-language network is the Canadian Television Network (CTV), which broadcasts both Canadian and U.S. programs as well as nightly newscasts.

For Francophone audiences there's Télé-Québec (TVA), which broadcasts news programs, movies, and shows from France, as well as dubbed American sitcoms and dramas.

Radio

Radio stations in Québec are mostly Francophone, with the exception of the English-language artists they play. Anglophones can tune into CBC Québec 1 (104.7 FM streaming), the city's only English-language radio station, for all their cultural, news, and educational programs. Tune into CHYZ (94.3 FM) to hear what the students at Université Laval are listening to. ÉNERGIE (98.9 FM) gives you top pop and Francophone hits, and Radio-Canada (106.3 FM) keeps you informed in French about news and culture.

WEIGHTS AND MEASURES

Electricity

Like the United States and Japan, Canada uses 110/120-volt, 60-cycle electrical power. Canadian electrical goods have a plug with two flat, vertical prongs and sometimes a third rounded prong, which acts as a ground.

Travelers from outside North America should bring a plug adapter for small appliances; a voltage converter may also be necessary.

Measurements

Canada uses the metric system of measurement. Distances are measured in kilometers, liquids in liters and milliliters, but height, strangely enough, is measured in feet.

Time

Québec City is on eastern standard time (EST/EDT), the same as New York and Toronto. Canada switches to daylight saving time (one hour later than standard time) from the second Sunday in March to the first Sunday in November. "Spring forward, fall back," is a simple way to remember how to set your clocks properly. In Québec the 24-hour clock is used for most schedules, including movies and trains.

Resources

Glossary

l'Abitation: the first settlement (habitation)

allongé: a long espresso coffee, the French name for an Italian *lungo*

Allophone: an immigrant to Canada whose native language is neither French nor English

Anglophone: a native English speaker

Bill 101: a Québec law that deals with French and English language issues

boîte à chansons: an intimate nightclub (literally, "music box") where you can hear singer/songwriters *(chansonniers)* play

boréal: the type of forest that is found in the province of Québec

branchée: plugged in, which translates to hip, or cool, in the French vernacular

brasserie: a brewery or pub

brioche: a type of sweet, eggy French bread

cabane à sucre: a sugar shack; this is where you go to see maple syrup tapped from trees and to eat maple-drenched treats

café: where you buy coffee as well as the drink itself; usually refers to an espresso

café filtre: drip coffee

calèche: a horse-drawn carriage

casse-croûtes: a Québécois snack bar generally specializing in poutine, hot dogs, and other Québécois snacks

chansonnier: a folk singer/songwriter

côte: hill; if a street has *"côte"* in its name, it's on a hill

coureurs de bois: early fur hunters and adventurers who helped explore North America

dépanneur: meaning "to help out"; a convenience store in Québec, commonly referred to as a *dép*

First Nations: indigenous nations in Canada other than the Métis and Inuit

Francophone: a native French speaker

frites: French fries

Inuit: northern indigenous peoples

joual: a popular form of slang

loonie: Canadian one-dollar coin

Métis: a post-contact indigenous group in Canada

Nouvelle France: the name given to Québec by the French; it also means New France

pâté chinois: a meat, potato, and vegetable pie similar to shepherd's pie

patriotes: the name given to patriots who led an uprising against the government in 1837; it's used today to denote those who are against federal rule

pont: a bridge

poudreuse: blowing snow

poutine: crispy French fries covered with fresh cheese curds and smothered in gravy—the unofficial food of Québec

quai: quay that juts out into the water

Quebecker: English name for all native citizens of the province of Québec

Québécois: the name for the Francophone population in the province as well as the language they speak; can also be the French term for all native citizens of the province of Québec

Refus Global (Total Refusal): a manifesto of a group of Québec artists that radically changed the face of modern Québec art

sacres: the name for Québécois swear words

sandwicherie: a place that makes sandwiches

sans gluten: gluten-free

sloche: slush made from melted snow

sovereigntists: those who want Québec to separate from the rest of Canada

stimés: hot dog with a steamed bun

Sulpicians: society of Catholic priests founded in Paris in 1641 who were part of the founding of Québec

table d'hôte: a fixed-price meal

tarte au sucre: sugar pie

terrasse: an outdoor patio

terroir: food products that come from the area, as in *terroir* cooking

tire sur la neige: maple syrup that has been frozen on snow, a popular treat during the sugaring-off season

toastés: hot dog with a toasted bun

toonie: a Canadian two-dollar coin

tourtière: a meat pie made with everything from pork and beef to game

tuque: winter hat

végétalien: vegan

végétarien: vegetarian

vernissage: gallery opening

viennoiseries: pastries and sweet breads usually eaten at breakfast

vieux: old, as in Vieux-Québec (Old Québec) and Vieux-Port (Old Port)

French Phrasebook

If you're uncomfortable about breaking out your rusty 10th-grade French, relax. In Québec City locals' English isn't as fluid as in Montréal, but those who work in tourism and hospitality speak it flawlessly. Even if you do feel confident with your French, the Québécois accent will take some getting used to, and the language you hear on the street won't have much to do with the words you read in this phrasebook. The Québécois also have a tendency to speak very fast, so don't be afraid to ask someone to slow down if you're having trouble understanding.

As has been explained throughout the guide, language is a central issue in Québec, so a good rule of thumb is to be polite; the Québécois are especially receptive to people who are at least trying to speak a little French, and they're always encouraging. Throw in a few easy French words here and there, like *bonjour* or *merci,* try to start all your conversations in French, and you'll be well on your way.

PRONUNCIATION

French is known for being difficult to pronounce—and as payback for creating such a difficult language, French-speakers are unable to properly pronounce any other language. When it comes to phonetic pronunciation, French is as bad as English. Most of the spellings and the pronunciations don't have much in common, which can make learning French difficult. Here are a few guidelines to get you started.

Vowels

Vowels in French can be confusing for an English speaker: the "a" is e, the "e" is i, and the "u" is from outer space. Here is the secret:

a pronounced a, as in "cat"

i pronounced ee, as in "free"

y pronounced the same way as i

o pronounced ah, as in "dog," or oh, as in "bone"

u This vowel has always been a tough one for English-speakers. The closest you can get would be to put your lips and tongue in position to say "oh" and try to say "ee" instead. Something like the ew in "stew" is not that far off.

e pronounced uh, as in "about." Before two or more consonants, it is pronounced eh as in "set." At the end of a word, such as *chaise* (chair), e is silent, except in words of one syllable like *je* (I), where it is pronounced uh.

Vowel Groups

To make things harder, French assembles certain letters to produce new sounds.

ai pronounced eh, as in "set," as well as ei

au pronounced oh, as in "bone," as well as eau

eu pronounced uh, as in "about." It is sometimes spelled **œu,** as in *œuf* or *sœur*

oi pronounced wa, as in "wagon"

ou pronounced oo, as in "foot"

Nasal Vowels

A typical aspect of French speech is nasal vowels, vowels pronounced through both the mouth and nose. They are as difficult for English-speakers to reproduce as the **u** and will require quite a bit of phonetic gymnastics before you get it right.

an, am pronounced ahn, as in "aunt"

en, em pronounced pretty close to ahn, combined with the on of "honk"

in where the a of "bag" is nasalized as in "anchor." You'll find more or less the same sound in many different spellings, such as **im, un, um, yn, ym, ain, aim, ein,** and **eim**

on, om pronounced on, as in "long"; a nasalized **o**

Accents

French has five different accents that stick to vowels and make French as exotic to read as it is to hear: In French they are called *accent aigu* (´), *accent grave* (`), *accent circonflexe* (^), *accent tréma* (¨), and the *cédille* (ç), which is only used with the letter **c.**

The circumflex and grave accents appear as **è, à, ù, ê, â, û, î,** and **ô.** Except for **ê** and **è,** which are pronounced eh as in "set," and **ô,** which always sounds like oh as in "bone," the accents don't change the pronunciation of the letters; they are mere decoration.

The acute accent, as in **é,** is pronounced ay as in "day," but shorter. The cedilla makes **c** sound like **s.**

Last but not least, the dieresis (*tréma*) separates two vowel sounds, such as ï in *naïve,* which is not pronounced nev, but as two separate syllables, na-ive.

Consonants

Most French consonants are similar to their English equivalents, even if there are a few differences. For example, *some* final consonants are silent; rather than pronouncing *vous* as "vooz," you'd say "voo." In general the following consonants are usually silent: **b, d, g, m, n, p, t, x,** and **z. S** is always silent in plurals but often pronounced otherwise. Others are generally pronounced: **c, f,** and **l. R** is usually pronounced, except in the endings **er** and **ier.**

c pronounced k as in "kick" before **a, o,** or **u,** and s as in "set" before **e, i,** or **y.** Combine **c** and **h,** as in *chance* (luck), and it is pronounced like sh as in "ship"

g pronounced g as in "god," except when placed before **e, i,** or **y,** when it is pronounced zh as in "measure." Combine it with **n,** as in *vigne* (vine), and it is pronounced like ny in "canyon"

h always silent

j pronounced zh as in "measure"

ll pronounced y as in "yes," in words like *famille*

r emphasized more strongly than in English and comes from the far back of the throat

BASIC EXPRESSIONS

Hello *Bonjour*

Hi *Salut*

Good-bye *Au revoir/Salut*

Good morning/afternoon *Bonjour*

Good evening *Bonsoir*

Good night *Bonne nuit*

How are you? (courteous) *Allez-vous?*

How are you doing? (colloquial) *Ça va?/Vas-tu?*

Fine, thank you. *Ça va bien, merci.*

And you? *Et vous?*

See you later. *À plus tard/À bientôt.*

Nice to meet you. *Enchanté.*

Yes *Oui*

No *Non*

Please *S'il vous plaît*

Thank you *Merci*

You're welcome *Bienvenu/De rien*

Excuse me *Excusez-moi*

Sorry *Pardon/Désolé* (*pardon* is for small mistakes, like bumping into someone; *désolé* is best used if you've made a larger error)

What's your name? *Comment vous appelez-vous?*

My name is . . . *Je m'appelle . . .*

Where are you from? *D'où venez-vous?*

I'm from . . . *Je viens de . . .*

Do you speak English? *Parlez-vous anglais?*

I don't speak French. *Je ne parle pas français.*

I don't understand. *Je ne comprends pas.*

I don't know. *Je ne sais pas.*

Can you please repeat? *Pourriez-vous répéter?*

What's it called? *Ça s'appelle?*

Would you like . . . ? *Voulez-vous . . . ?*

TERMS OF ADDRESS

In French, the most polite way to address a stranger is by using the *vous* form of "you," as opposed to *tu,* even though *vous* is the plural second person—it never hurts to err on the side of politesse.

I *je*

you *tu*

he *il*

she *elle*

we *nous*

you (plural) *vous*

they *ils/elles* (*ils* is for a group of men, or a mixed group; *elles* is for a group of women)

Mr./Sir *monsieur*

Mrs./Madame *madame*

Miss *mademoiselle* (best used only for young girls—*madame* is preferable for anyone you'd refer to as "Ms." in English)

young man *jeune homme*

young woman *jeune fille*

child *enfant*

brother/sister *frère/sœur*

father/mother *père/mère*

son/daughter *fils/fille*

husband/wife *mari/femme*

friend *ami/amie*

boyfriend/girlfriend *copain/copine*

married *marié/mariée*

single *célibataire*

divorced *divorcé/divorcée*

QUESTIONS

When? *Quand?*

What? *Quoi?*

What is it? *Qu'est-ce que c'est?*

Who? *Qui?*

Why? *Pourquoi?*

How? *Comment?*

Where is . . . ? *Où est . . . ?*

What's it called? *Ça s'appelle?*

Would you like . . . ? *Voulez-vous . . . ?*

GETTING AROUND

Where is . . . ? *Où est . . . ?*

How far away is . . . ? *À quelle distance est . . . ?*

How can I get to . . . ? *Puis-je aller à . . . ?*

bus *bus*

car *voiture*

train *train*

bus station *la station d'autobus*

train station *la gare de trains*

airport *l'aéroport*

What time do we leave? *À quelle heure est le départ?*

What time do we arrive? *À quelle heure arrive-t-on?*

a one-way ticket *un aller simple*

a round-trip ticket? *un aller retour*

Can you take me to this address? *Pourriez-vous m'emmener à cette adresse?*

north *nord*
south *sud*
east *est*
west *ouest*
left/right *gauche/droite*
straight ahead *tout droit*
entrance *entrée*
exit *sortie*
first *premier*
last *dernier*
next *prochain*

ACCOMMODATIONS

Are there any rooms available? *Avez-vous des chambres disponibles?*
I'd like to make a reservation. *J'aimerais faire une reservation.*
I want a single room. *J'aimerais une chambre simple.*
Is there a double room? *Y a-t-il une chambre double?*
private bathroom *salle de bains privée*
key *clé*
one night *une nuit*
Can you change the sheets/towels? *Pourriez-vous changer les draps/les serviettes?*
Could you please wake me up? *Pourriez-vous me réveiller?*
Is breakfast included? *Est-ce que le petit déjeuner est inclus?*

FOOD

to eat *manger*
to drink *boire*
breakfast *déjeuner*
lunch *dîner*
dinner *souper*
Can I see the menu? *Puis-je voir le menu?*
We're ready to order. *Nous sommes prêts à commander.*
Can I have some more wine? *Puis-je avoir un peu plus de vin?*
Can you bring me the bill please? *Pourriez-vous apporter l'addition?*
Is the service/the tip included? *Est-ce que le service est compris?*
I'm a vegetarian. *Je suis végétarien.*
It was delicious. *C'était délicieux.*
hot *chaud*
cold *froid*
sweet *sucré*
salty *salé*
bread *pain*
rice *riz*
Enjoy! *Bon appétit!*

Meat and Fish

meat *viande*
beef *bœuf*
sweetbreads (veal) *ris de veau*
pork *porc*
lamb *agneau*
sweetbreads (lamb) *ris d'agneau*
chicken *poulet*
ham *jambon*
fish *poisson*
salmon *saumon*
mussels *moules*
oysters *huîtres*
shrimp *crevette*
tuna *thon*
rare *saignant*
medium *à point*
well done *bien cuit*
roasted *rôti*
boiled *bouilli*
grilled *grillé*
fried *frit*

Eggs and Dairy

milk *lait*
cream *crème*
butter *beurre*
cheese *fromage*
ice cream *crème glacée*
egg *œuf*
hard-boiled egg *œuf dur*
over-easy eggs *œufs tournés*
scrambled eggs *œufs brouillés*
poached egg *œuf poché*

Vegetables and Fruits

vegetables *légumes*
carrot *carotte*
tomato *tomate*
potato *patate/pomme de terre*
cucumber *concombre*
pepper *poivron*
mushrooms *champignons*
eggplant *aubergine*
peas *petits pois*
cabbage *chou*

apple *pomme*
pear *poire*
banana *banane*
orange *orange*
lemon *citron*
grape *raisin*
strawberry *fraise*
blueberry *bleuet*
raspberry *framboise*

Seasoning and Spices

sugar *sucre*
salt *sel*
black pepper *poivre*
onion *oignon*
garlic *ail*
olive oil *huile d'olive*
vinegar *vinaigre*
cinnamon *cannelle*
basil *basilic*
parsley *persil*
mint *menthe*
ginger *gingembre*

Drinks

drinks *boissons*
beer *bière*
wine *vin*
wine list *la carte des vins*
cheers! *à votre santé!/santé!*
water *eau*
ice *glace*
juice *jus*
filtered coffee *café filtre*
coffee with milk *café au lait*
black coffee *café noir*

SHOPPING

money *argent*
ATM *guichet automatique*
credit card *carte de crédit*
to buy *acheter*
to shop *magasiner*
I don't have change. *Je n'ai pas de monnaie.*
more *plus*
less *moins*

a good price *un bon prix*

sales *soldes*

How much does it cost? *Combien ça coûte?*

That's too expensive. *C'est trop cher.*

discount *rabais*

Can I try it on? *Est-ce que je peux l'essayer?*

It's too tight. *C'est trop serré.*

It's too big. *C'est trop grand.*

Can I exchange it? *Est-ce que je peux l'échanger?*

HEALTH AND SAFETY

Can you help me? *Pouvez-vous m'aider?*

I don't feel well. *Je ne me sens pas bien.*

I'm sick. *Je suis malade.*

Is there a pharmacy close by? *Y a-t-il une pharmacie pas loin?*

Can you call a doctor? *Pouvez-vous appeler un docteur?*

I need to go to the hospital. *Je dois aller à l'hôpital.*

medicine *médicament*

condom *condom, préservatif*

Is this neighborhood safe? *Est-ce que ce quartier est sécuritaire?*

Help! *À l'aide!, Au secours!*

Call the police! *Appeler la police.*

thief *voleur*

COMMUNICATIONS

to talk, to speak *parler*

to hear, to listen *écouter, entendre*

to make a phone call *faire un appel téléphonique*

cell phone *cellulaire*

What's your phone number? *Quel est ton numéro de téléphone?*

What's your email address? *Quelle est ton adresse électronique?*

collect call *appel à frais virés*

Do you have Internet? *Avez-vous Internet ici?*

post office *bureau de poste*

letter *lettre*

stamp *timbre*

postcard *carte postale*

NUMBERS

0 *zéro*

1 *un*

2 *deux*

3 *trois*

4 *quatre*

5 *cinq*

6 *six*

7 *sept*
8 *huit*
9 *neuf*
10 *dix*
11 *onze*
12 *douze*
13 *treize*
14 *quatorze*
15 *quinze*
16 *seize*
17 *dix-sept*
18 *dix-huit*
19 *dix-neuf*
20 *vingt*
21 *vingt-et-un*
30 *trente*
40 *quarante*
50 *cinquante*
60 *soixante*
70 *soixante-dix*
80 *quatre-vingt*
90 *quatre-vingt dix*
100 *cent*
101 *cent un*
200 *deux cent*
500 *cinq cent*
1,000 *mille*
2,000 *deux mille*

TIME

What time is it? *Quelle heure est-il?*
It's 2 o'clock. *Il est deux heures.*
It's 2:15. *Il est deux heures et quart.*
It's 2:30. *Il est deux heures et demie.*
It's 2:45. *Il est deux heures quarante-cinq.*
in two hours *dans deux heures*
now *maintenant*
before *avant*
after *après*
late *tard*
early *tôt*
When? *Quand?*

DAYS AND MONTHS

day *jour*
night *nuit*

morning *matin*
afternoon *après-midi*
yesterday *hier*
tomorrow *demain*
today *aujourd'hui*
week *semaine*
month *mois*
year *année*
Monday *lundi*
Tuesday *mardi*
Wednesday *mercredi*
Thursday *jeudi*
Friday *vendredi*
Saturday *samedi*
Sunday *dimanche*
January *janvier*
February *février*
March *mars*
April *avril*
May *mai*
June *juin*
July *juillet*
August *août*
September *septembre*
October *octobre*
November *novembre*
December *décembre*

SEASONS AND WEATHER

season *saison*
spring *printemps*
summer *été*
autumn *automne*
winter *hiver*
weather *temps/météo*
sun *soleil*
It's sunny. *Il fait du soleil.*
rain *pluie*
It's raining. *Il pleut.*
snow *neige*
It's snowing. *Il neige.*
snowstorm *tempête de neige*
ice *glace/verglas*
It's hot. *Il fait chaud.*
It's cold. *Il fait froid.*

Suggested Reading

HISTORY AND GENERAL INFORMATION

Dickinson, John A., and Brian Young. *A Short History of Québec.* Montréal: McGill-Queen's University Press, 1993, revised 2008. Originally written in 1992, this book is now into its fourth edition and offers a comprehensive overview of the province's social and economic development from pre-European to modern times. This latest edition includes reflections on the Bouchard-Taylor Commission on Accommodation and Cultural Differences, which examined attitudes toward immigration and immigrants in the province.

Grescoe, Taras. *Sacré Blues: An Unsentimental Journey through Quebec.* Toronto: Macfarlane Walter & Ross, 2001. Montréal author Taras Grescoe's modern account of Québec explores the stranger side of the province's pop culture, takes readers to a Francophone country-and-western festival, meets up with UFO-obsessed followers of Raël, and, of course, deconstructs a Montréal Canadiens hockey game. The book won the Québec Writers' Federation First Book Award and the Mavis Gallant Prize for Nonfiction in 2001.

Lacoursière, Jacques, and Robin Philpot. *A People's History of Québec.* Montréal: Baraka Books, 2009. First published in French, this concise book looks at the history of the province through the people who discovered, explored, and inhabited it. The focus is on day-to-day life and offers little-known details, like the despicable "mixed dancing" at times of celebration and early settlers' love of *charivari,* a loud, rambunctious party through the streets.

FICTION AND MEMOIRS

Carrier, Roch. *The Hockey Sweater.* Montréal: Tundra Books, 1979. This semi-autobiographical children's picture book is one of the most memorable Canadian stories. It tells the tale of a boy in small-town Québec who orders a Canadiens hockey sweater from the Eaton's catalogue only to receive a Toronto Maple-Leaf jersey. Full of subtle comments on Québec and the rest of Canada, it's a touching story that has been immortalized by an NFB film.

MacLennan, Hugh. *Two Solitudes.* Toronto: McClelland & Stewart, 1945. The title of this book has become emblematic of the country's French/English cultural and linguistic divide. Set between World War I and 1939, the book takes place in Saint-Marc-des-Érables, a small Québec town, and the booming, predominantly English city of Montréal. Centered on Paul Tallard, a Québécois at home with both languages, the book follows him on a quest to find his own identity and a way of defining the Canadian experience.

Proulx, Monique. *Les Aurores Montréales.* Toronto: Douglas & McIntyre, 1997. Twenty-seven short stories make up this collection that takes place in pre- and post-referendum Québec. Weaving in and out of Montréal, the stories look at the lives of Quebeckers and how they are affected by the changing times.

Tremblay, Michel. *Les Belles Sœurs.* Vancouver: Talonbooks, revised ed., 1992. Arguably the most important Québécois writer of his generation, Tremblay was only 23 years old when he wrote this play in 1965. First presented in 1968 at Théâtre du Rideau Vert, it ushered in a new era of Québécois theater. Written in *joual* (working-class slang), the play is set in the triplexes of Montréal's Plateau and follows the exploits of an extended family.

Internet Resources

Foodie in Québec City
www.foodiequebec.com
This English-language blog covers all aspects of the food and restaurant scene in Québec City and beyond.

Food Nouveau
www.foodnouveau.com/quebeccity
Québec City-based Marie Asselin is a recipe developer and food stylist. The city-specific section of her blog features curated lists of her favorite poutines, brunches, coffee shops, breweries, and more.

Québec Original
www.quebecoriginal.com
The province's official tourism website has comprehensive information on anything and everything to do with the province, from national parks to festivals to kid-friendly fun.

Said the Gramophone
www.saidthegramophone.com
This music blog offers an interesting insider take on the Montréal, Québec, and Toronto music scenes.

Voir
www.voir.ca
The online component to the Francophone alternative weekly, Voir has event listings, restaurant reviews, and a weekly webcast that takes you behind the scenes of the weekly photo shoot and gives you a rundown of the week's biggest events.

Index

F

G

H

IJ

KL

M

NOP

QR

Restaurants Index

Nightlife Index

Shops Index

Hotels Index

Photo Credits

Title page photo: © Vlad Ghiea | Dreamstime.com

All interior photos © Andrea Bennett, except: page 2 (top right) © Peanutroaster | Dreamstime.com, (bottom) © Industryandtravel | Dreamstime.com; page 14 (top left) © Christian De Grandmaison | Dreamstime.com, (bottom) © Isabel Poulin | Dreamstime.com; page 17 © Wangkun Jia | Dreamstime.com; page 19 (bottom right) © Aladin66 | Dreamstime.com; page 21 © Will Keats-Osborn, page 26 © Jiawangkun | Dreamstime.com; page 29 (top) © Wangkun Jia | Dreamstime.com, (bottom) © Elena Duvernay | Dreamstime.com; page 30 © Samantha Ong | Dreamstime.com; page 37 (bottom) © Meunierd | Dreamstime.com; page 42 © Ritu Jethani | Dreamstime.com; (top right) © Daniel Logan | Dreamstime.com; page 61 © Will Keats-Osborn; (bottom) © Aquarium du Québec/ Steve Deschênes; page 79 (bottom) © Courtesy of Auberge Saint-Antoine; page 92 © Will Keats-Osborn; page 97 (top) © Fairmont Château Frotenac, page 98 © Michel Johnson/ le Draue; page 108 (top right) © Will Keats-Osborn; page 136 (bottom) © Francis Gagnon OTC; page 138 © Martinmark | Dreamstime.com; page 170 (top right) © Will Keats-Osborn; page 183 (bottom) © Fairmont le Château Frontenac; page 190 (bottom) © Courtesy of Auberge Saint-Antoine; page 193 (top) © Alain Blanchette/Le Massif, (bottom) © Will Keats-Osborn; page 203 (top) © Will Keats-Osborn, (bottom) © Mont-Sainte-Anne; page 211 (top) © Photo GREMM/WhalesOnline.org, (bottom) © Alain Blanchette/Le Massif

MAP SYMBOLS

▮	Sights	⊛	National Capital	▲	Mountain		Major Hwy
▮	Restaurants	⊙	State Capital	✦	Natural Feature		Road/Hwy
▮	Nightlife	○	City/Town		Waterfall		Pedestrian Friendly
▮	Arts and Culture	★	Point of Interest		Park	- - - - - -	Trail
▮	Sports and Activities	•	Accommodation		Archaeological Site		Stairs
▮	Shops	▼	Restaurant/Bar	T	Trailhead	···········	Ferry
▮	Hotels	▪	Other Location	P	Parking Area		Railroad

CONVERSION TABLES

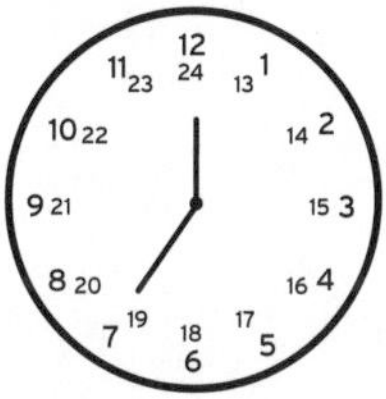

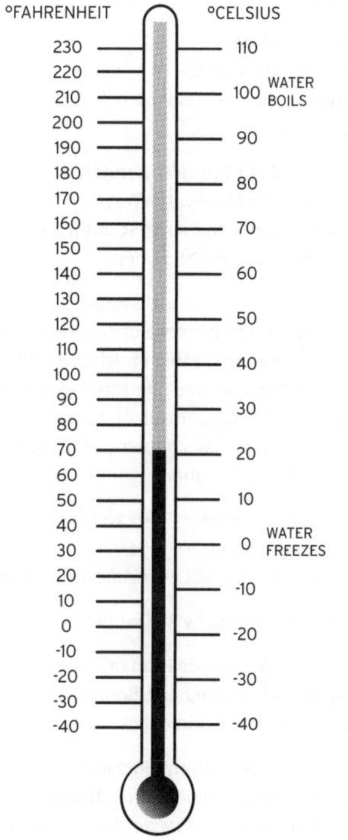

°C = (°F - 32) / 1.8
°F = (°C x 1.8) + 32
1 inch = 2.54 centimeters (cm)
1 foot = 0.304 meters (m)
1 yard = 0.914 meters
1 mile = 1.6093 kilometers (km)
1 km = 0.6214 miles
1 fathom = 1.8288 m
1 chain = 20.1168 m
1 furlong = 201.168 m
1 acre = 0.4047 hectares
1 sq km = 100 hectares
1 sq mile = 2.59 square km
1 ounce = 28.35 grams
1 pound = 0.4536 kilograms
1 short ton = 0.90718 metric ton
1 short ton = 2,000 pounds
1 long ton = 1.016 metric tons
1 long ton = 2,240 pounds
1 metric ton = 1,000 kilograms
1 quart = 0.94635 liters
1 US gallon = 3.7854 liters
1 Imperial gallon = 4.5459 liters
1 nautical mile = 1.852 km

12 24 1 13 2 14 3 15 4 16 5 17 6 18 7 19 8 20 9 21 10 22 11 23

°FAHRENHEIT
230 220 210 200 190 180 170 160 150 140 130 120 110 100 90 80 70 60 50 40 30 20 10 0 -10 -20 -30 -40

°CELSIUS
110 100 WATER BOILS 90 80 70 60 50 40 30 20 10 0 WATER FREEZES -10 -20 -30 -40

MOON QUÉBEC CITY
Avalon Travel
Hachette Book Group
1700 Fourth Street
Berkeley, CA 94710, USA
www.moon.com

Editor: Kathryn Ettinger
Series Manager: Leah Gordon
Copy Editor: Deana Shields
Graphics and Production Coordinator: Lucie Ericksen
Cover Design: Faceout Studios, Charles Brock
Interior Design: Domini Dragoone
Moon Logo: Tim McGrath
Map Editor: Albert Angulo
Cartographers: Albert Angulo, Brian Shotwell
Indexer: Greg Jewett

ISBN-13: 978-1-63121-493-6

Printing History
1st Edition — 2015
2nd Edition — January 2019
5 4 3 2 1

Front cover photo: Château Frontenac overlooking Lower Town © Michael Snell/RobertHarding
Back cover photo: Les Fortifications in Upper Town © Martinmark | Dreamstime.com

Printed in China by RR Donnelley

5